AF587960

Sorel Etrog

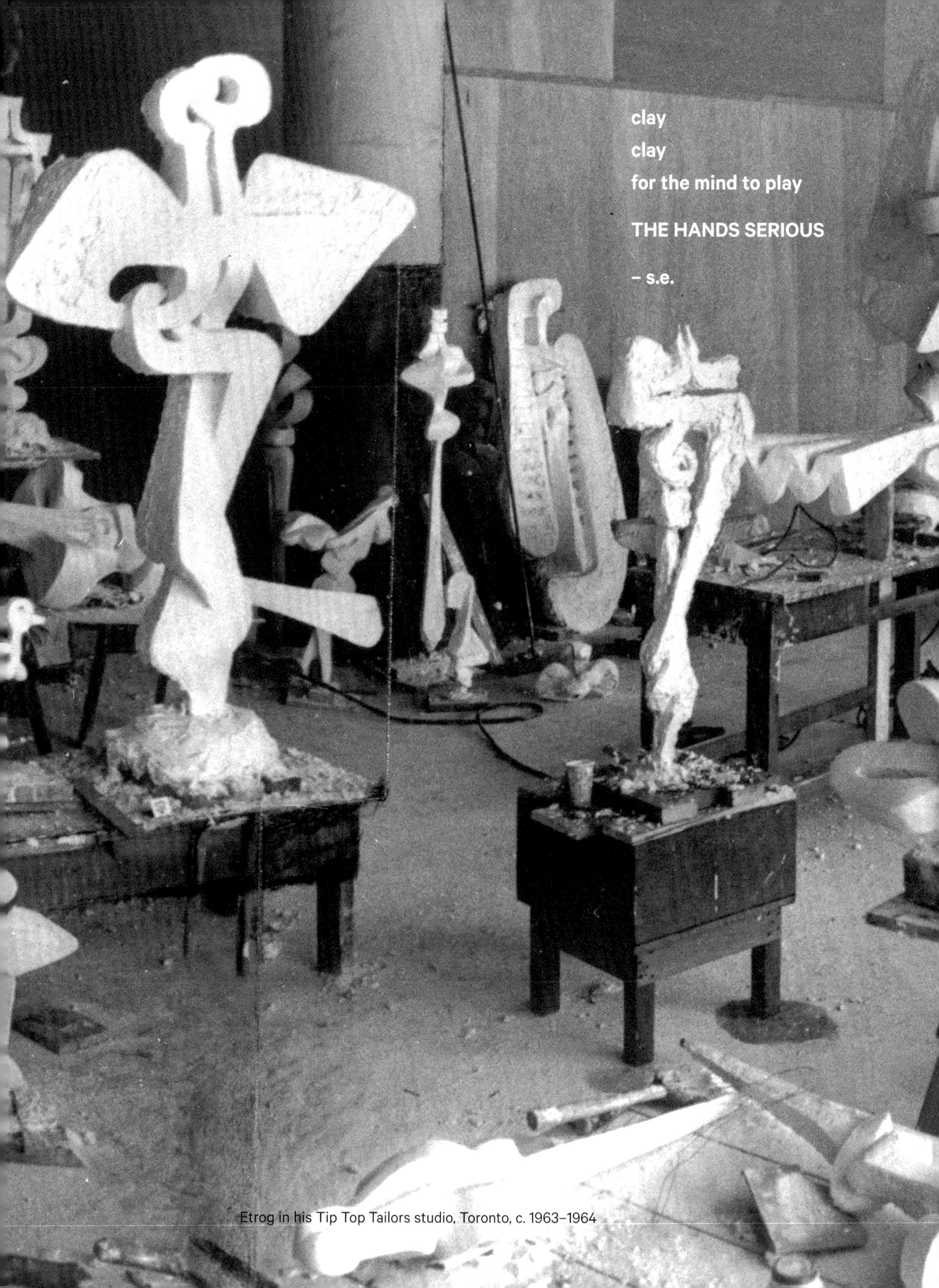

clay
clay
for the mind to play
THE HANDS SERIOUS

– s.e.

Etrog in his Tip Top Tailors studio, Toronto, c. 1963–1964

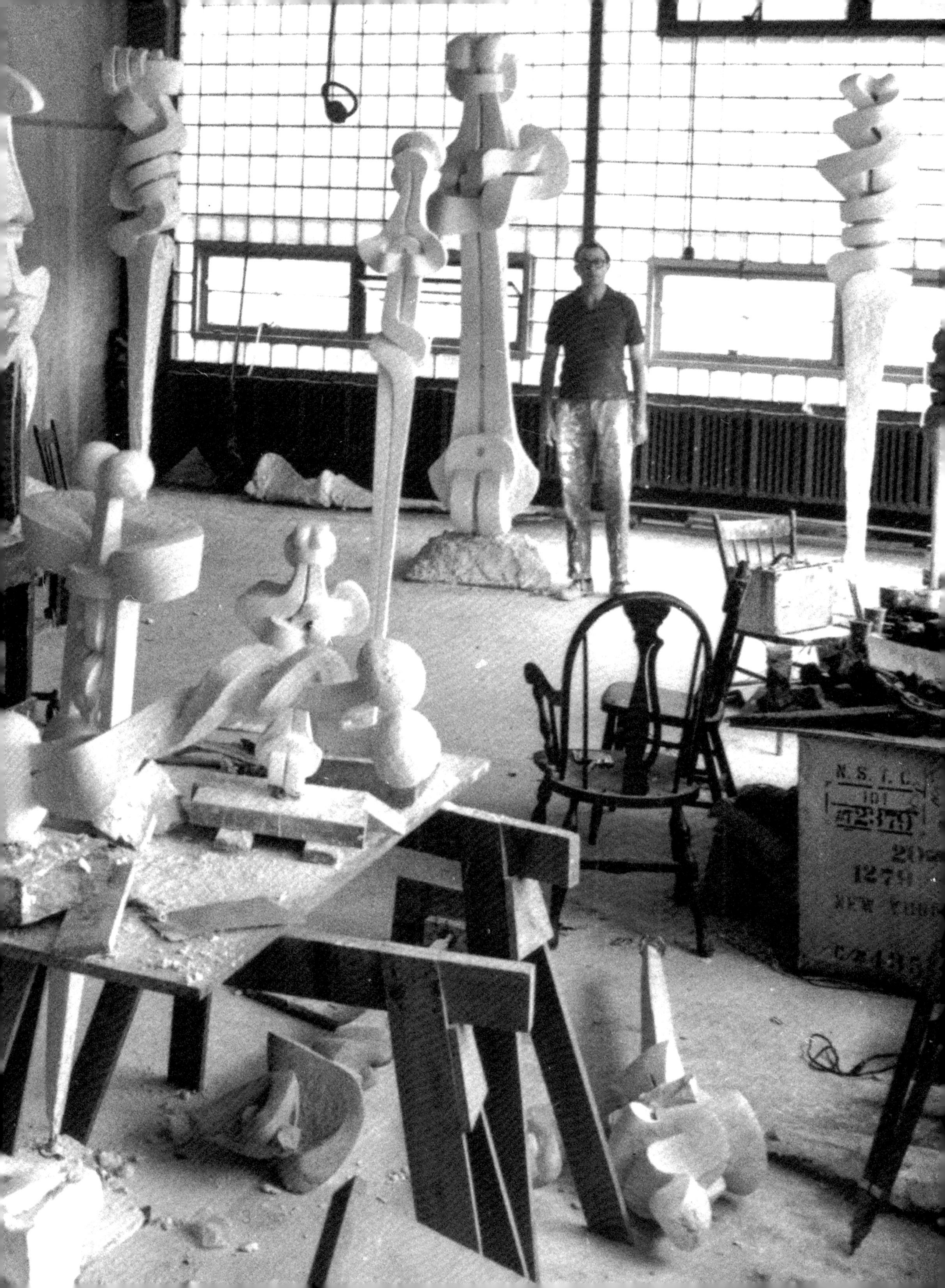
101
#2379
1279

Sorel Etrog
Five Decades

Edited by
Ihor Holubizky

Art Gallery of Ontario

Dedicated to the memory of Samuel J. Zacks (1904–1970)

Etrog (centre) with Ayala and Samuel J. Zacks, Gallery Moos, Toronto, 1959

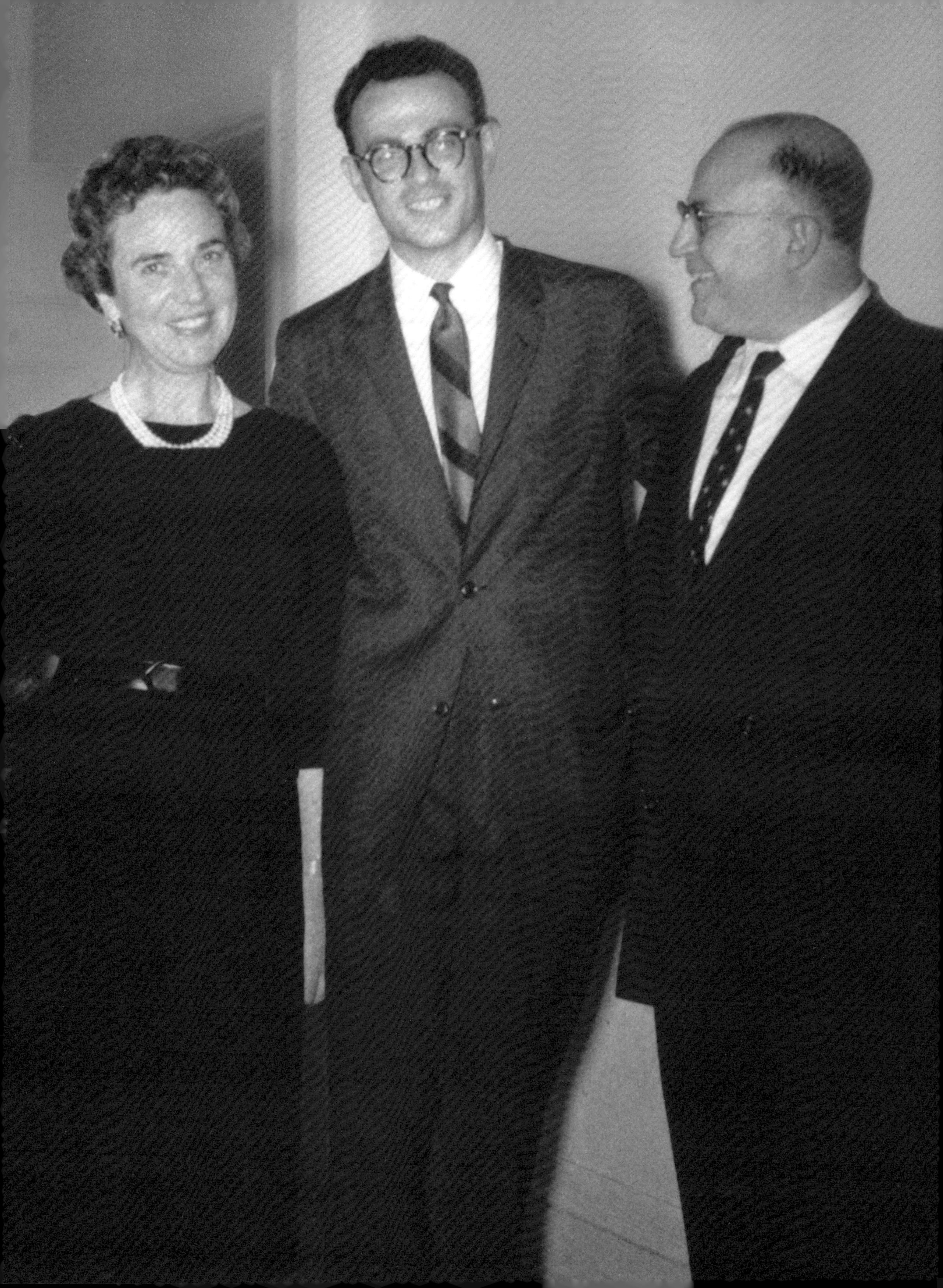

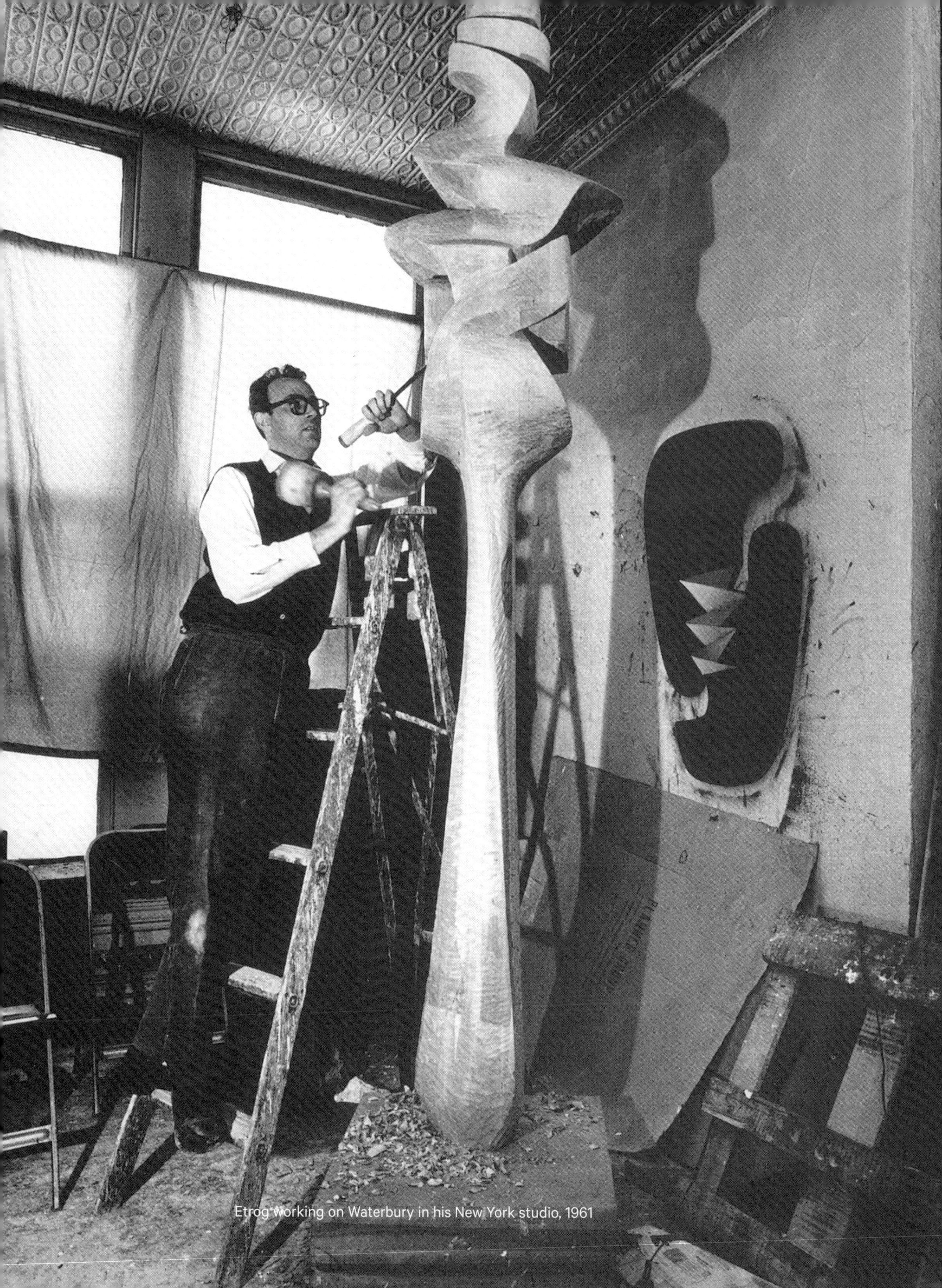

Etrog working on Waterbury in his New York studio, 1961

10 Matthew Teitelbaum
13 Ihor Holubizky
16 Works
93 Sir Philip Hendy
94 Theodore Allen Heinrich
100 William J. Withrow
102 Florian Rodari
107 Marshall McLuhan
112 Gary Michael Dault
116 List of Works
122 Public Collections
124 Selected Bibliography

Matthew Teitelbaum
Foreword

Sorel Etrog was among a handful of émigré artists on the Toronto art scene—along with Kosso Eloul, Augustin Filipovic, Gershon Iskowitz, Christiane Pflug and Anton van Dalen—who, by the mid-1960s, had made a significant contribution to the languages of contemporary art in Canada. Etrog arrived here from Europe bearing deep personal experiences of life with other touchstones informing his work. His references to other traditions enriched the conversation in a relatively insulated world and suggested a connectedness that was largely unimagined. Within his generation Etrog has been the most internationally connected of artists and has returned over and over again to make his home in Toronto, where he still lives today.

He connected here to there certainly, one geography to another, and working relentlessly across disciplines has also enabled him to connect painting, sculpture, poetry, film and book illustration in sustained and inventive ways. Indeed, from an artist whose work engages repeatedly with interlocking forms, on some overarching level his instinct and motivation has always been about finding ways to connect. Not surprising perhaps for an immigrant whose sensibility is motivated by the idea of a search.

This exhibition began with two challenges: How could we represent Etrog's work in our permanent collection at the Art Gallery of Ontario in a way that would appropriately document the breadth of his activity? And how would we create an exhibition that ensures, as best we might, that the work comes alive for a younger generation of viewers who may be unfamiliar with this most international of Canadian artists?

On the first point, we have worked closely with Sorel and his studio assistant to acquire key works from each stage of his career, comprising his constructions, drawings, paintings and sculpture. Sorel has also committed the gift of his extraordinary archives to the Art Gallery of Ontario, which will be a treasure for researchers for generations to come.

On the second point, we strived to respond to a couple of fundamental questions: How do we present Sorel's work in a way that brings his contribution truly into the present? How do we address his relationships with key thinkers of his time—Marshall McLuhan, Samuel Beckett and Eugène Ionesco, among others—and mark not only the development of his own artistic voice but also the ideas he shared with them? The result is an exhibition which, in both content and organization, addresses a key idea of our time, namely the interdisciplinarity of practice. A film cascades into a painting, while book illustration abuts set designs, and sculpture scaled for public spaces engages with Etrog's poetry. It is a rich journey through a restless yet expressively driven career that both challenges and inspires visitors.

I would like to thank Ihor Holubizky, the editor of this publication and originator of the structure of the accompanying exhibition, which AGO staff brought to fruition after Ihor was unable to continue in his role as guest curator. I wish to acknowledge Dennis Reid, former Chief Curator, Research at the AGO, for recognizing the significance of Etrog's work and laying the groundwork for this project to emerge. I also want to extend my thanks to Florian Rodari, whose essay displays keen insights and revelations about Etrog's *Bulls* series, and Gary Michael Dault, who has enriched this catalogue with a piece that is at once personal and deferential towards Etrog and his work. Many thanks also go out to William Withrow and the families of Sir Philip Hendy, Theodore Allen Heinrich and Marshall McLuhan, who have graciously allowed us to reprint excerpts from archival essays on the multiple embodiments of Etrog's career.

This exhibition would not have been fully realized nor as comprehensive a record of Etrog's career had it not been for the generous loans of Etrog's artworks from Sonja Bata, Jay Hennick, Canadian Apartment Properties Real Estate Investment Trust and the Sarick Collection.

My sincerest gratitude goes out to every one of the generous and enthusiastic supporters of the Sorel Etrog exhibition. Special thanks must go to Al and Malka Green for their exemplary and early commitment to the project. We are also deeply grateful to BloombergSen; Lloyd Fogler and Fogler, Rubinoff; The Jay and Barbara Hennick Family Foundation; Albert & Temmy Latner Family Foundation; Steven & Lynda Latner; Samuel & Esther Sarick; Charles & Rose Tabachnick; and Sonja Bata. Your contributions have allowed us to not only set but also fulfill lofty expectations for both the exhibition and its accompanying publication.

I commend the efforts of numerous AGO employees for their contribution to this project—in particular Laura Comerford, the project manager of the exhibition, for putting together an exceptional tribute to Sorel, as well as Jim Shedden and Daniel Naccarato of the Publishing team, whose commitment to excellence is evident throughout this book.

In addition, I would like to acknowledge the collaborative efforts of Sorel's assistant, Eva Varga, who was instrumental to the completion of both the exhibition and the publication. I would also like to thank Sorel's long-time friend and publisher Howard Aster for the valuable advice he provided to our Publishing team. Most of all, I wish to extend my deepest thanks to Sorel himself for his ongoing vision and generous support that has spanned decades, and for a body of work that remains as relevant today as ever.

Our hope is that audiences, in viewing this exhibition, will combine the spirit of celebration with the excitement of discovery. By revisiting a well-known and beloved artist in new ways, through paths that open up new contexts in which to understand his contribution, our hope is that Sorel's sustained international career will be more fully understood.

Matthew Teitelbaum
Michael and Sonja Koerner Director, and CEO
Art Gallery of Ontario

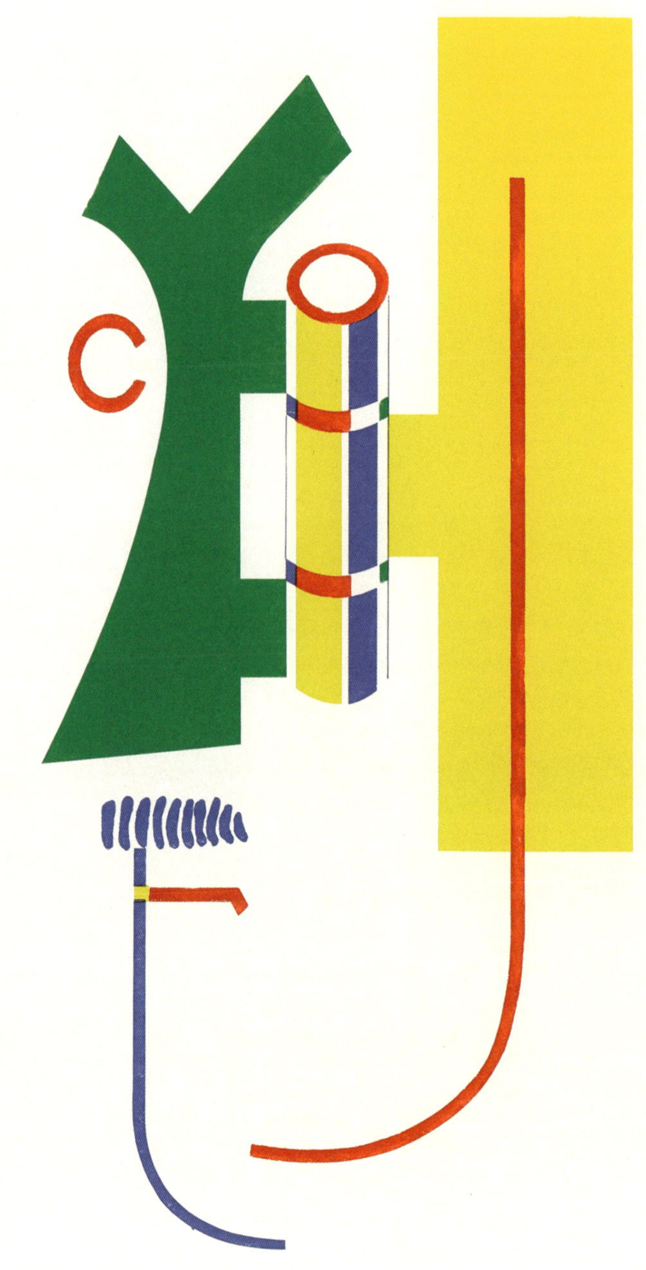

JOYCE CENTENARY FESTIVAL TORONTO

1982

etrop

Ihor Holubizky
Five Decades

This exhibition offers a unique and rich view into Sorel Etrog's work, life and times over five decades, exploring the complexity and diversity of each though his sculptures, paintings, works on paper, book and text works and his rarely seen but remarkable 1975 film *Spiral*.

A convention of most retrospectives is to order works by time and themes, and to insist on an ever-evolving style, adaptation and causality through a chain of influences (the simplistic Darwinian model), which the biographical form also impresses upon us. To do so, however, can flatten works of art—like a flower pressed dry between the pages of a book—and all the more so for Sorel Etrog whose work is multi-dimensional and spatial, both literally and figuratively.

To extrapolate from Etrog's recurring terms, there are the links, hinges and spirals. On the one hand there is a tangible link to the European avant-garde between the wars and a hinge to the past, the Mediterranean world of antiquity and non-Western culture; the hinge, metaphorically, brings the past into direct contact with the present. The spiral can be seen as his associations and collaborations with European writer-playwrights Samuel Beckett and Eugène Ionesco and in Toronto with Marshall McLuhan, figures who are credited with shaping a post-1950 cultural and philosophical consciousness. Etrog's literary and cultural interests extend and spiral to other moderns as well—T.S. Eliot, James Joyce and Tristan Tzara, to name a few.

The exhibition methodology, therefore, is an orchestration of processional routes and the opportunity for purposeful wandering: a moment to pause, which leads to another. The aggregate experience, to quote Clive Dilnot, is an "enigma of things [which] reveal other, potentially rich, even paradoxical subtexts of relationships and continuities."[1] Such a methodology also offers a museum model that Roger G. Kennedy termed the Iconostasis—"an assemblage of objects not [only] to be looked at but looked through, significant for what they represent."[2] We take this view-through to the streets of Toronto where Etrog sculptures are mounted in many public spaces. Don't think of them merely as objects of type and style, but as utterances in a Beckett play. We are not, however, pawns in an absurdist endgame, but better able/enabled to consider the paradoxes of life and art. Where do they link, hinge or spiral?

The paradoxical aspect of Etrog's inventiveness, and erudite resistance to what some may think art should be or look like, is unquestionably evident in his passion for words and ideas. He accepted University of Toronto professor Robert O'Driscoll's invitation to mark the 100th anniversary of James Joyce's birth in 1982, and wrote of it as "a dada experience, a chance encounter with a non-chronological chronology, a collage of thoughts and experiences in a dream chamber. I couldn't imagine at the time that for months ahead I would live under a Joyce and Dada spiel-spell—'a plotsome to getsome'—as Joyce said."[3]

The relevance of Etrog's work rests in the thoughts that matter. Artists think, make and activate. In this exhibition *we* can think, make and activate, and enter the dream chamber.

Dr. Ihor Holubizky is senior curator at the McMaster Museum of Art in Hamilton, Ontario.

1. Clive Dilnot, "The Enigma of Things," in *Kunst & Museumjournaal*, Eindhoven 5 (5), 1994, p. 21

2. Roger G. Kennedy, "Some Thoughts about National Museums at the End of the Century," in *Museum Studies: An Anthology of Contexts*, ed. Bettina Messias Carbonell (Oxford: Blackwell Publishing, 2004), p. 304

3. Sorel Etrog and John Cage, *Dream Chamber and About Roratorio*, ed. Robert O'Driscoll (Toronto: Black Brick Press, 1982), p. 63

Works

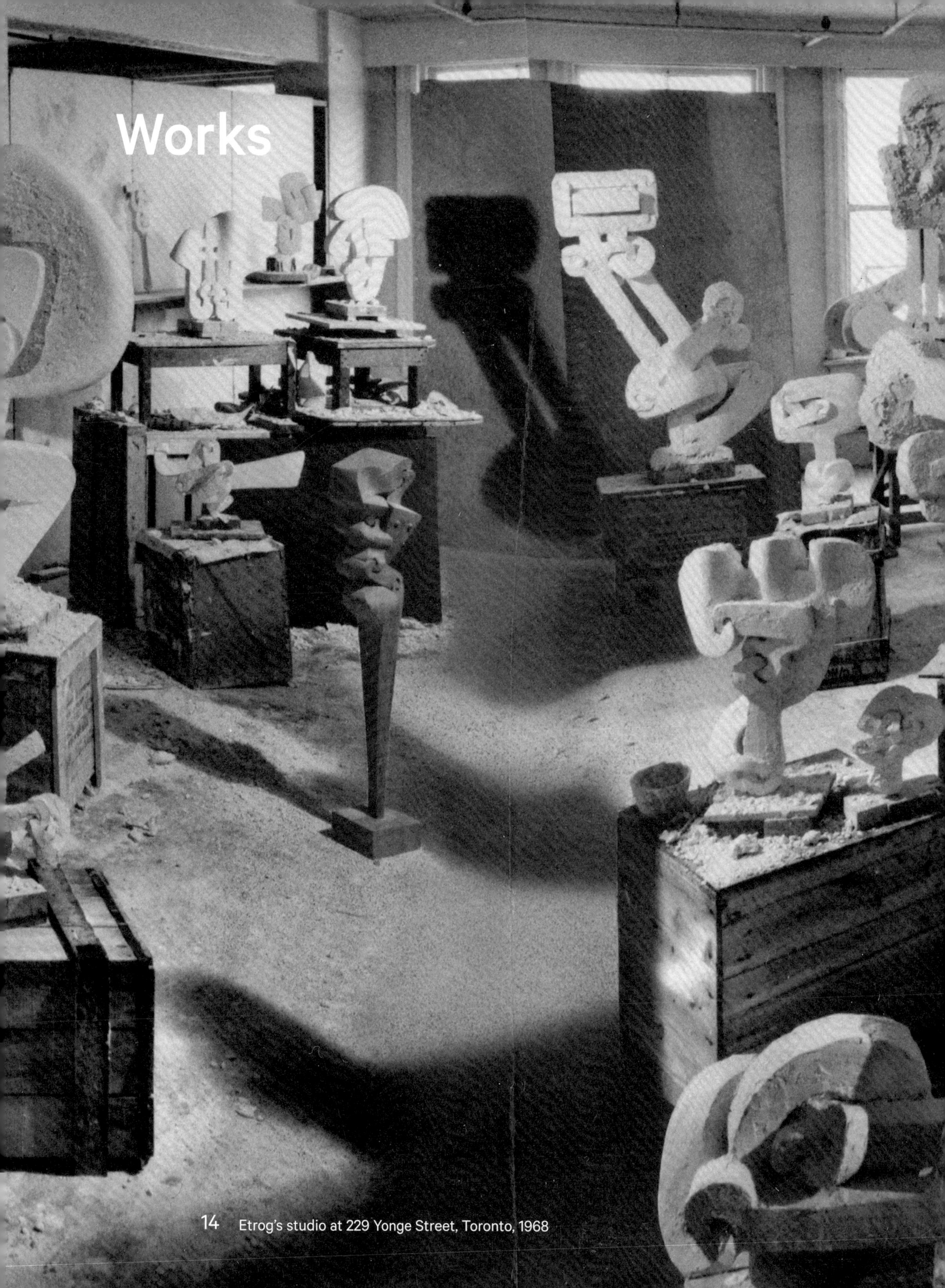

 Etrog's studio at 229 Yonge Street, Toronto, 1968

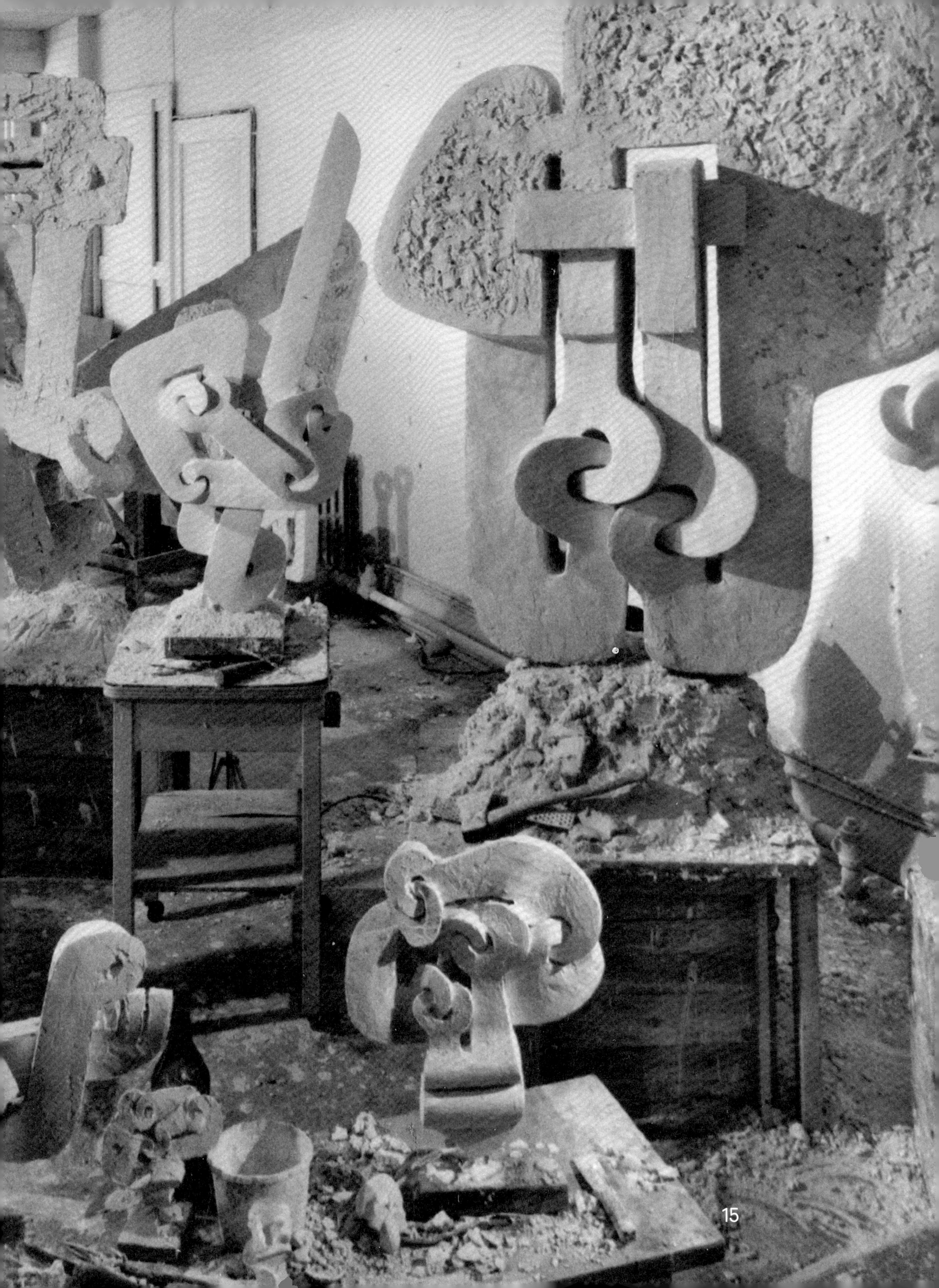

15

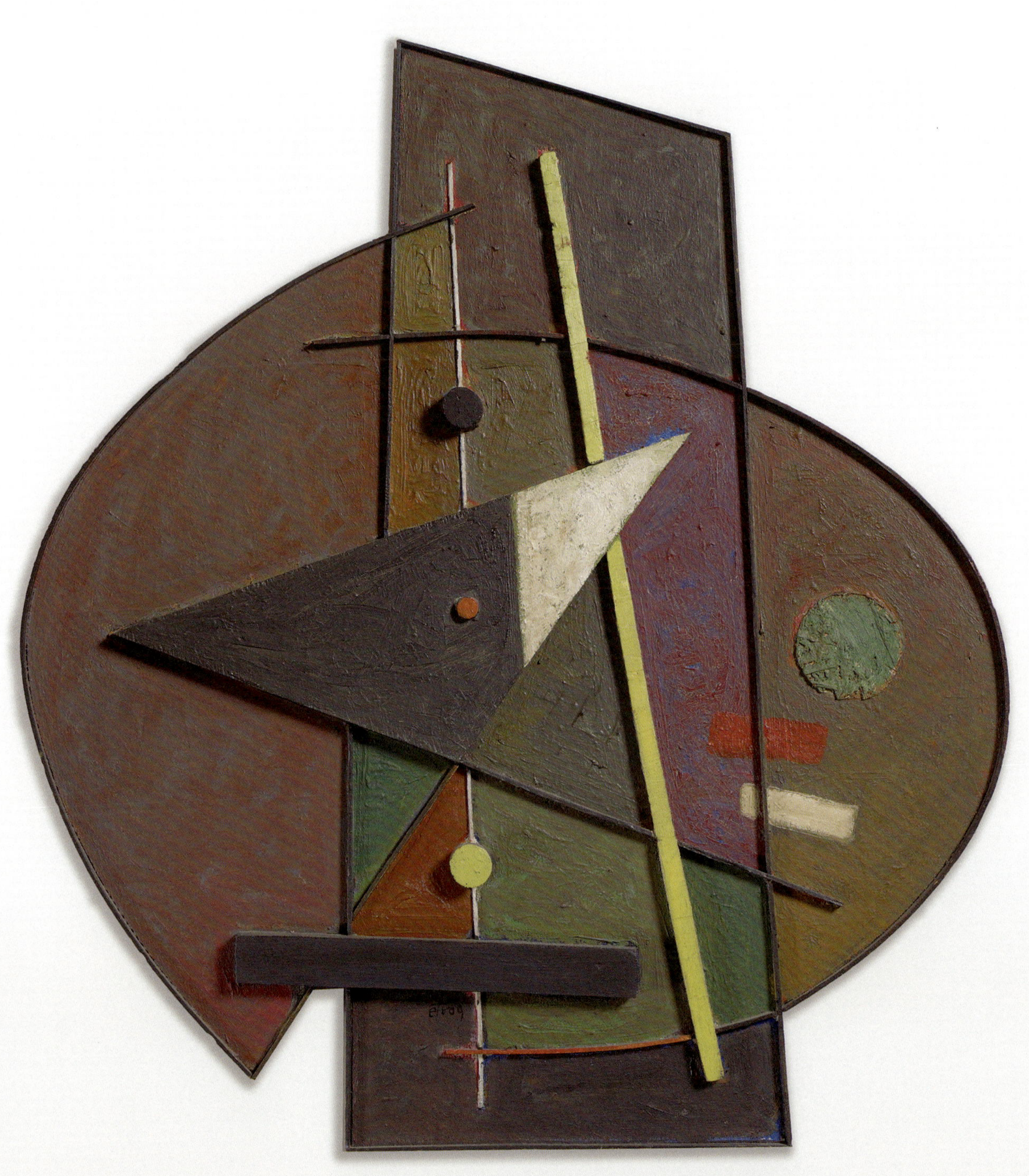

16 Society of Triangles, 1954–1955

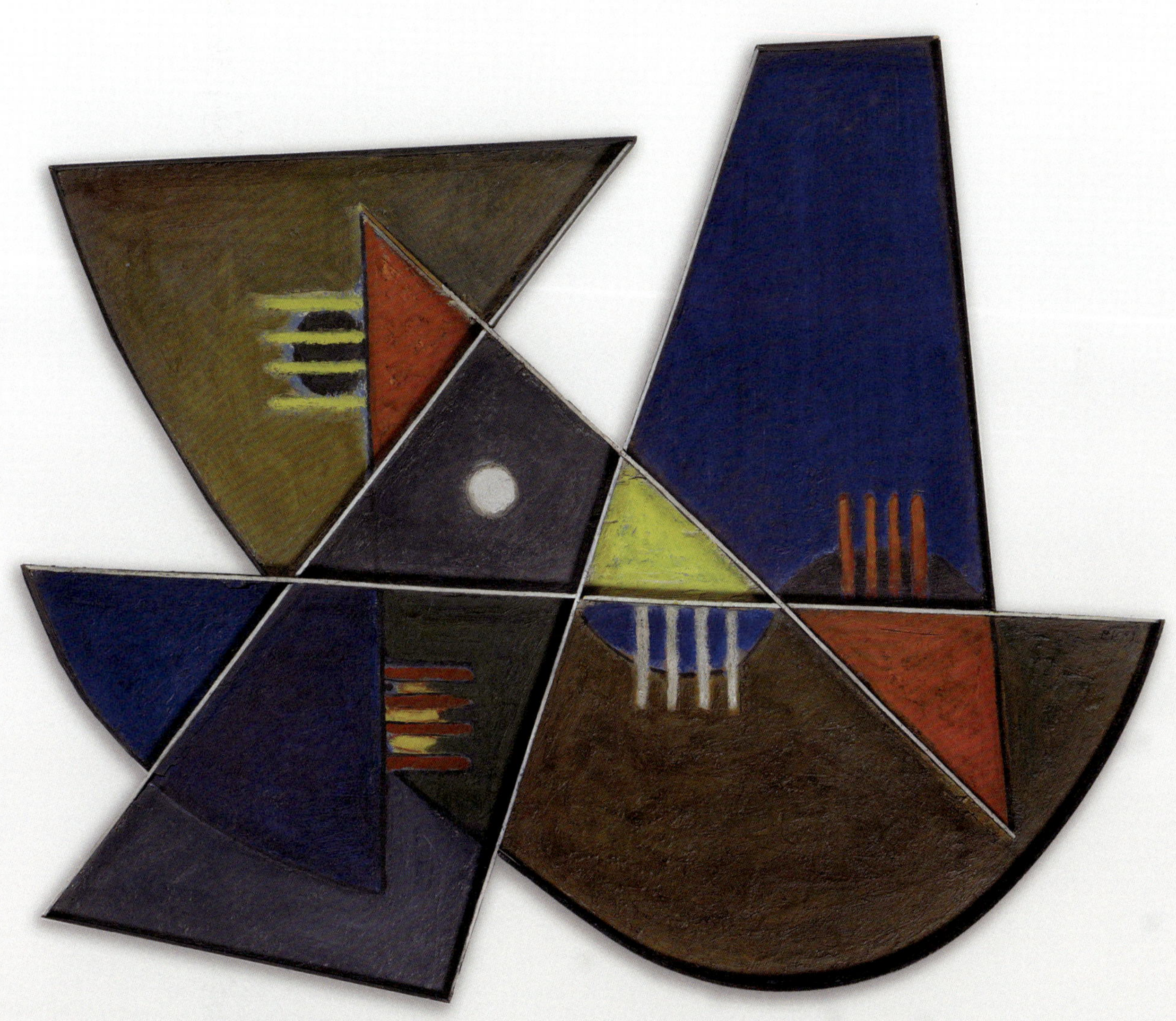

String Quartet (Bartok), 1955

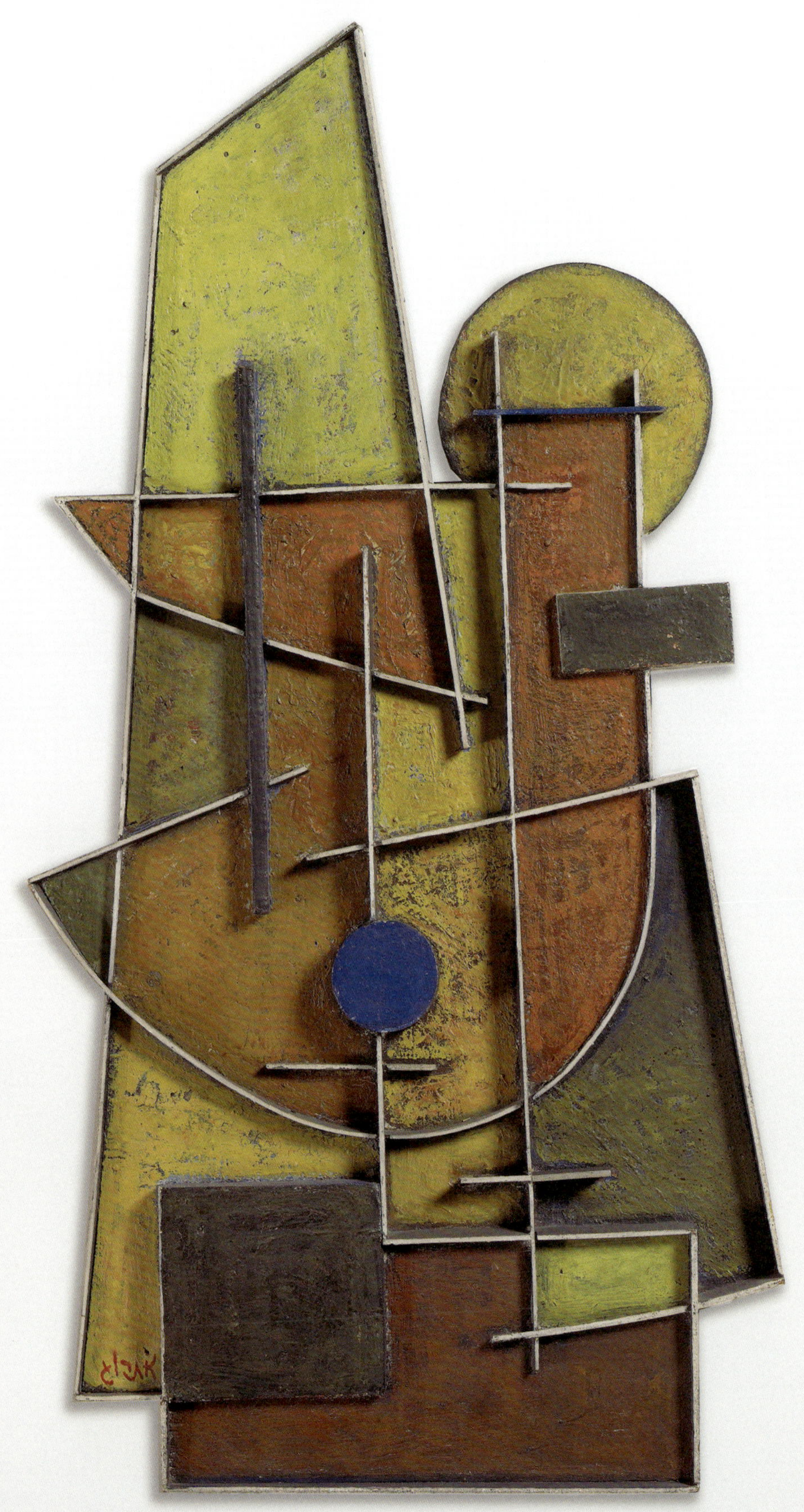

18 White Scaffolding, 1956–1958

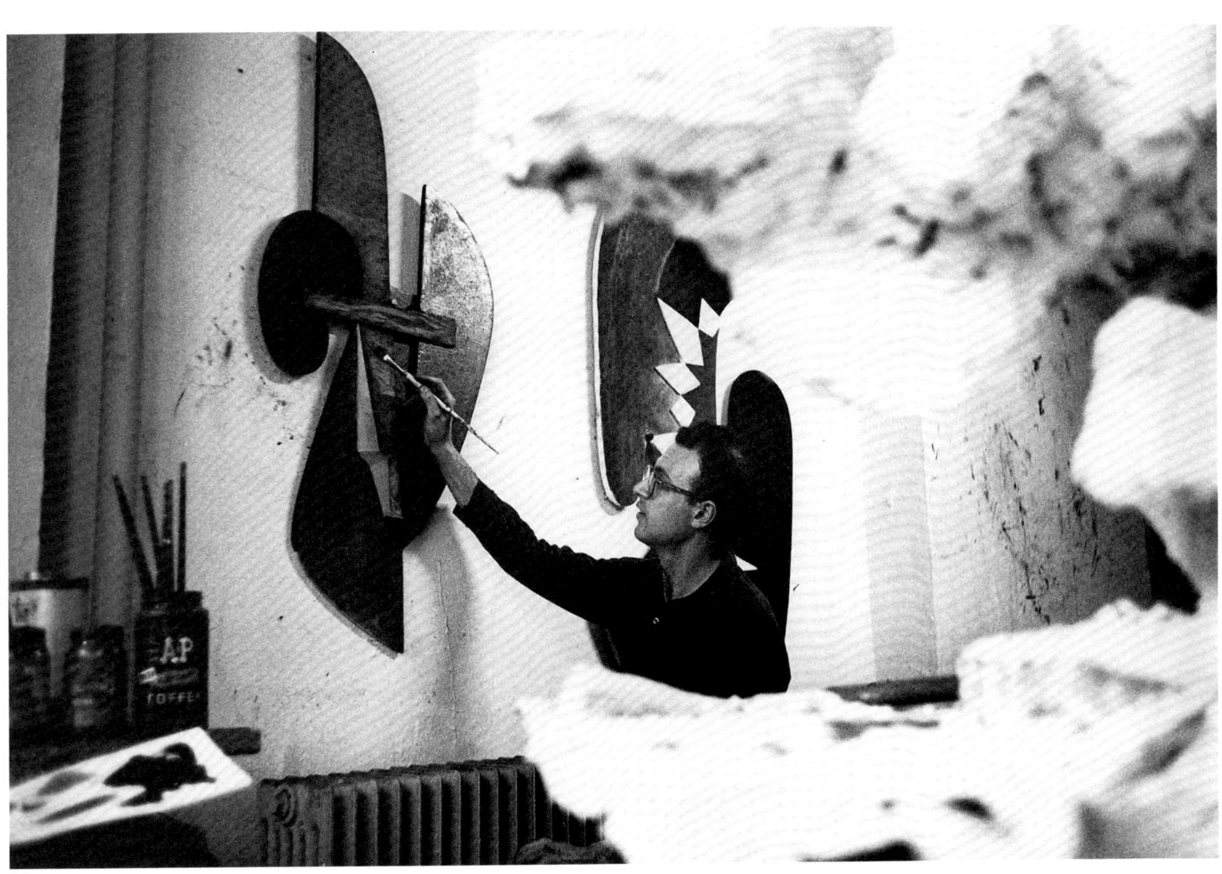

Etrog painting in his New York studio, c. 1958–1959

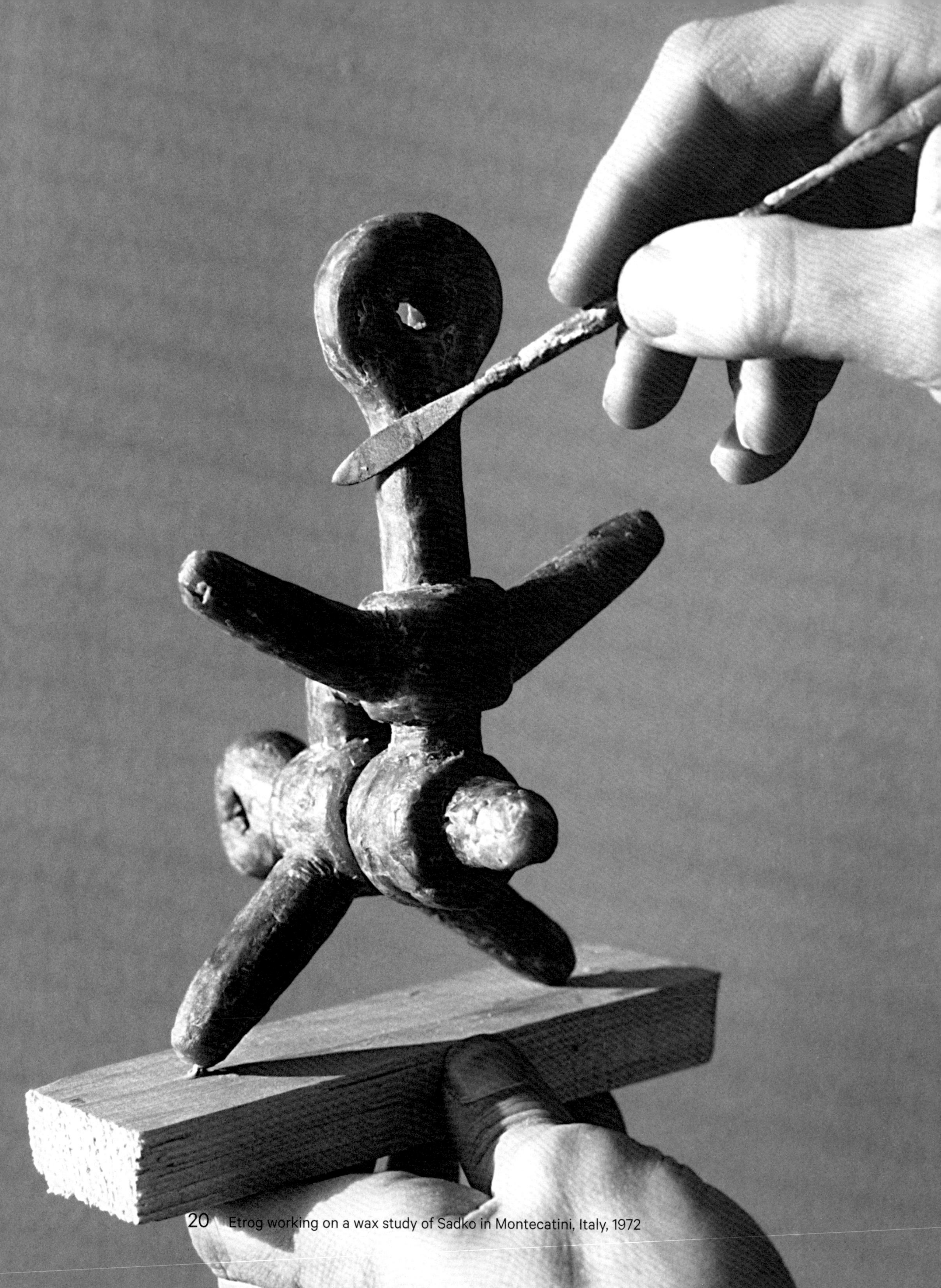

 Etrog working on a wax study of Sadko in Montecatini, Italy, 1972

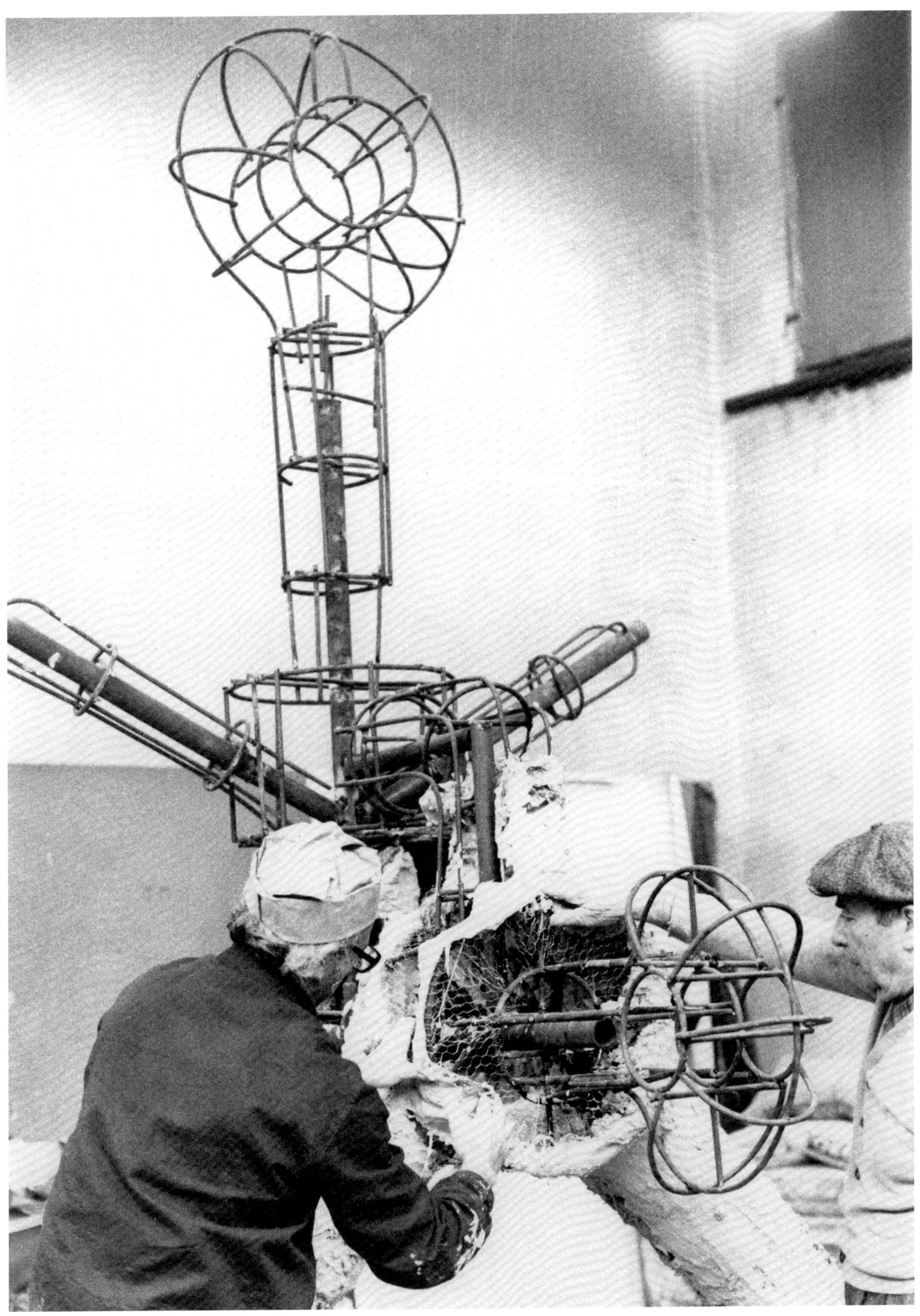

Etrog working on the plaster for Sadko in Montecatini, Italy

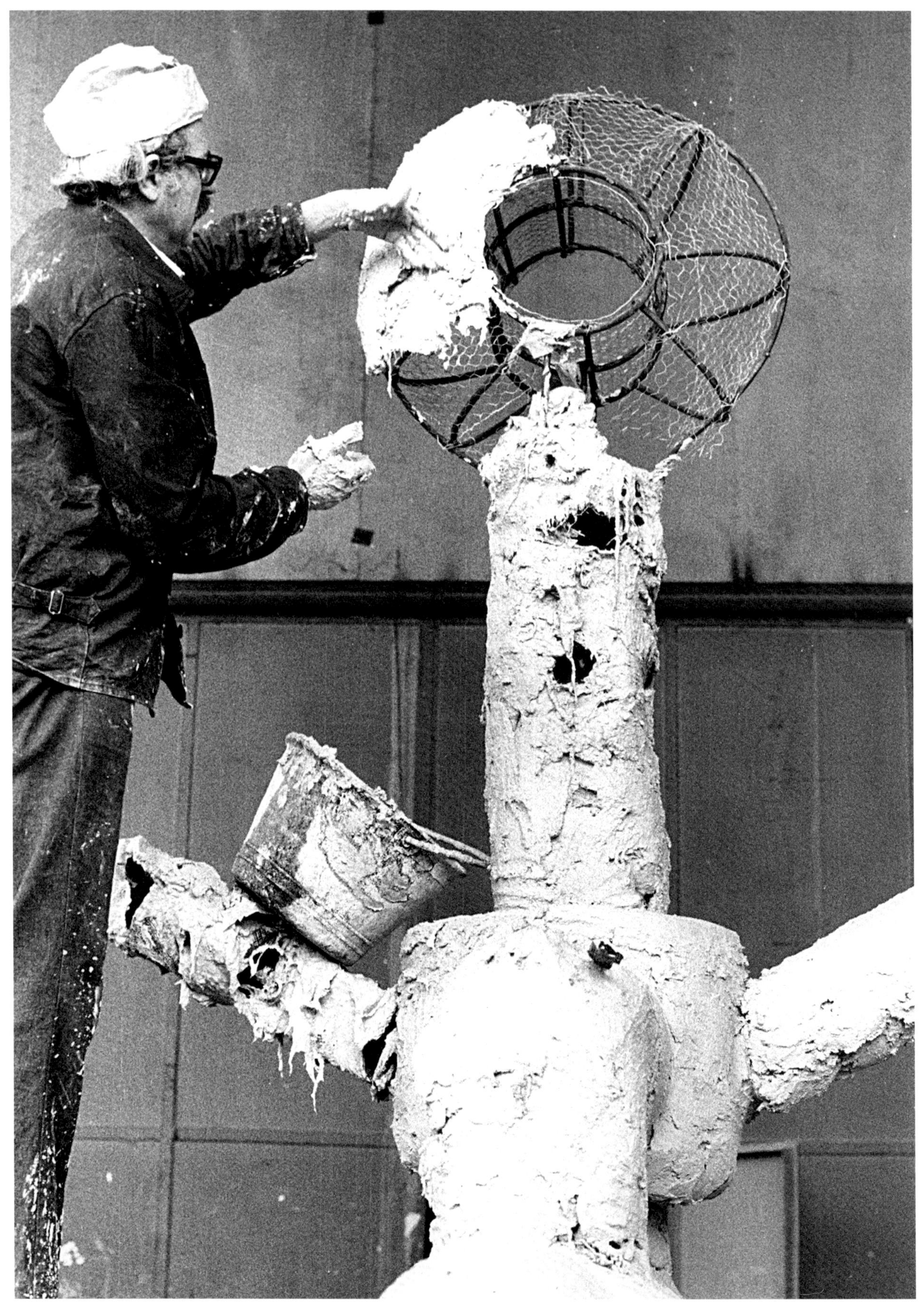

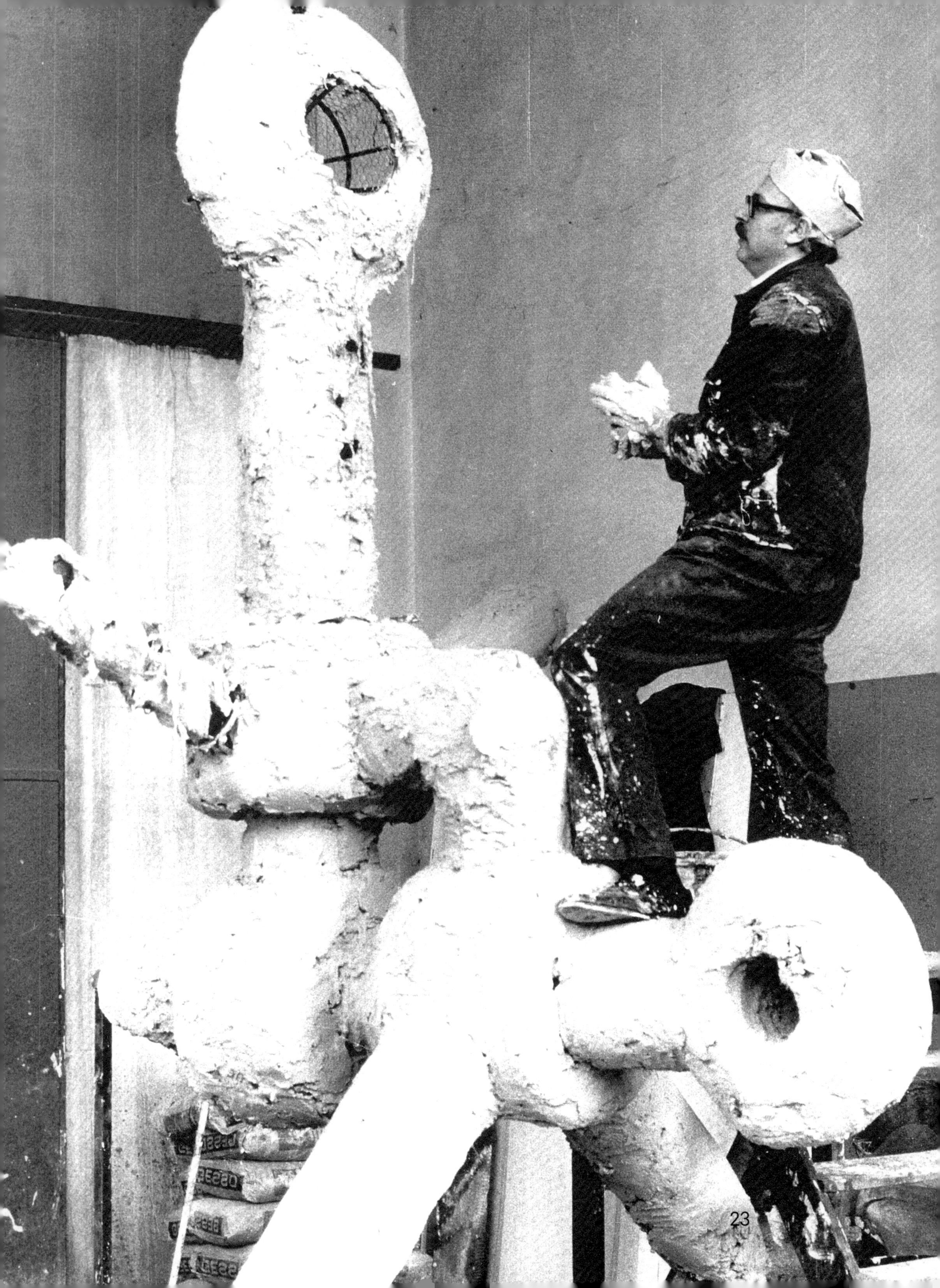

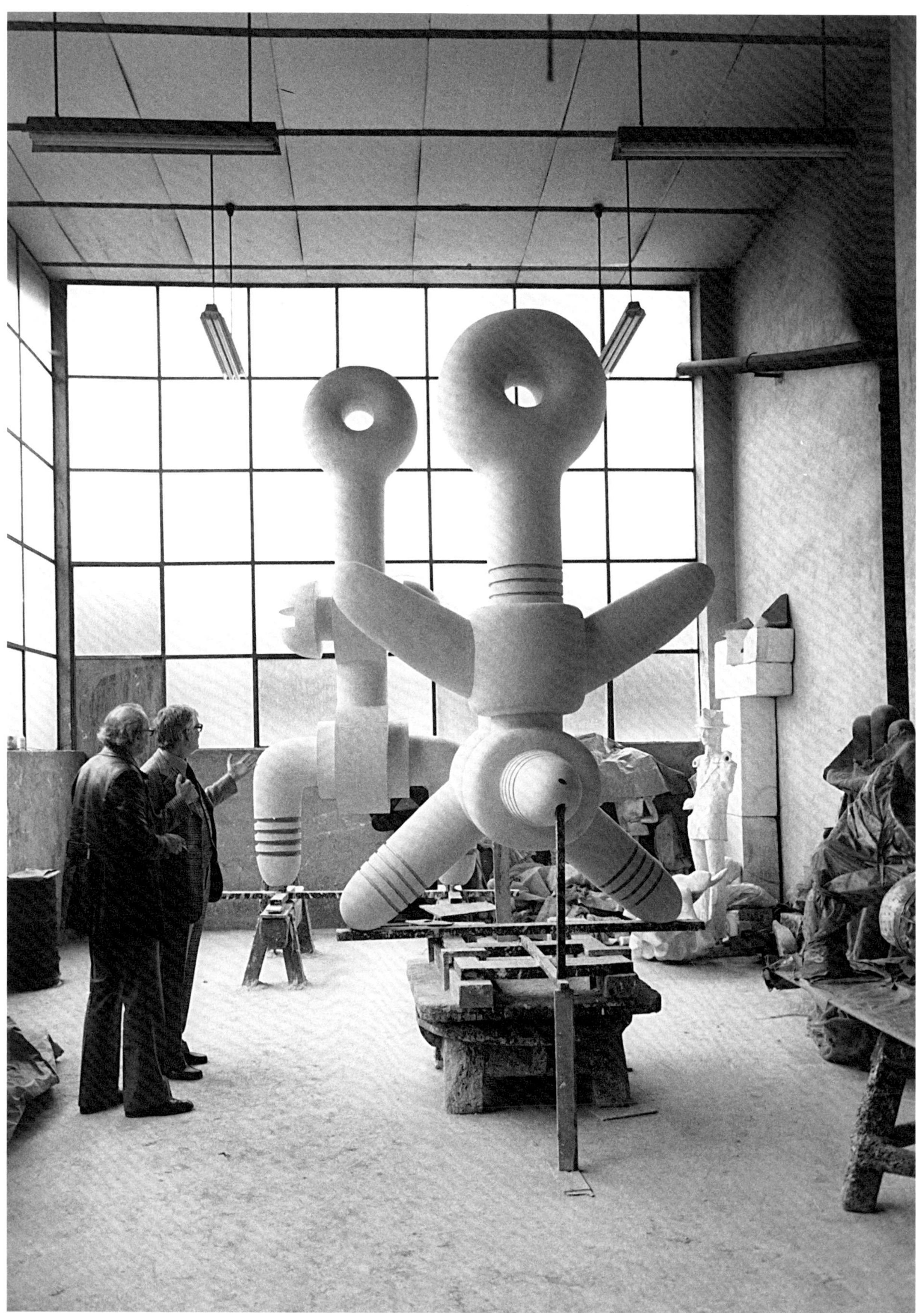

 Etrog's Sadko and Kabuki in the Michelucci Foundry, Montecatini, Italy, c. 1972

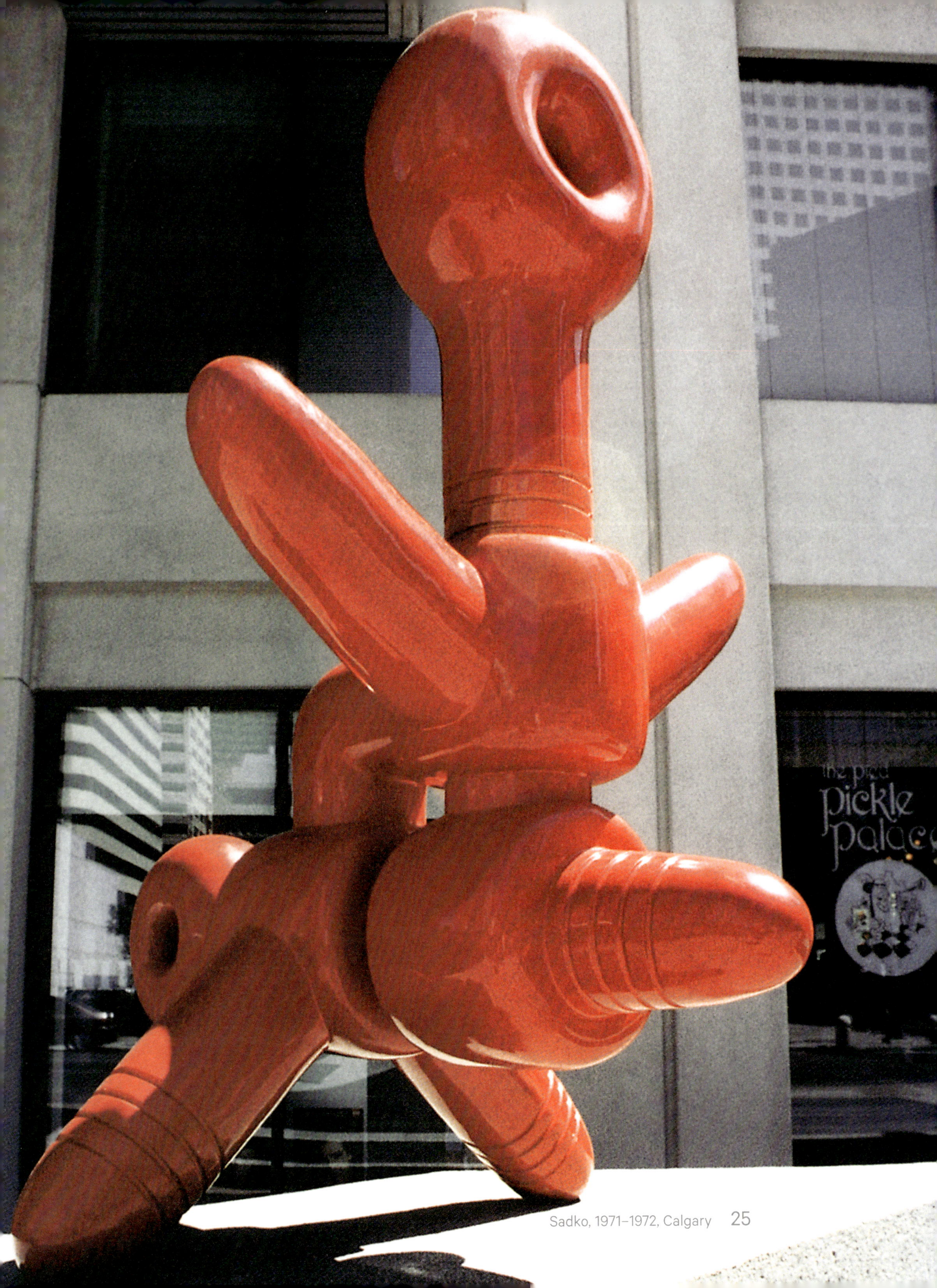

Sadko, 1971–1972, Calgary

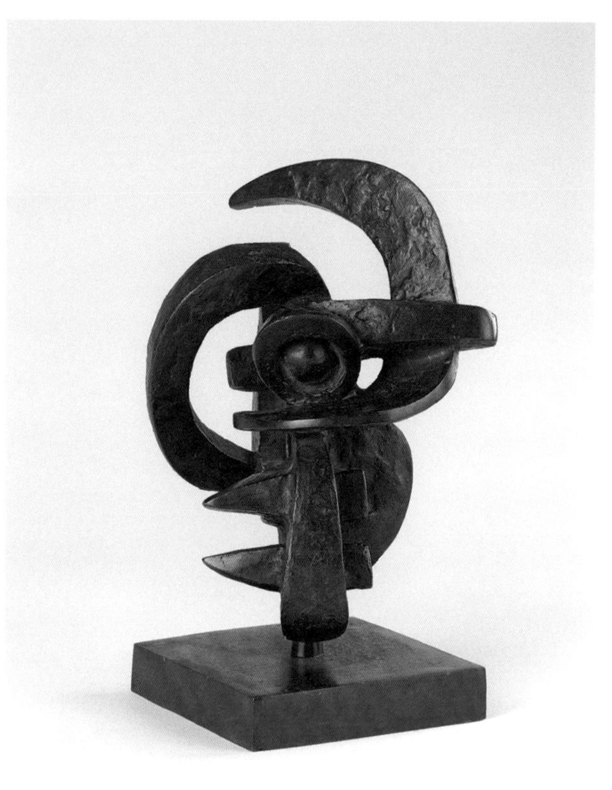

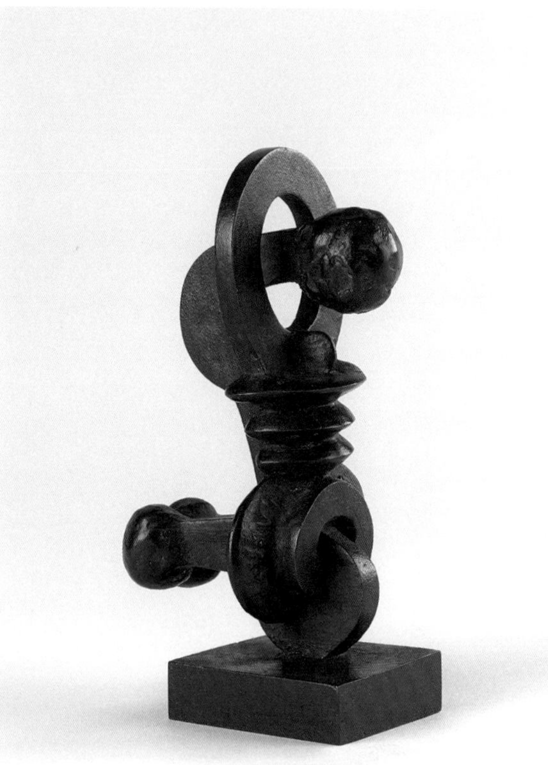

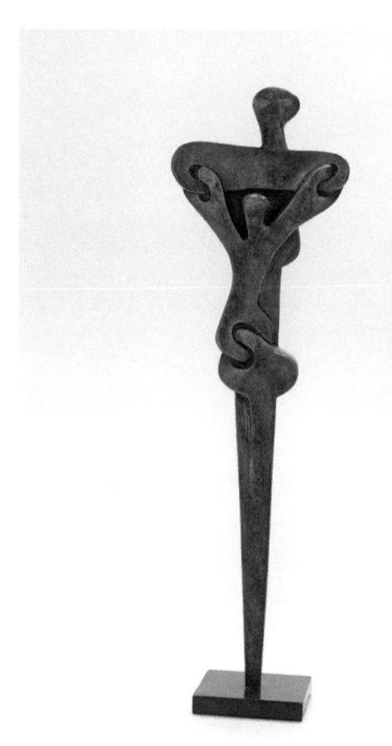

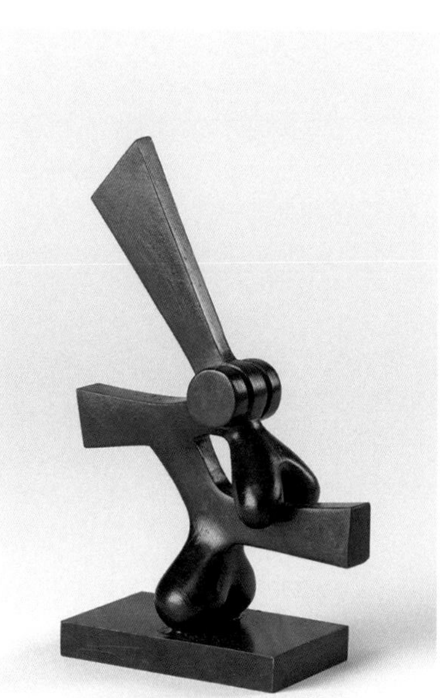

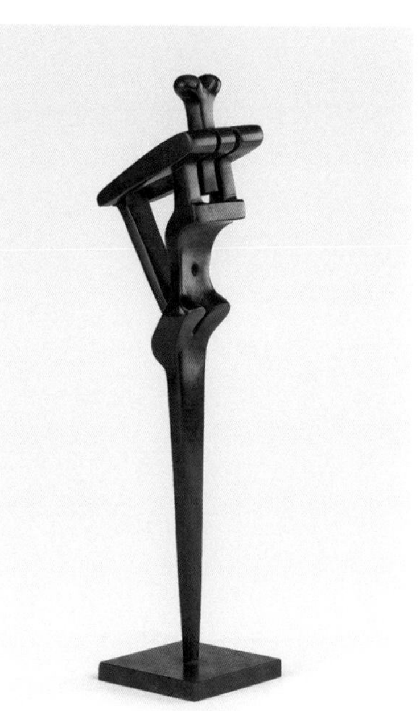

Barbarian Head, 1959; Corinth, 1959
Homage to Cimabue, 1968; Crusader II, 1976; Bashota, 1972

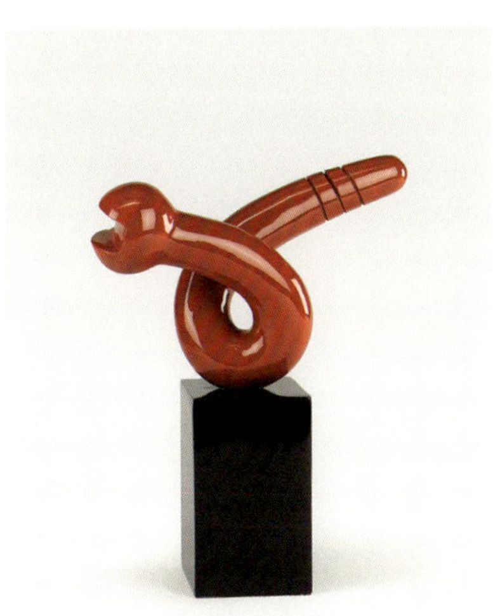
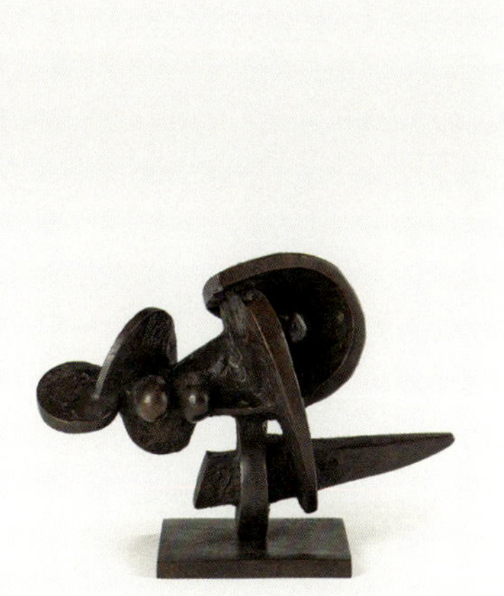
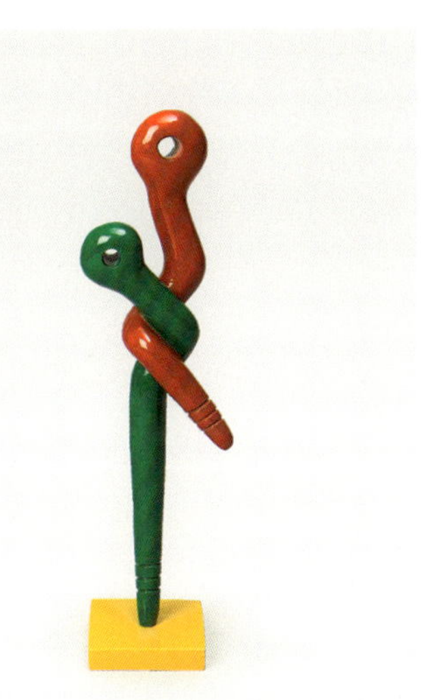
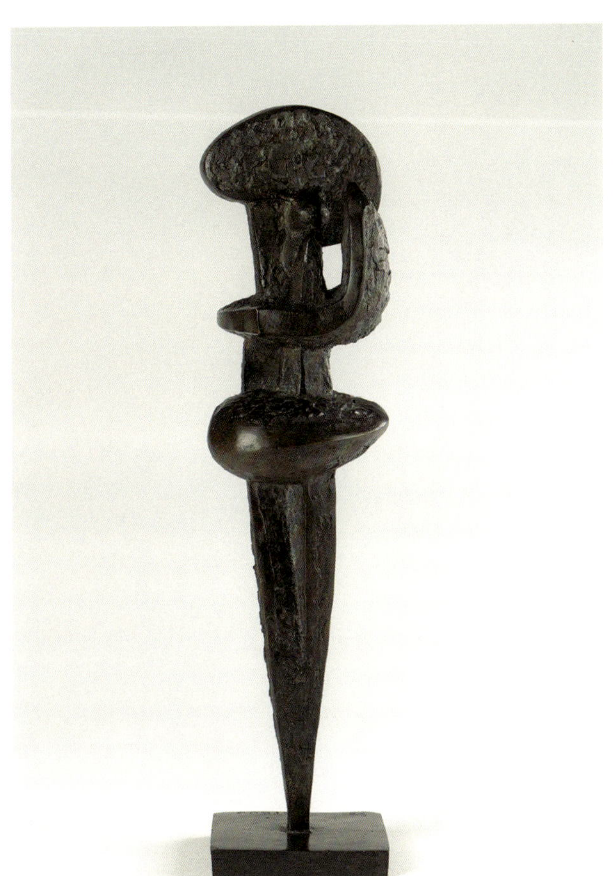
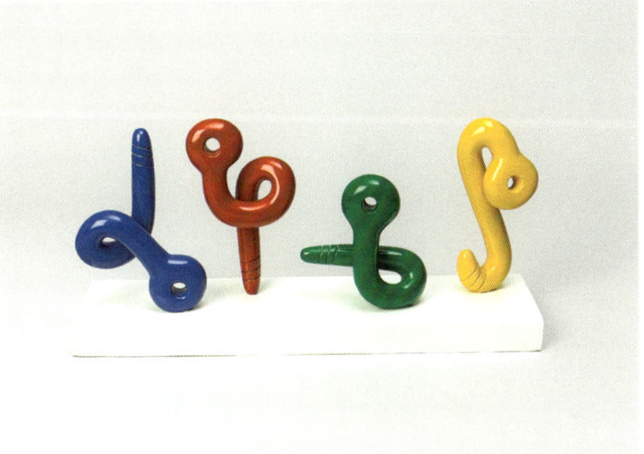
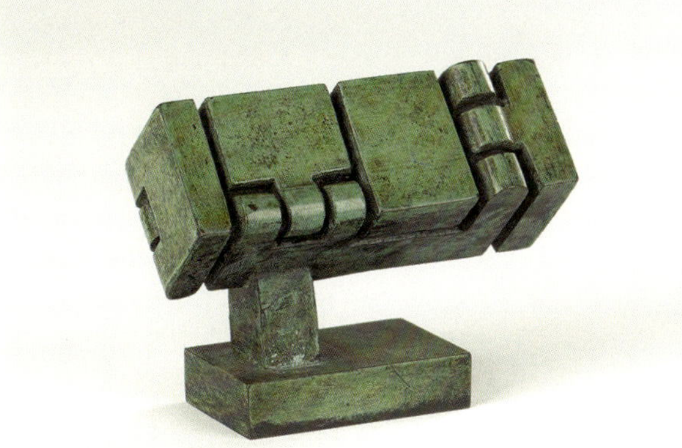

Buffon, 1973; War Remembrance, 1959; Cybelle, 1972
Haielet, 1959; Quartet, 1972; Antitete, 1976

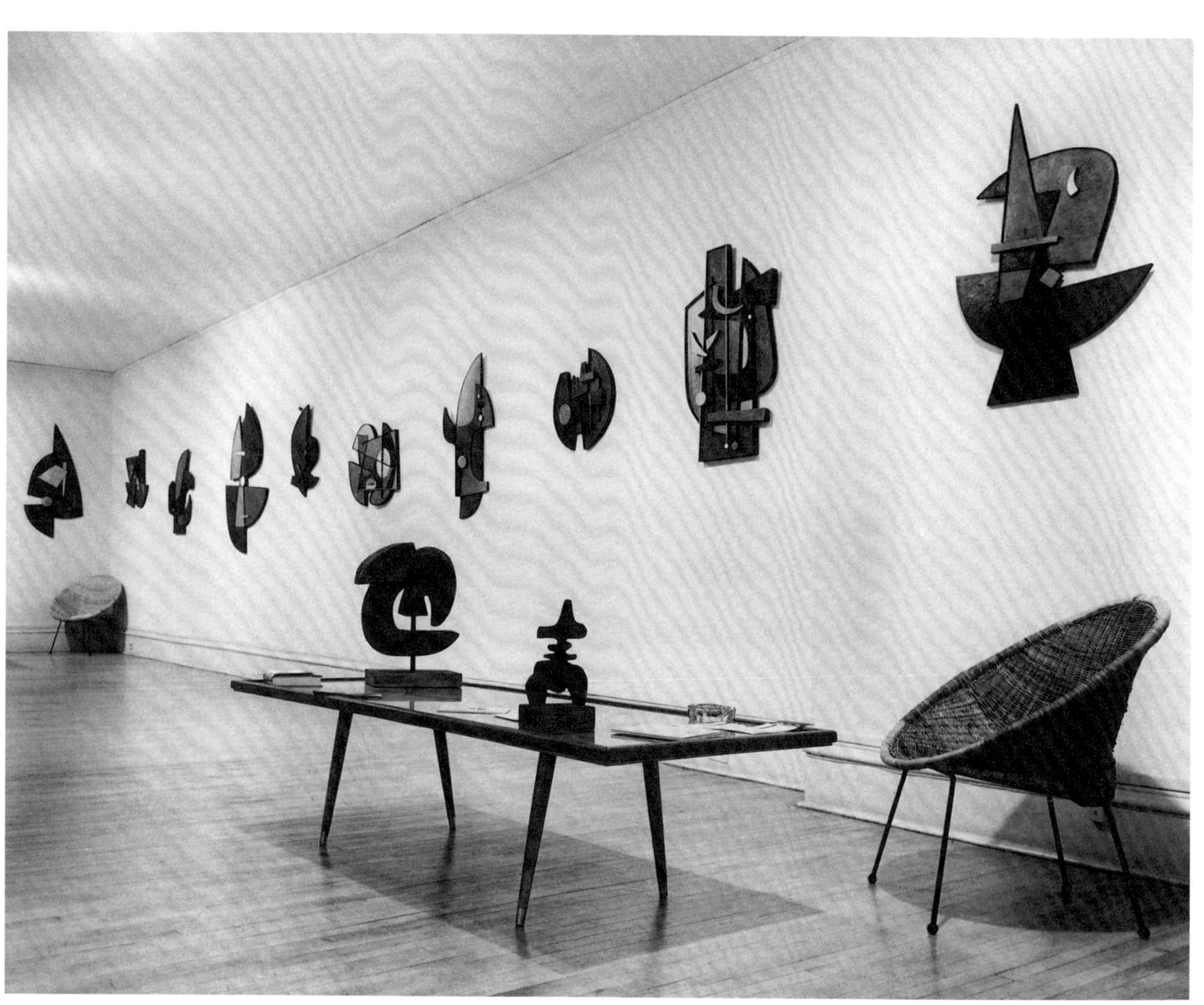

28 Etrog's exhibition of painted constructions at Gallery Moos, Toronto, 1959

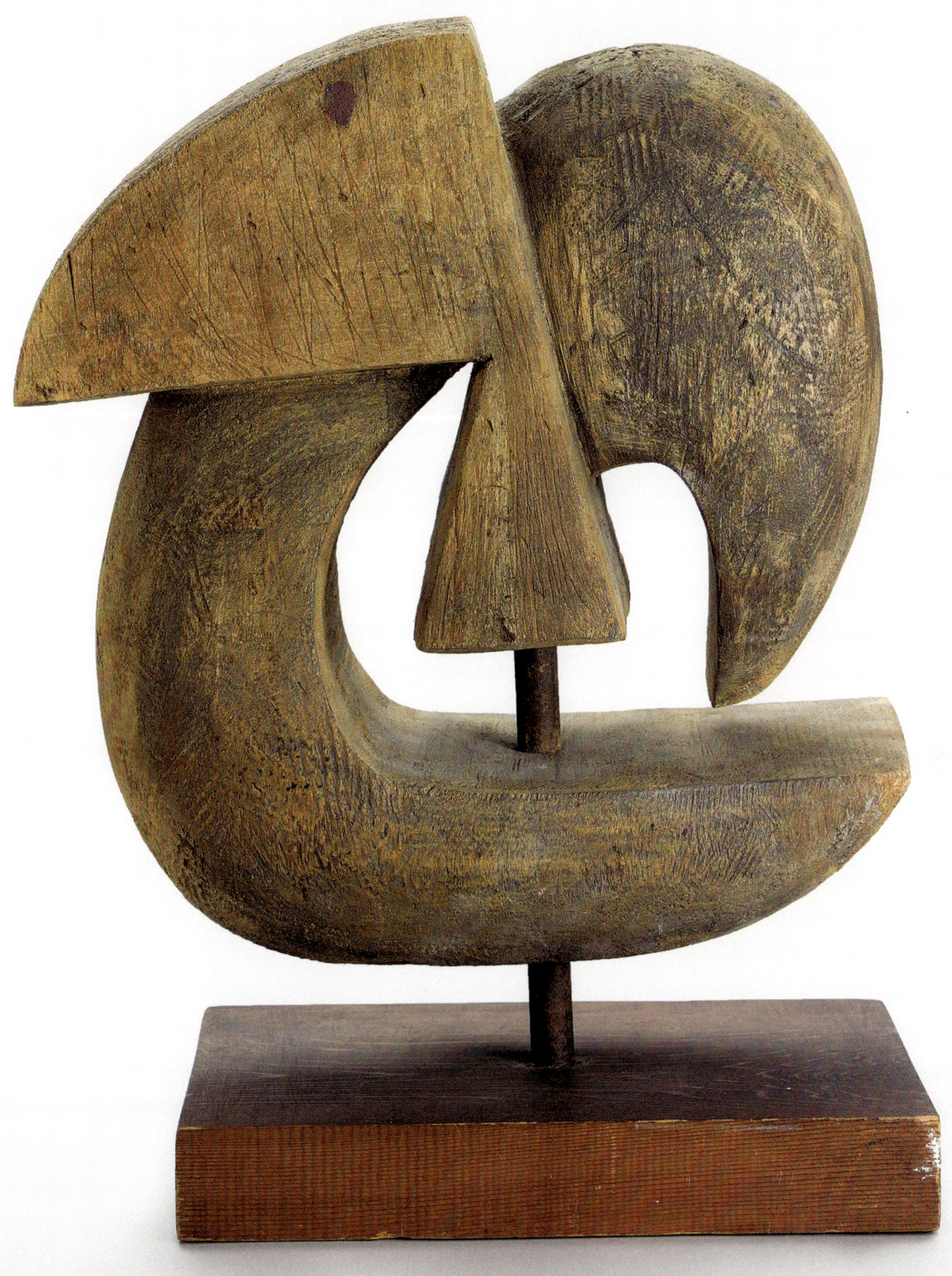

The Golem, 1959

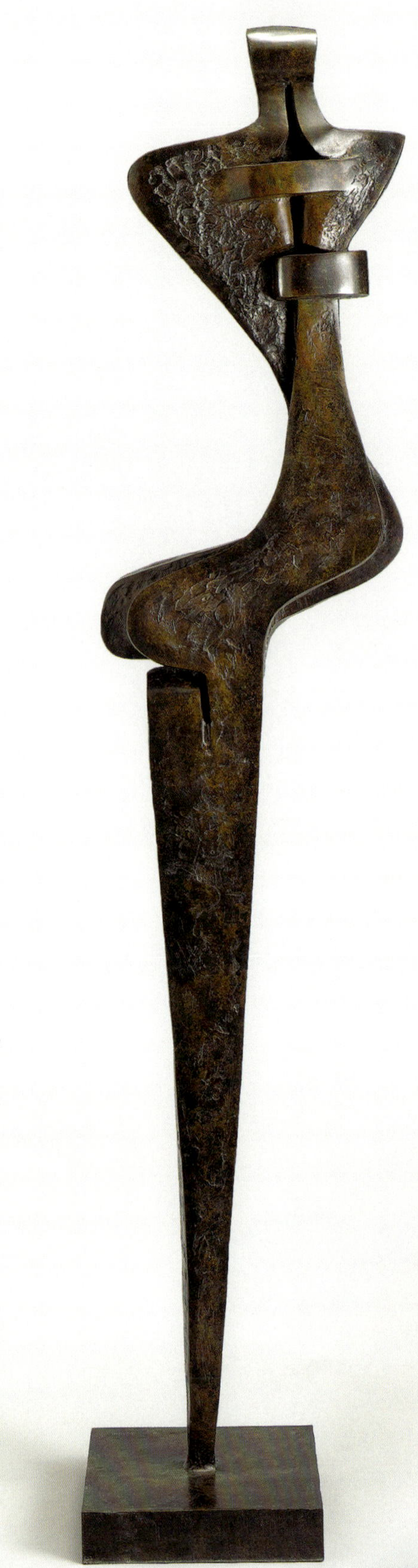

30 The Jester, 1962–1964

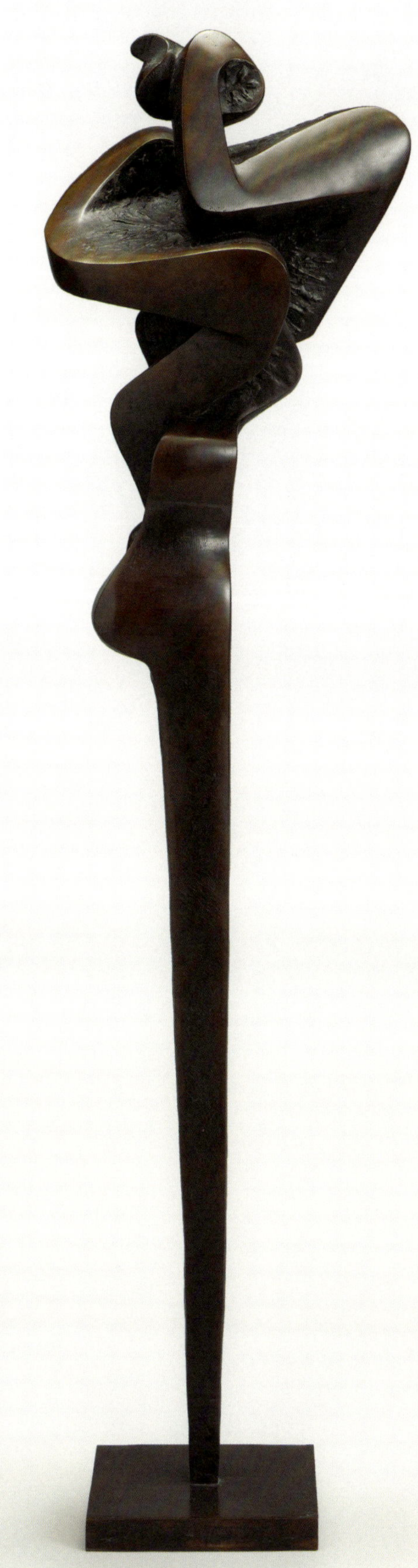

Ritual Dancer, 1960–1962

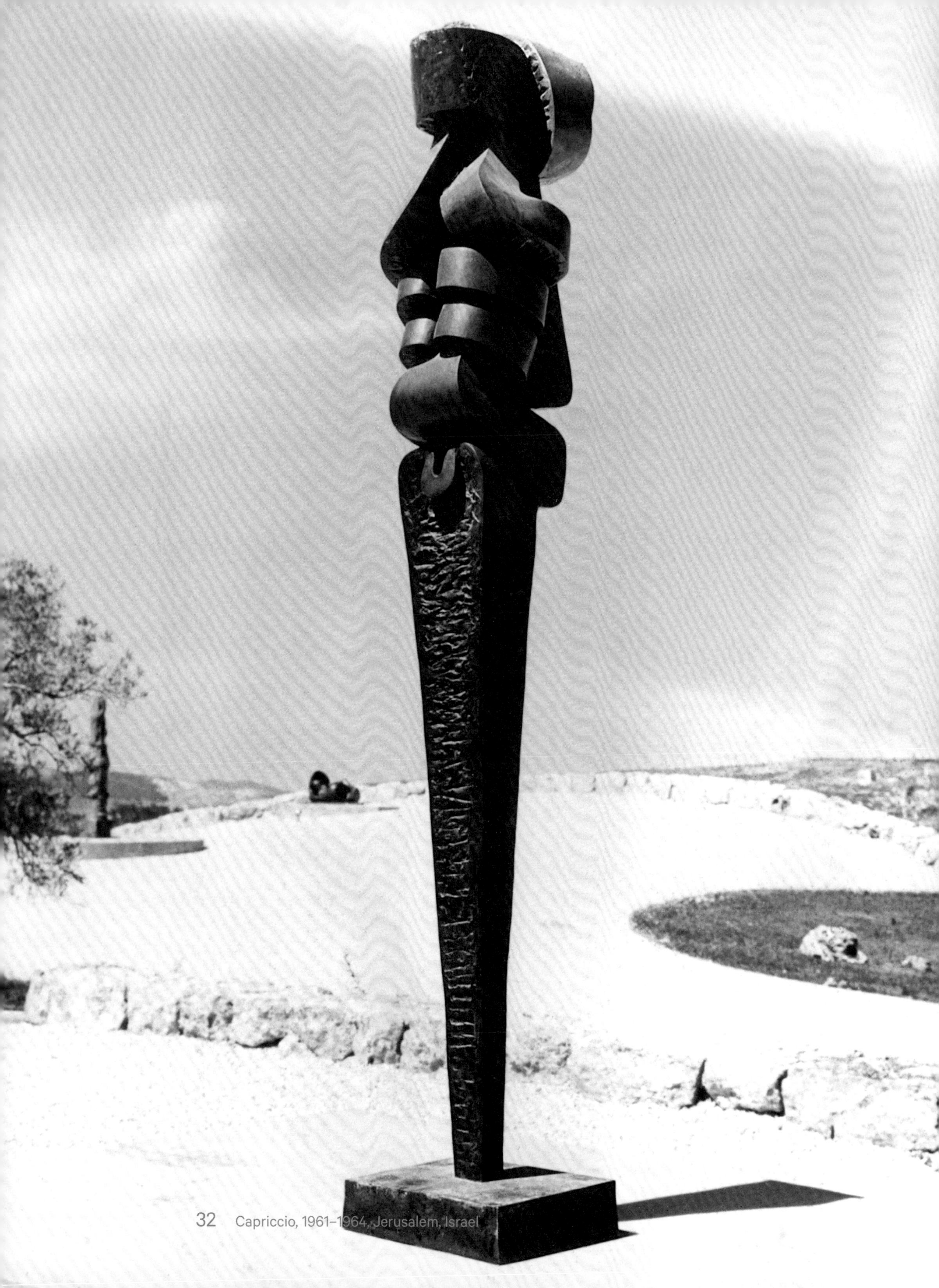

32 Capriccio, 1961–1964, Jerusalem, Israel

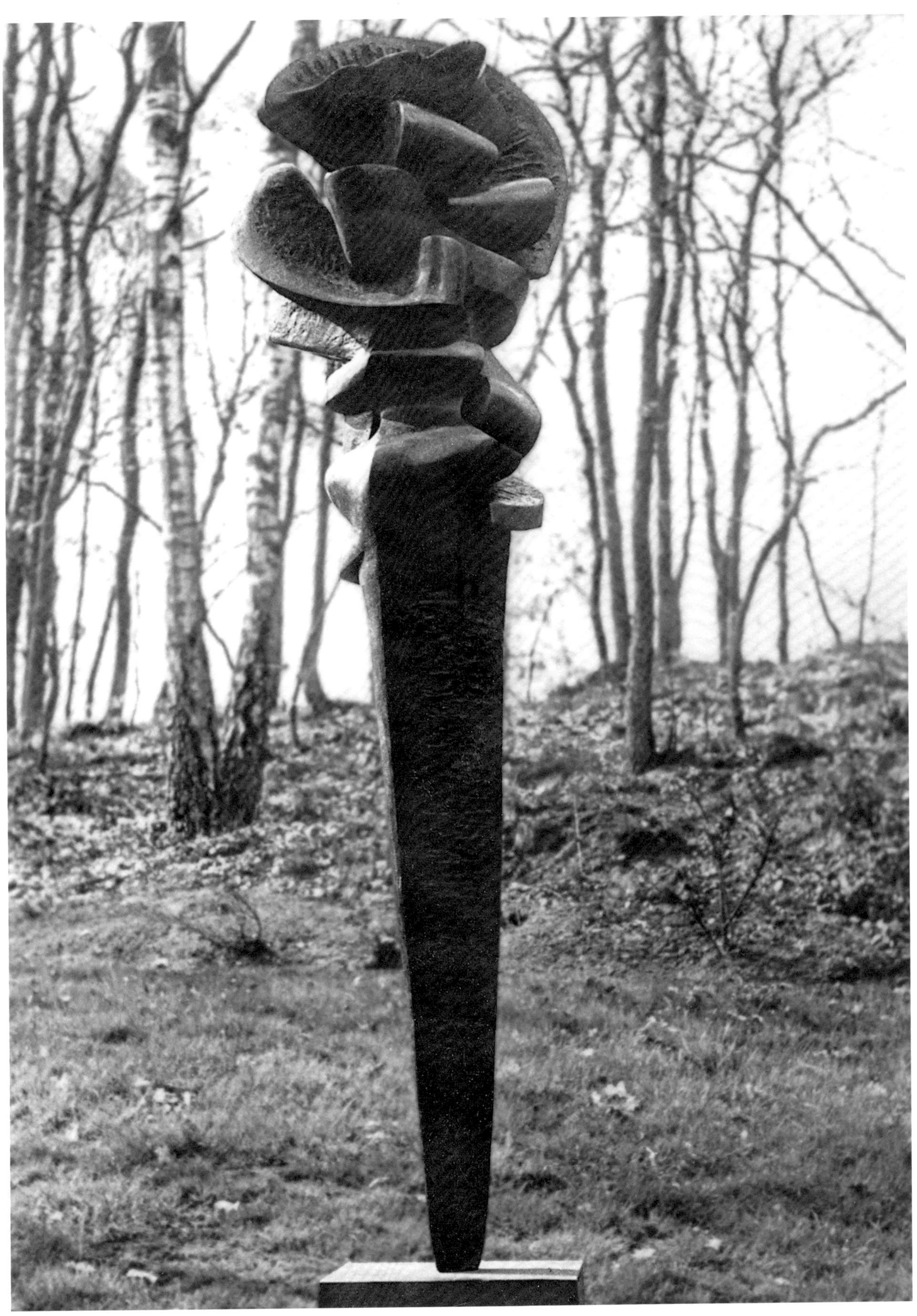

Complexes of a Young Lady, 1965, Otterlo, Netherlands

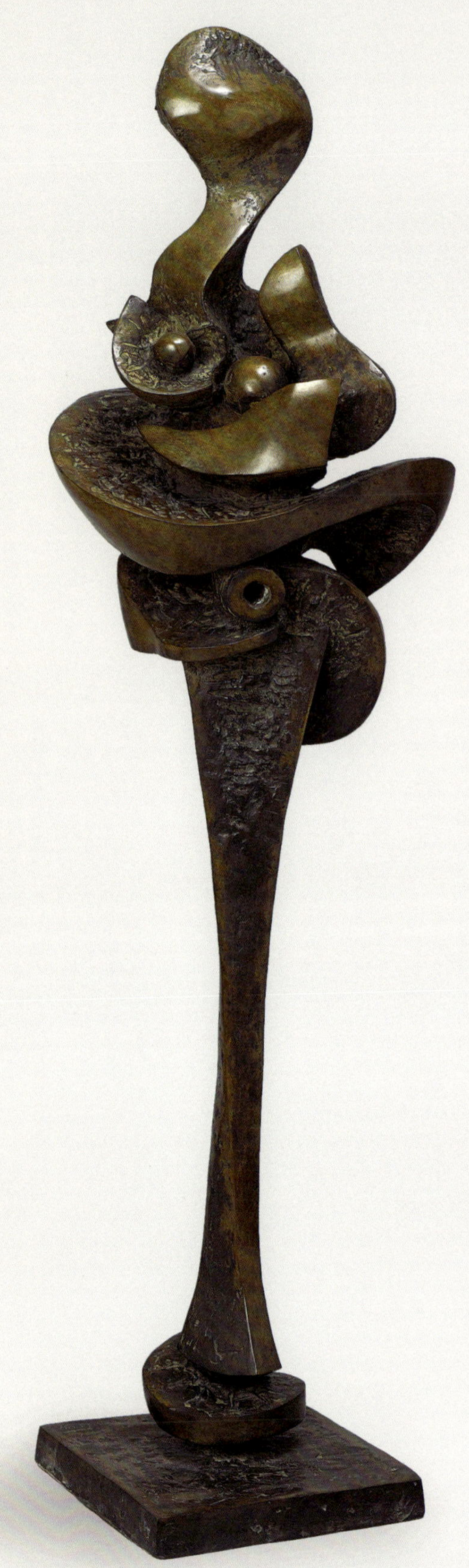

34 Blossom, 1960–1961

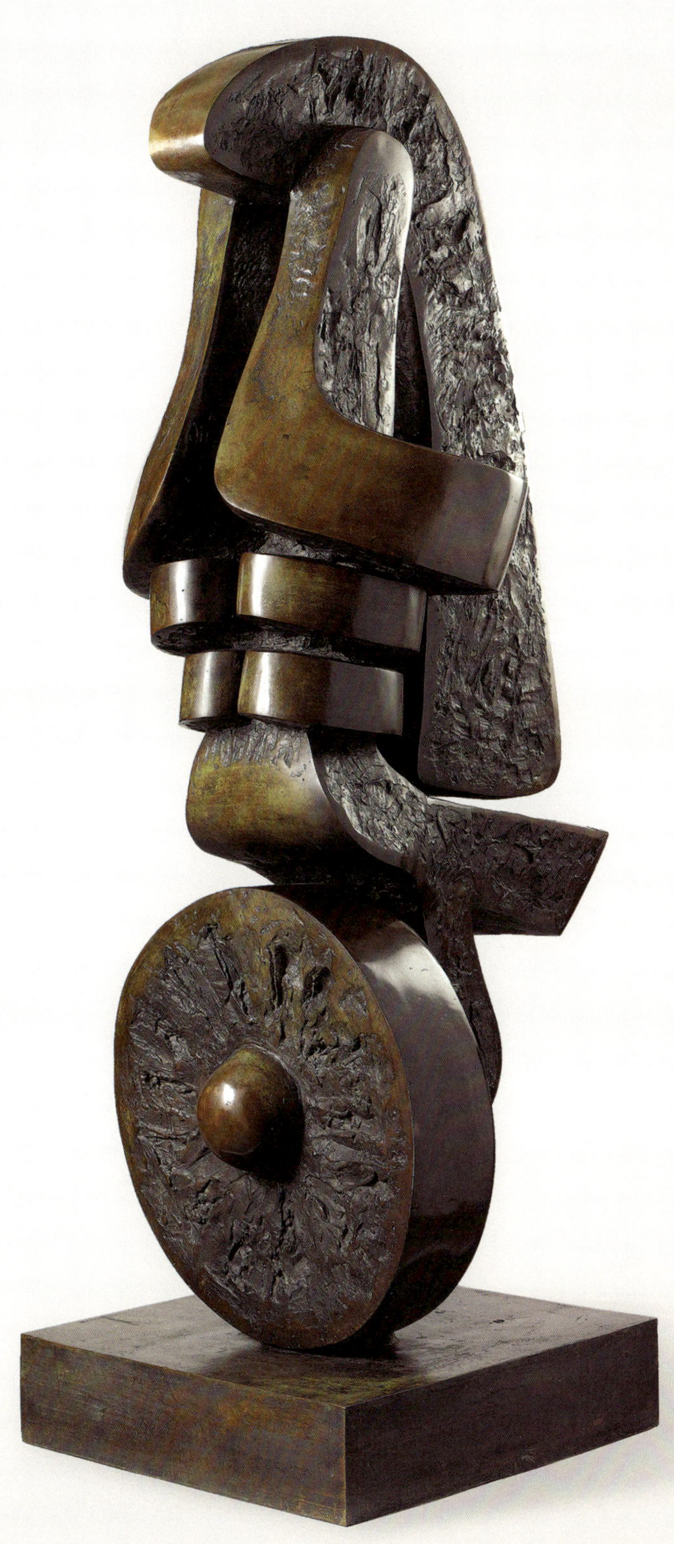

Sunbird II, 1962–1964

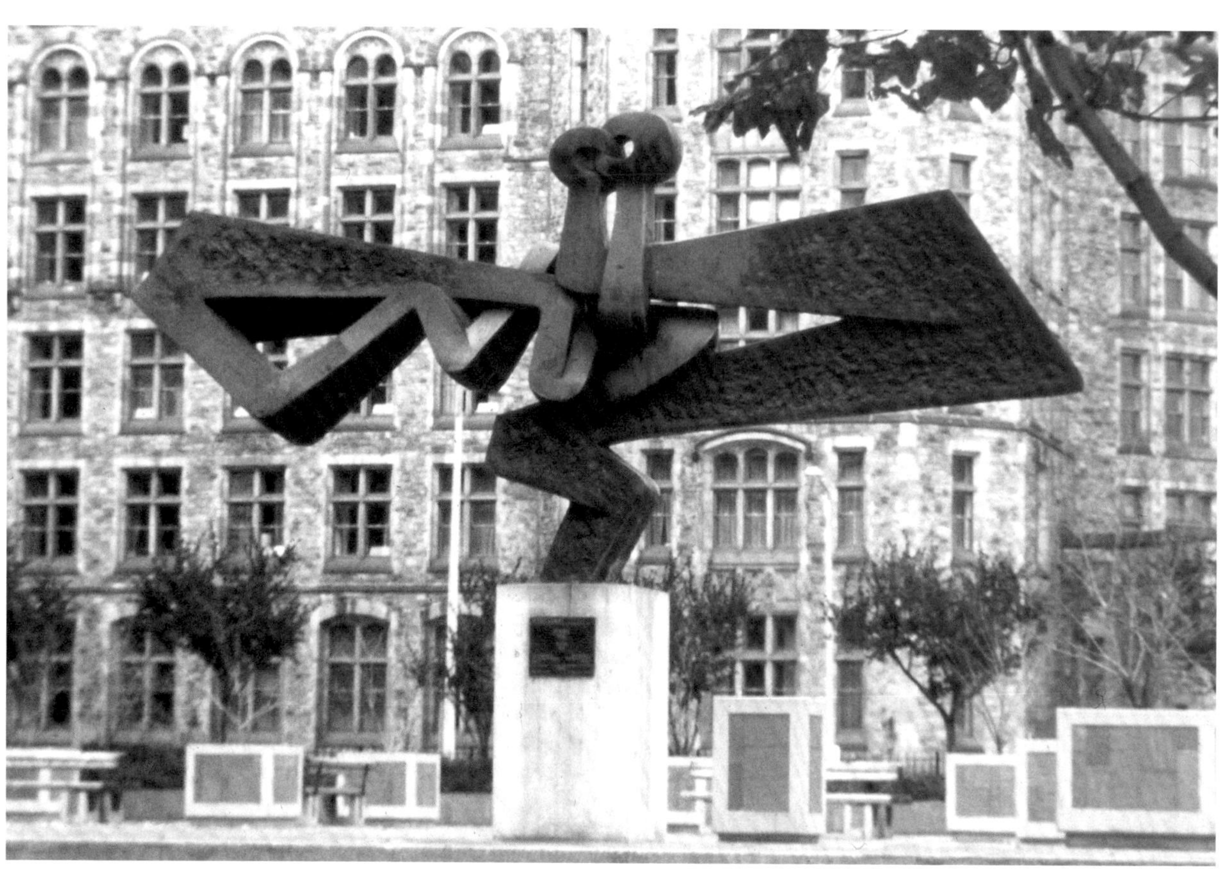

 Flight No. 1, 1963–1964, Ottawa

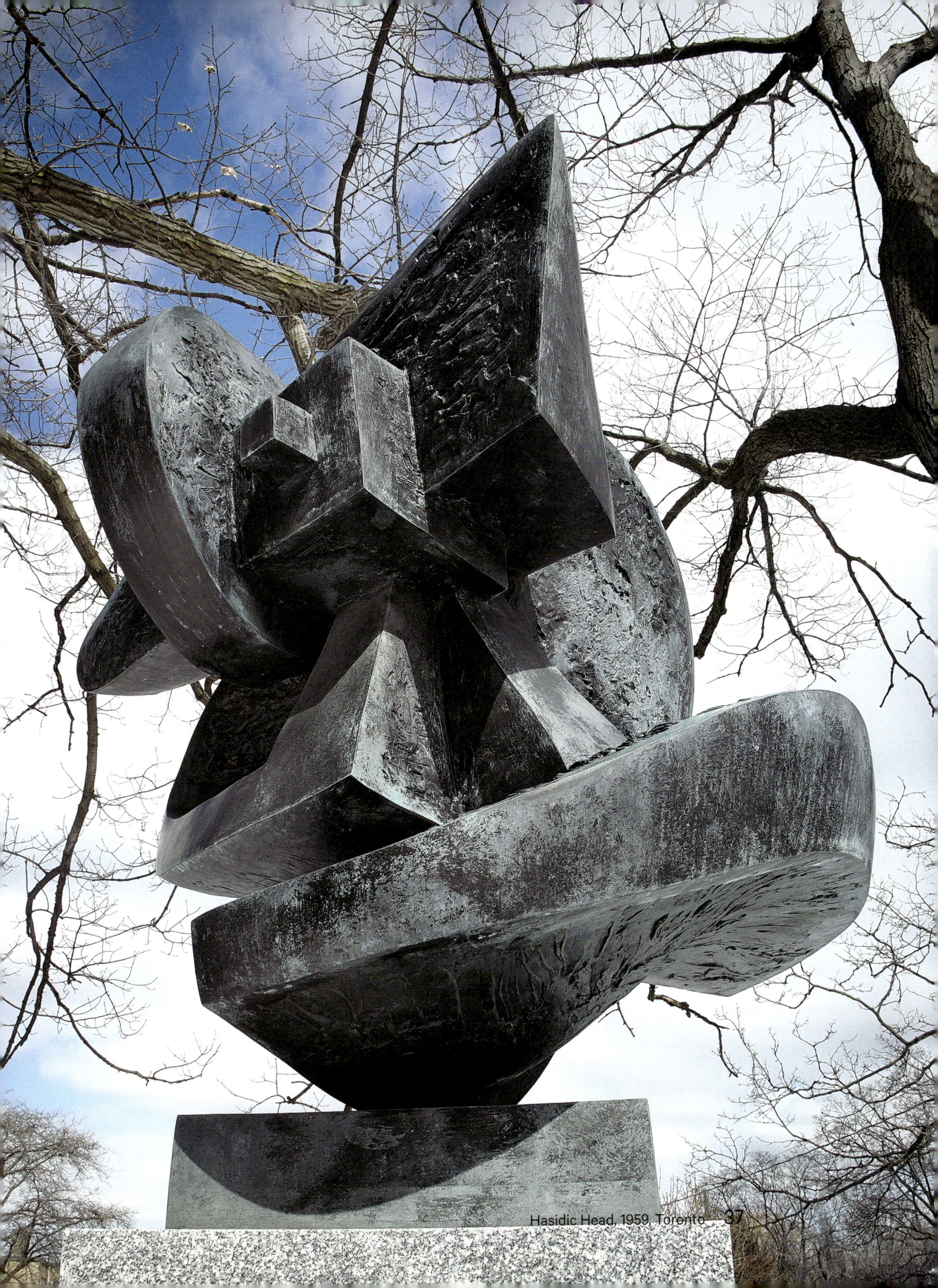

Hasidic Head, 1959, Toronto

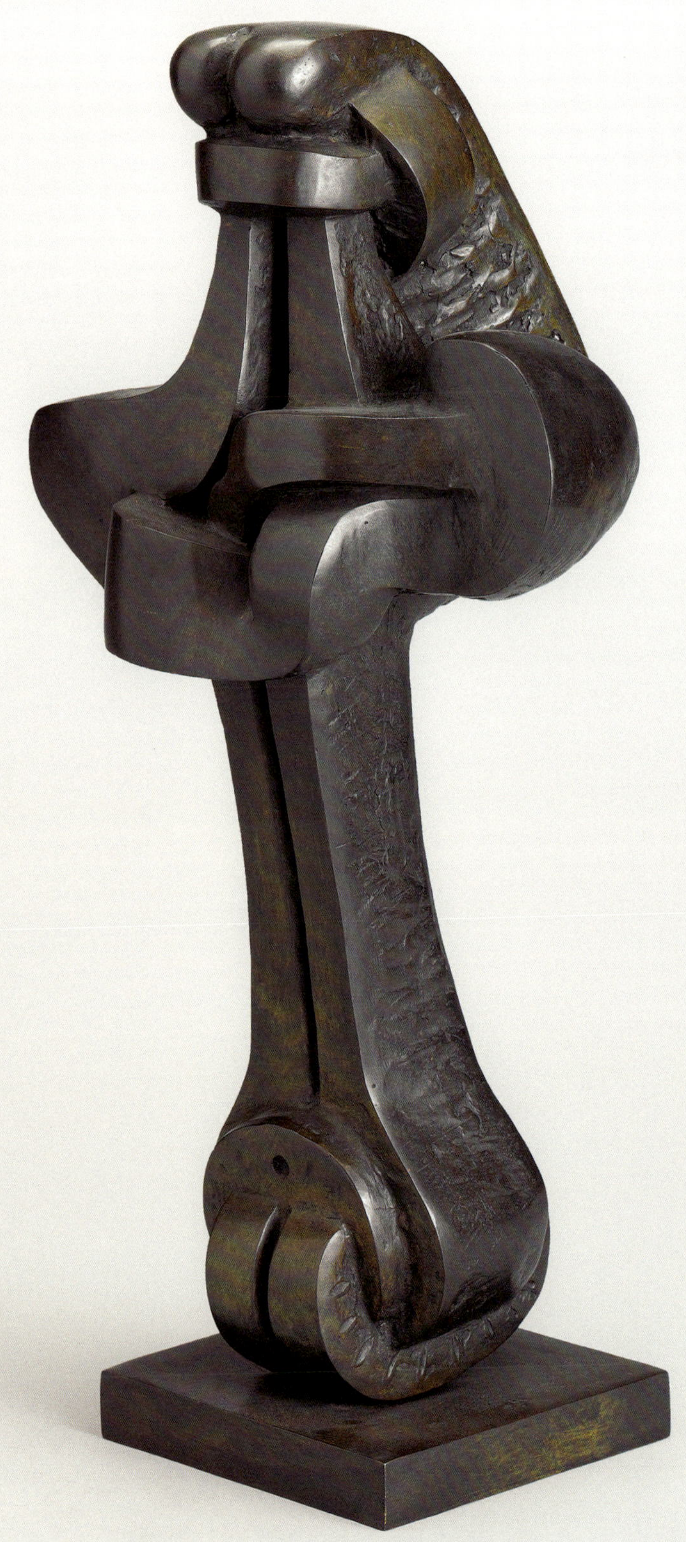

38 Mother and Child, 1962–1964

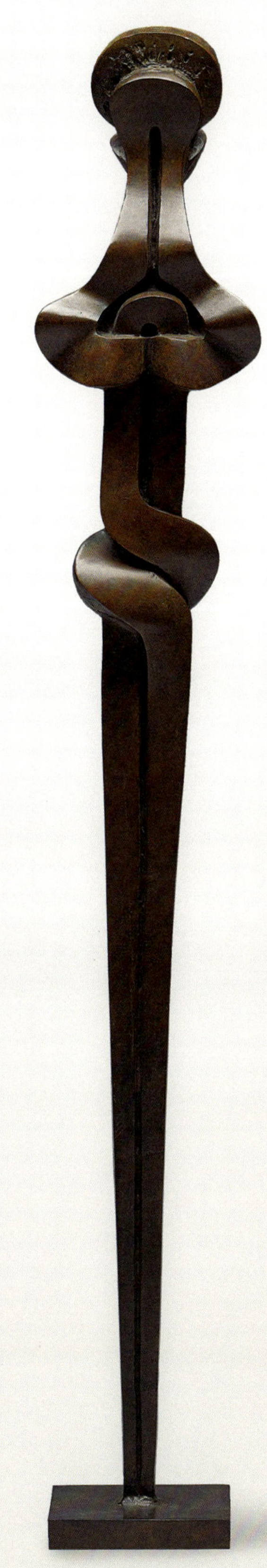

Standing Figure (Madonna), 1962–1964

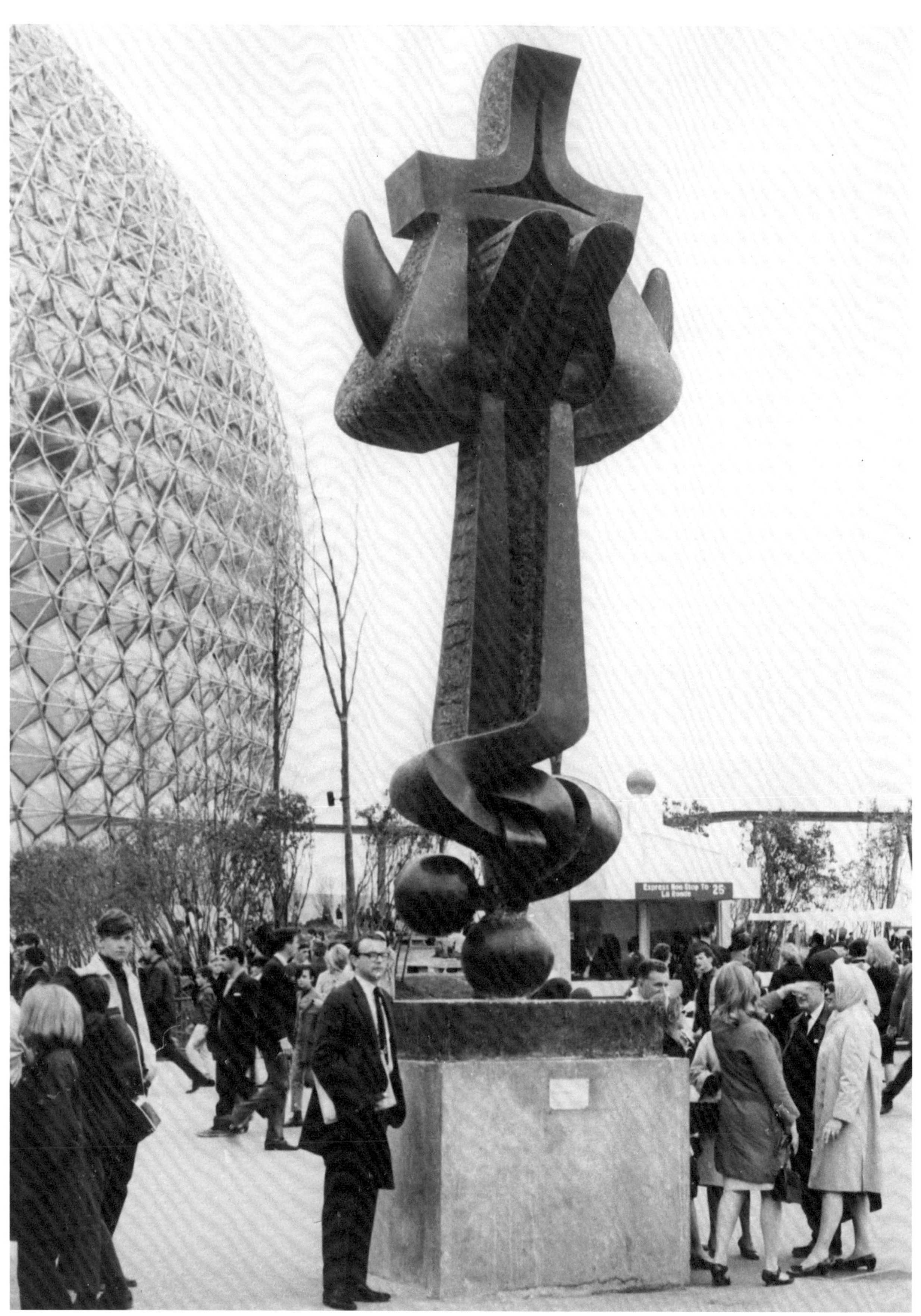

 Moses, 1964, Montreal

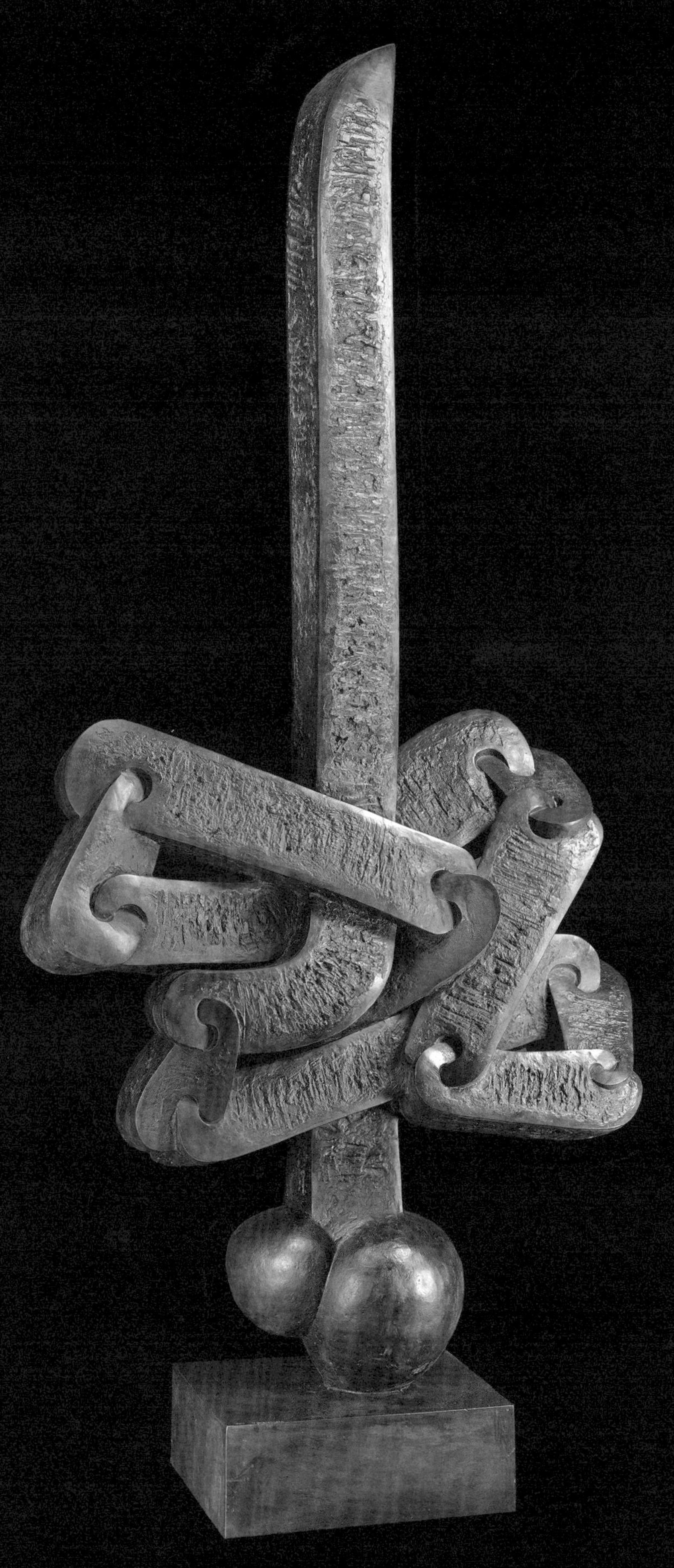

Pulcinella, 1964–1966

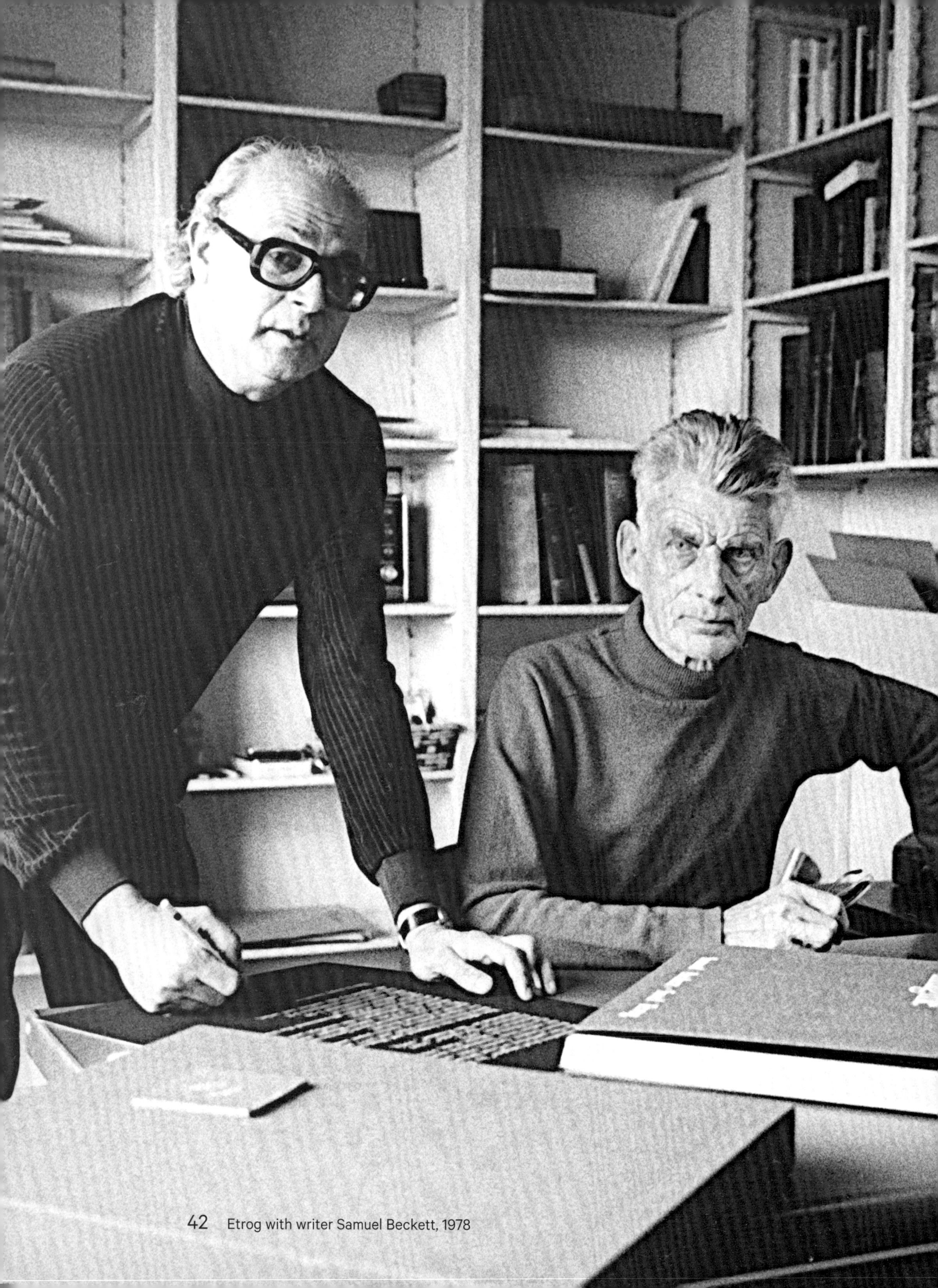

 Etrog with writer Samuel Beckett, 1978

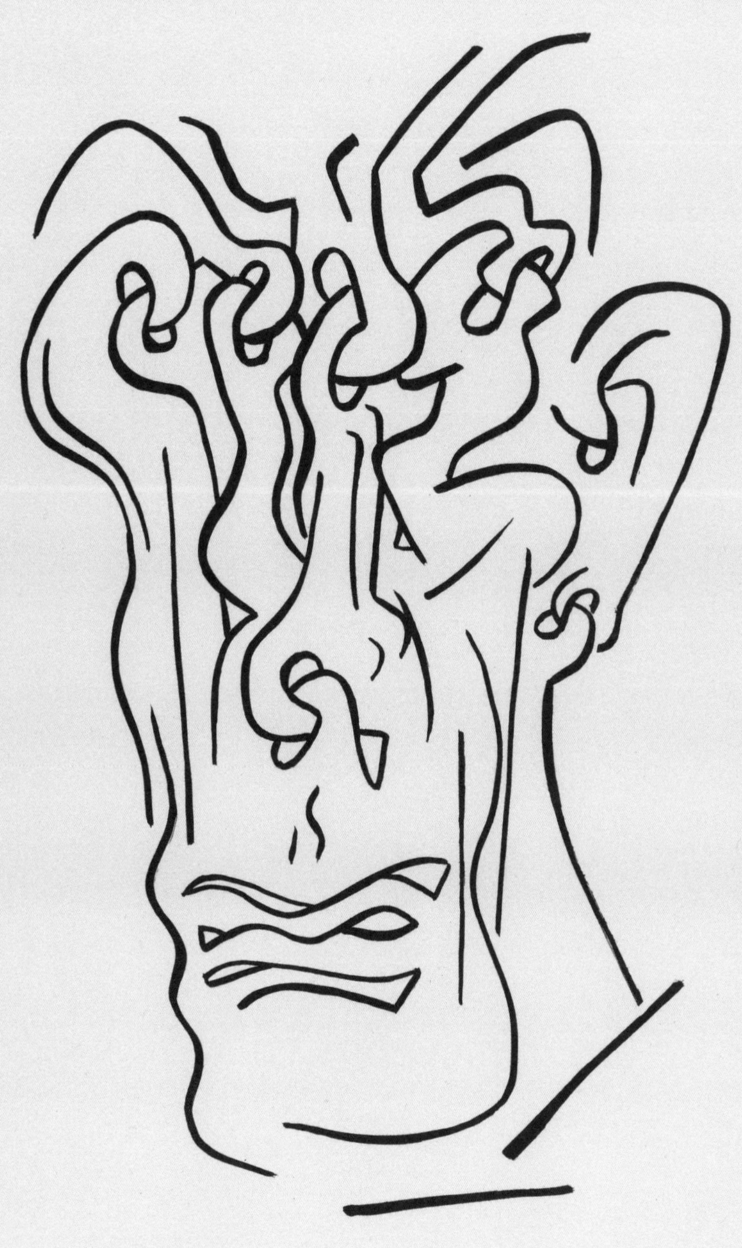

No trace anywhere
of life, you say, pah,
no difficulty there,
imagination not dead
yet, yes, dead, good,
imagination dead
imagine.

No trace anywhere
of life, you say, pah,
no difficulty there,
imagination not dead
yet, yes, dead, good,
imagination dead
imagine.

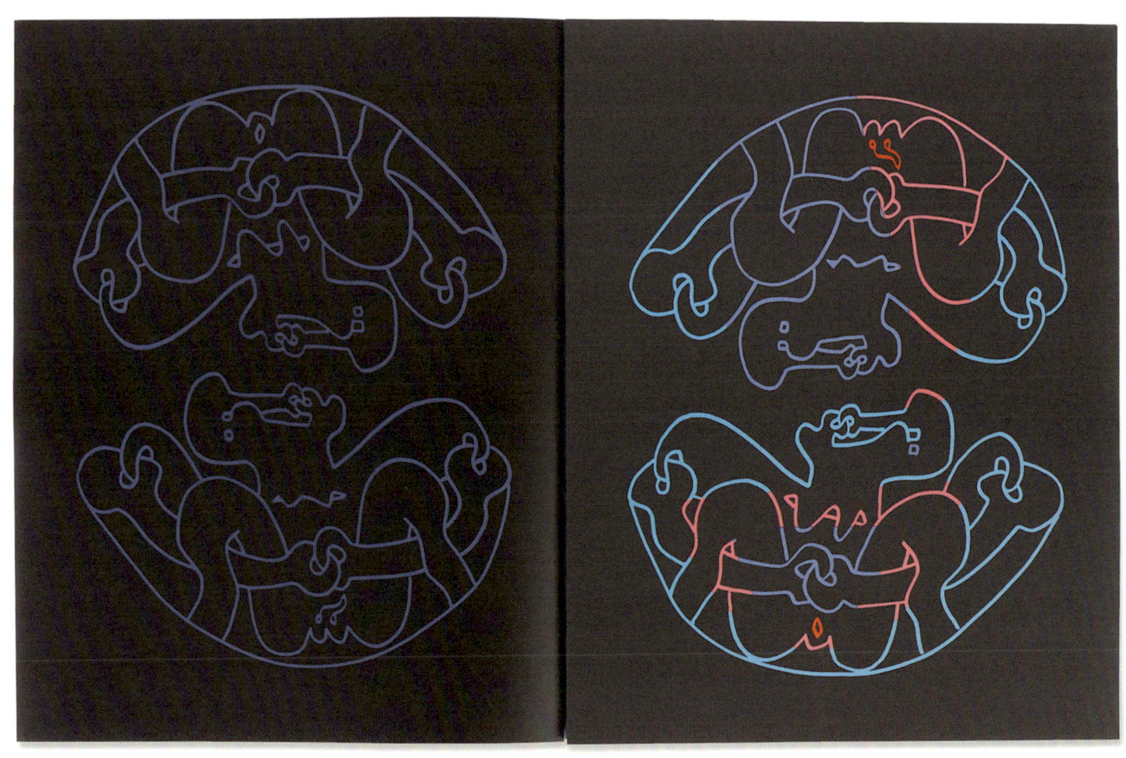

all vibrates, ground, wall, vault,
bodies, ashen or leaden or between
the two, as may be. But on the
whole, experience shows, such
uncertain passage is not common.
And most often, when the light
begins to fail, and along with it the
heat, the movement continues
unbroken until, in the space of
some twenty seconds, pitch black is
reached and at the same instant
say freezing-point. Same remark
for the reverse movement, towards
heat and whiteness. Next most

all vibrates, ground, wall, vault,
bodies, ashen or leaden or between
the two, as may be. But on the
whole, experience shows, such
uncertain passage is not common.
And most often, when the light
begins to fail, and along with it the
heat, the movement continues
unbroken until, in the space of
some twenty seconds, pitch black is
reached and at the same instant
say freezing-point. Same remark
for the reverse movement, towards
heat and whiteness. Next most

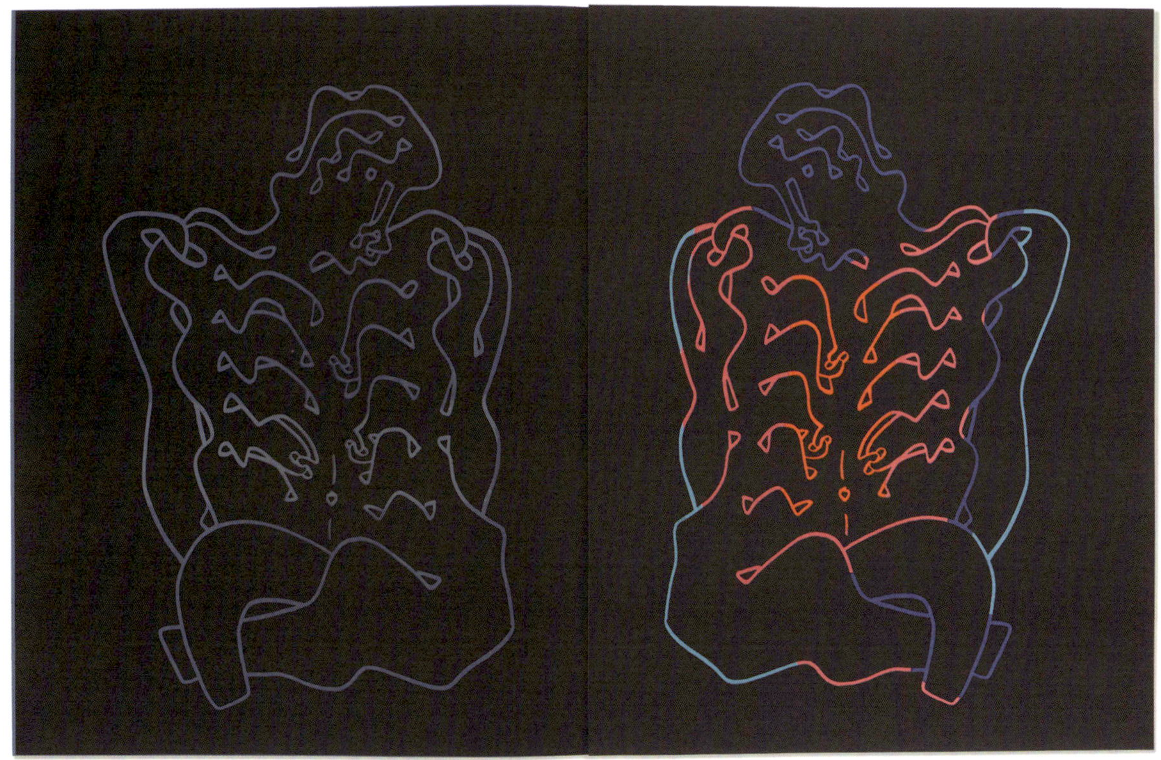

Mais
celles
qui
n'existent
pas
n'ont pas
de
nom.

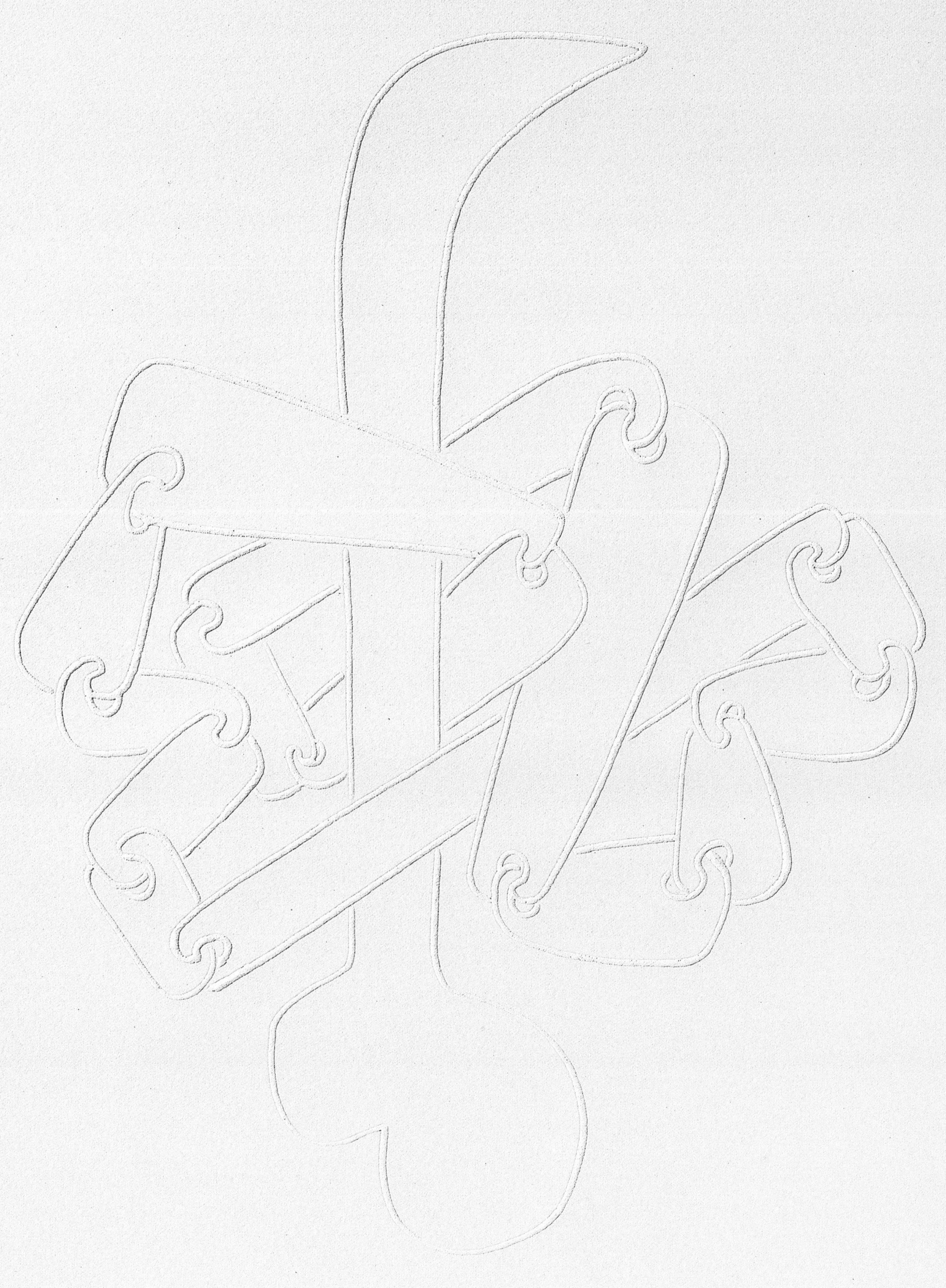

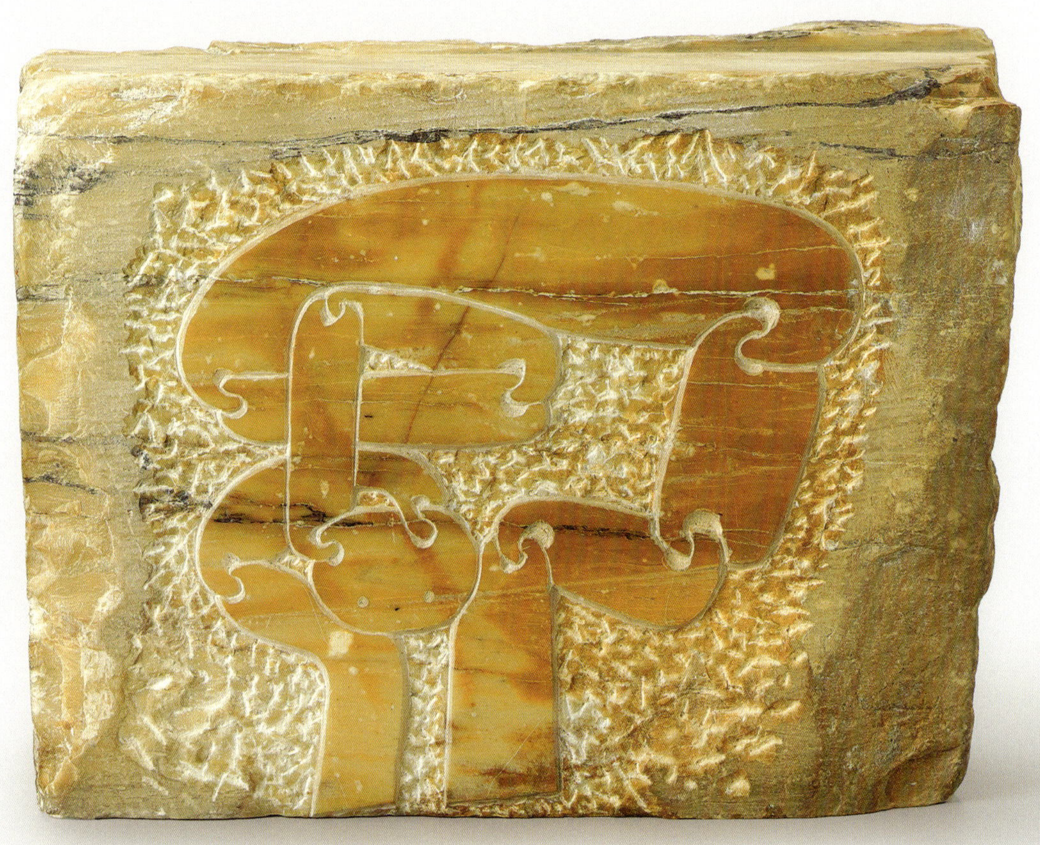

48 Giallo di Sienna, 1966–1967

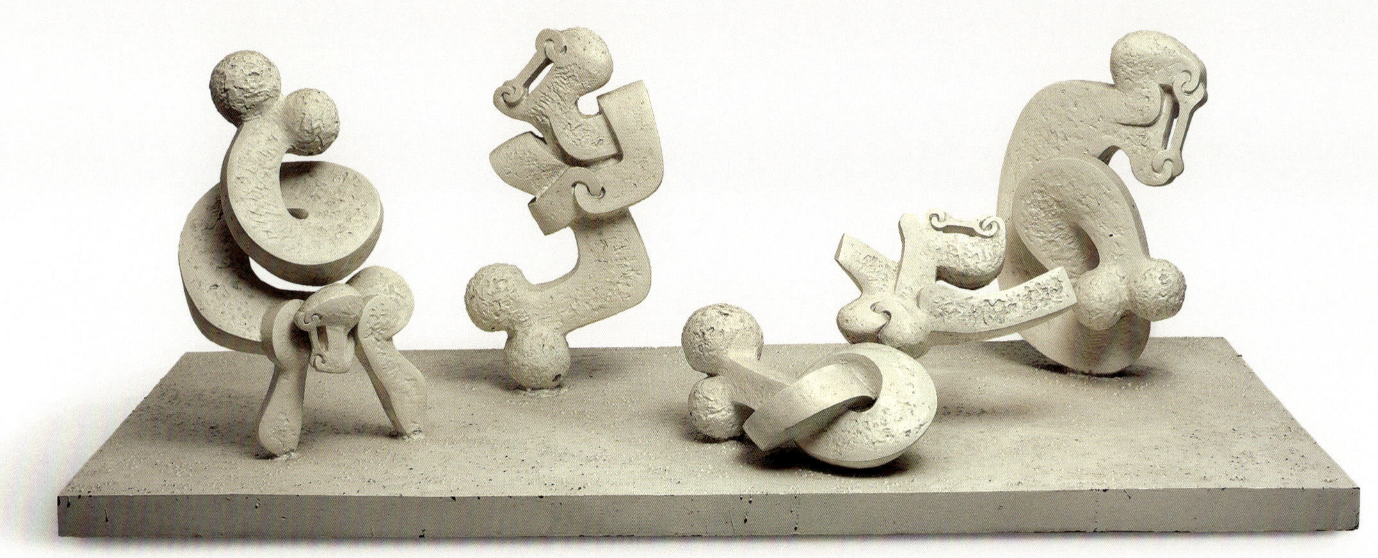

Quartet, 1969

GALLERIES

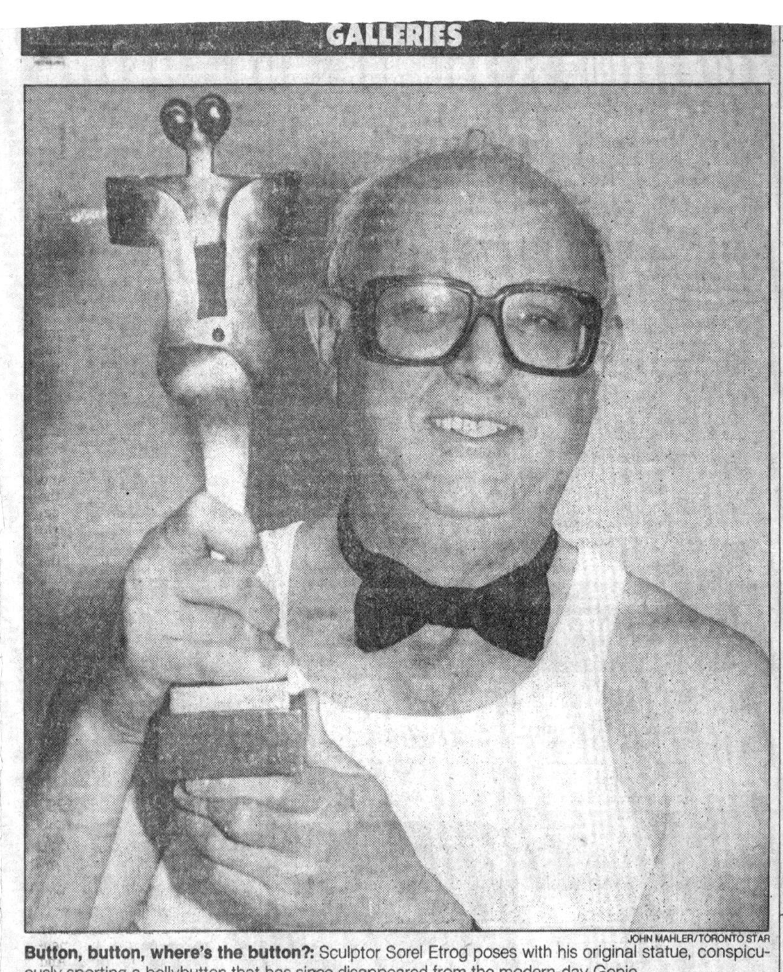

JOHN MAHLER/TORONTO STAR

Button, button, where's the button?: Sculptor Sorel Etrog poses with his original statue, conspicuously sporting a bellybutton that has since disappeared from the modern-day Genie.

Sorry, Oscar, but art award goes to your cousin Genie

Continued from page D1

at the pinnacle of his career. He was exhibiting regularly in Europe and North America and was already in the collections of many major international museums, including the Guggenheim and the Museum of Modern Art in New York.

Oscar, on the other hand, sprung

CHRISTOPHER HUME

Art

awards officials failed to notify him about the change. He read about it first in this newspaper.

Etrog, the Hebrew word for a bitter citrus fruit used by Jews in the Sukkoth ceremony, was dropped because it hadn't caught on with the public. The academy wanted something "meaningful, bilingual, catchy and marketable,"

1968: The Etrog is born. 1980: The Etrog is renamed the Genie Award.
2012: RIP…The Genie Awards become the Canadian Screen Awards.

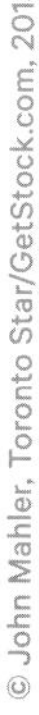

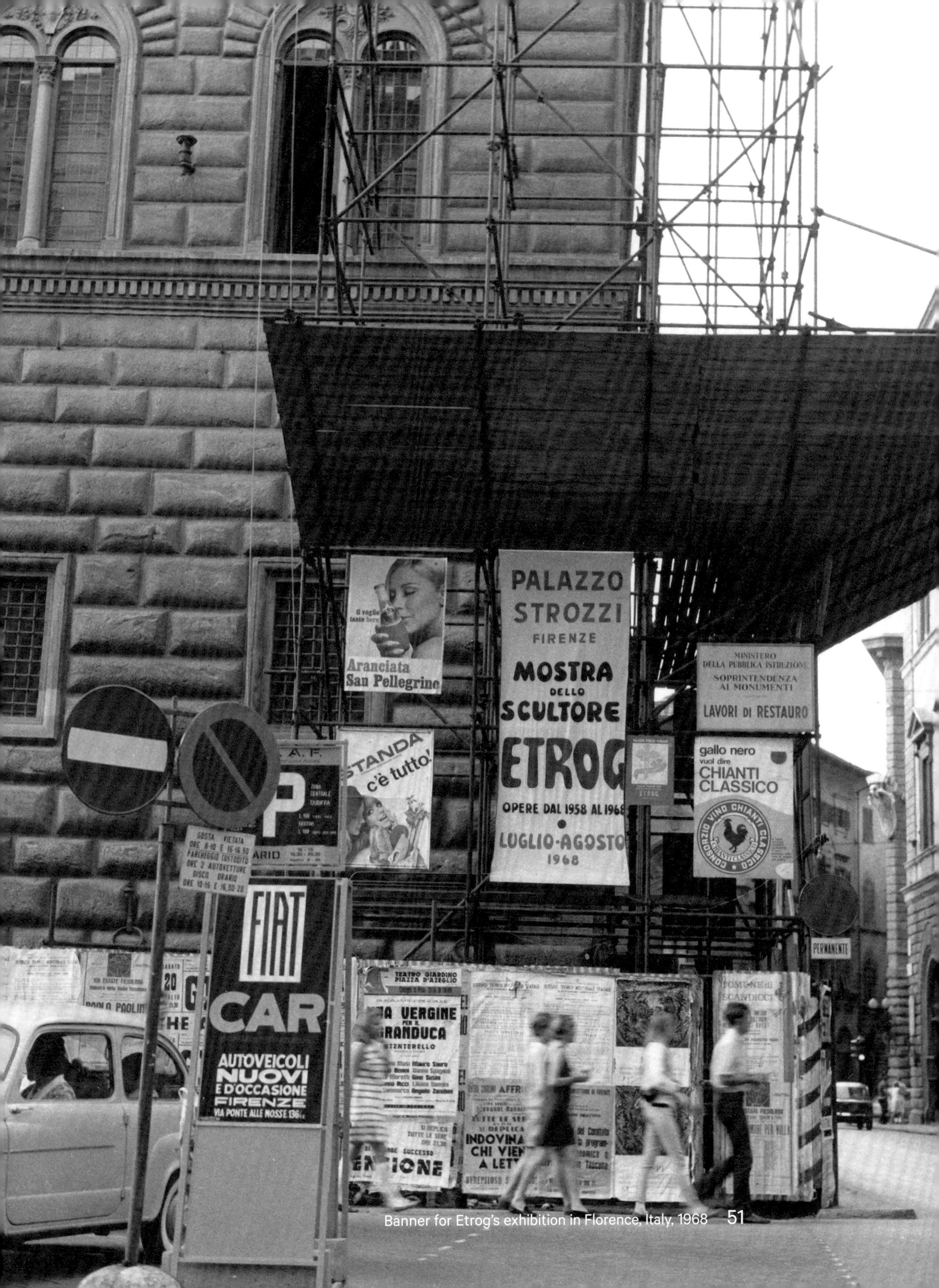

Banner for Etrog's exhibition in Florence, Italy, 1968

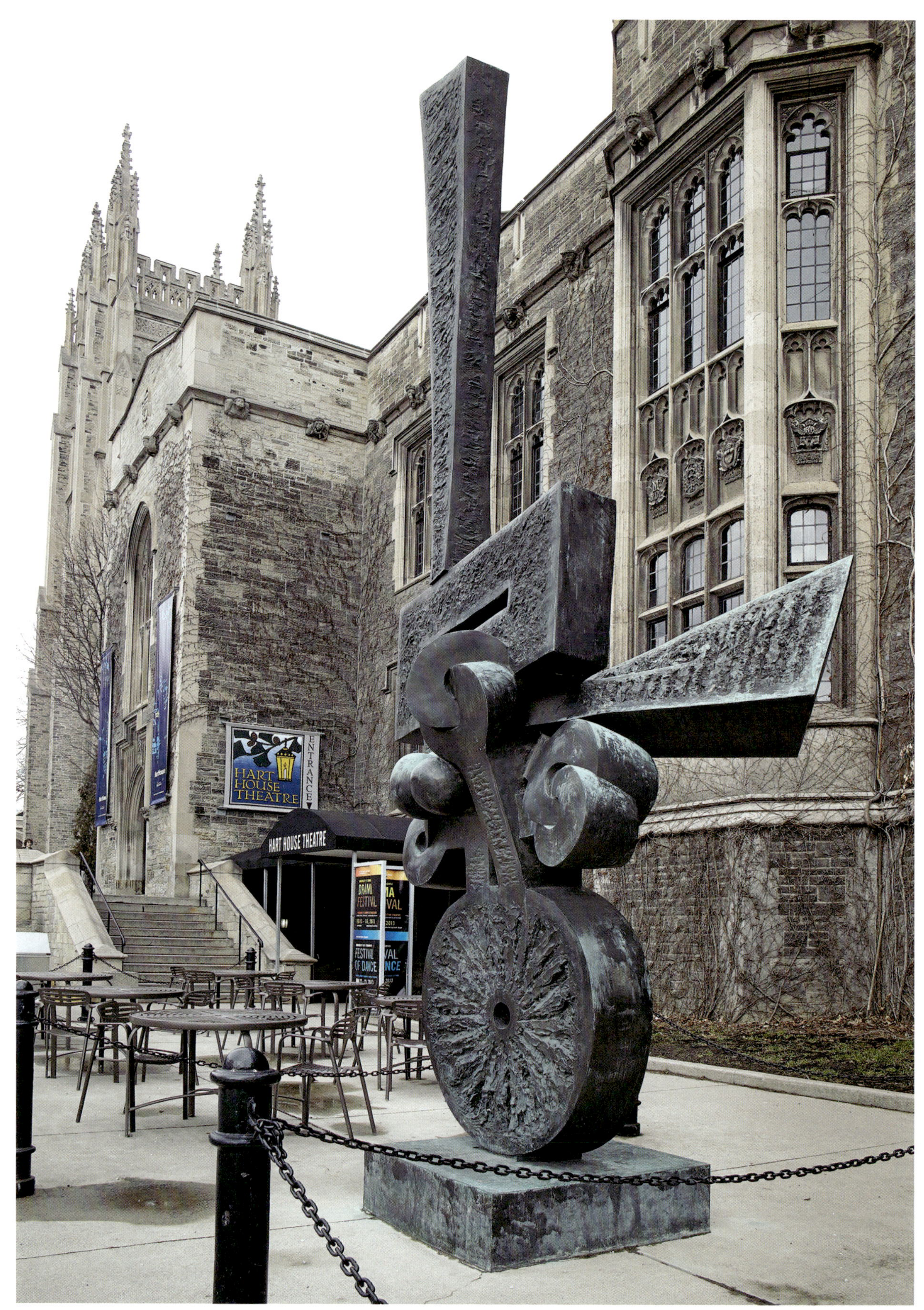

 Survivors Are Not Heroes, 1967, Toronto

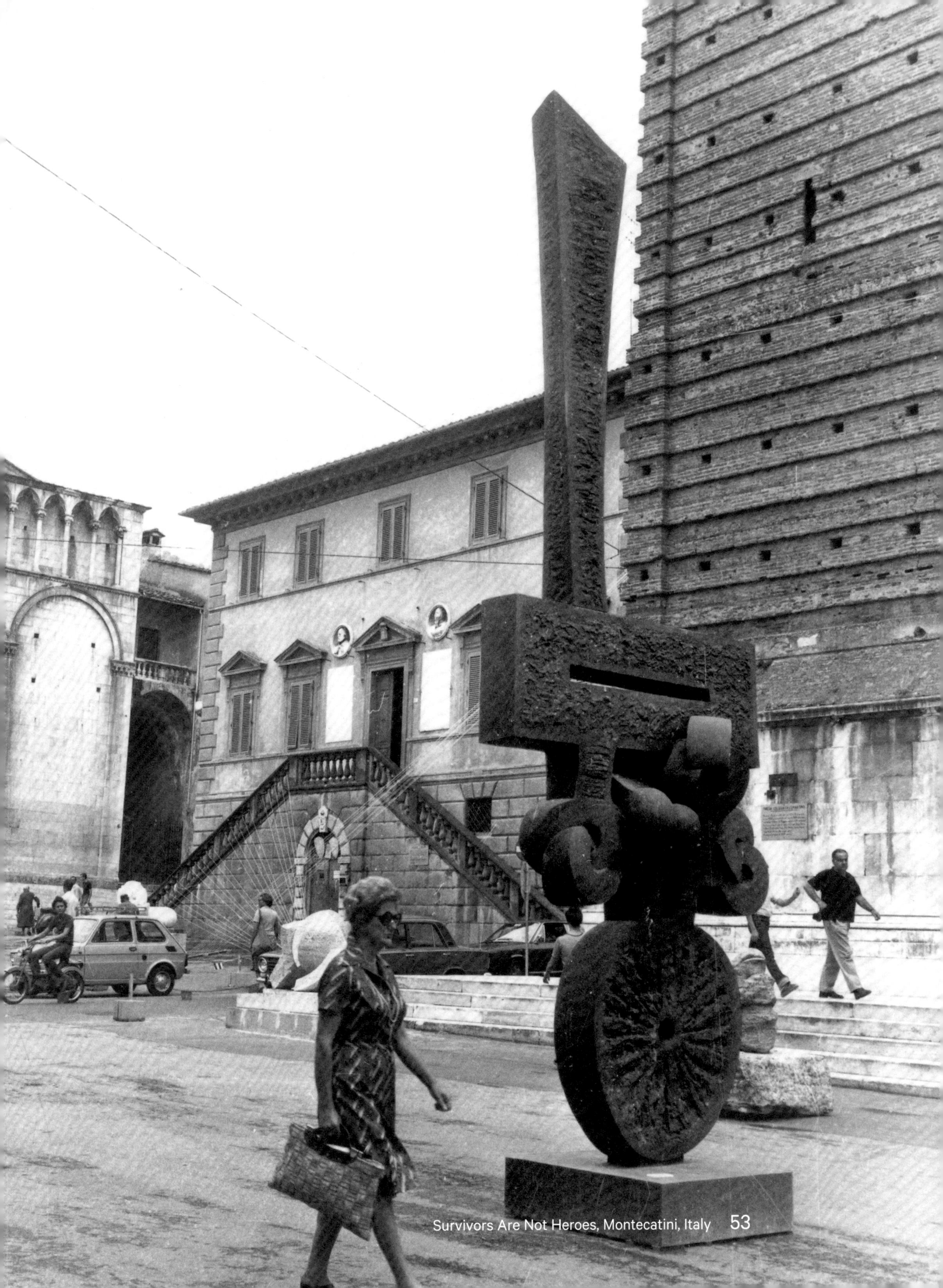

Survivors Are Not Heroes, Montecatini, Italy

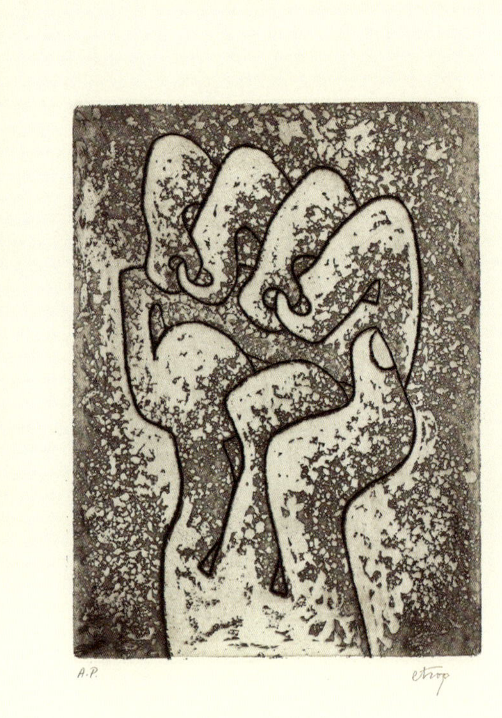

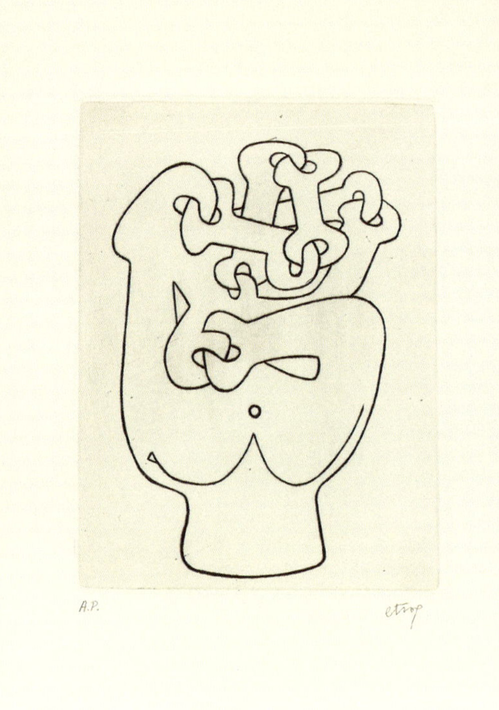

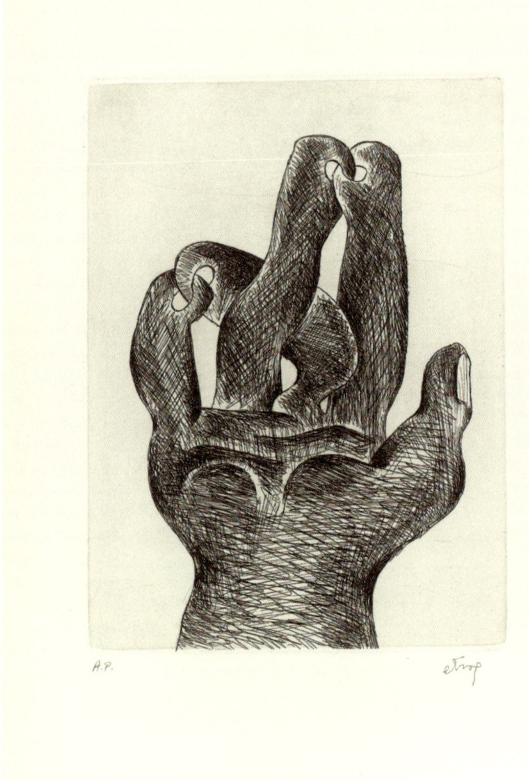

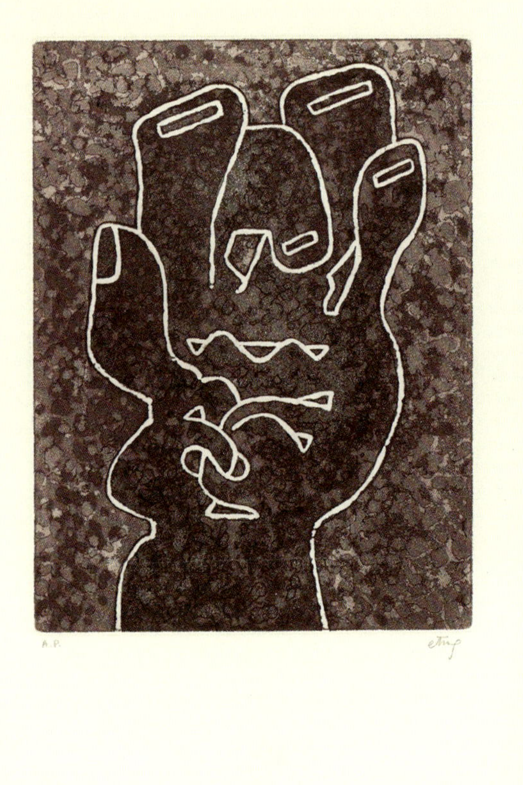

Hand IV, 1969; Hand II, 1969
Hand VII, 1969; Hand VIII, 1969

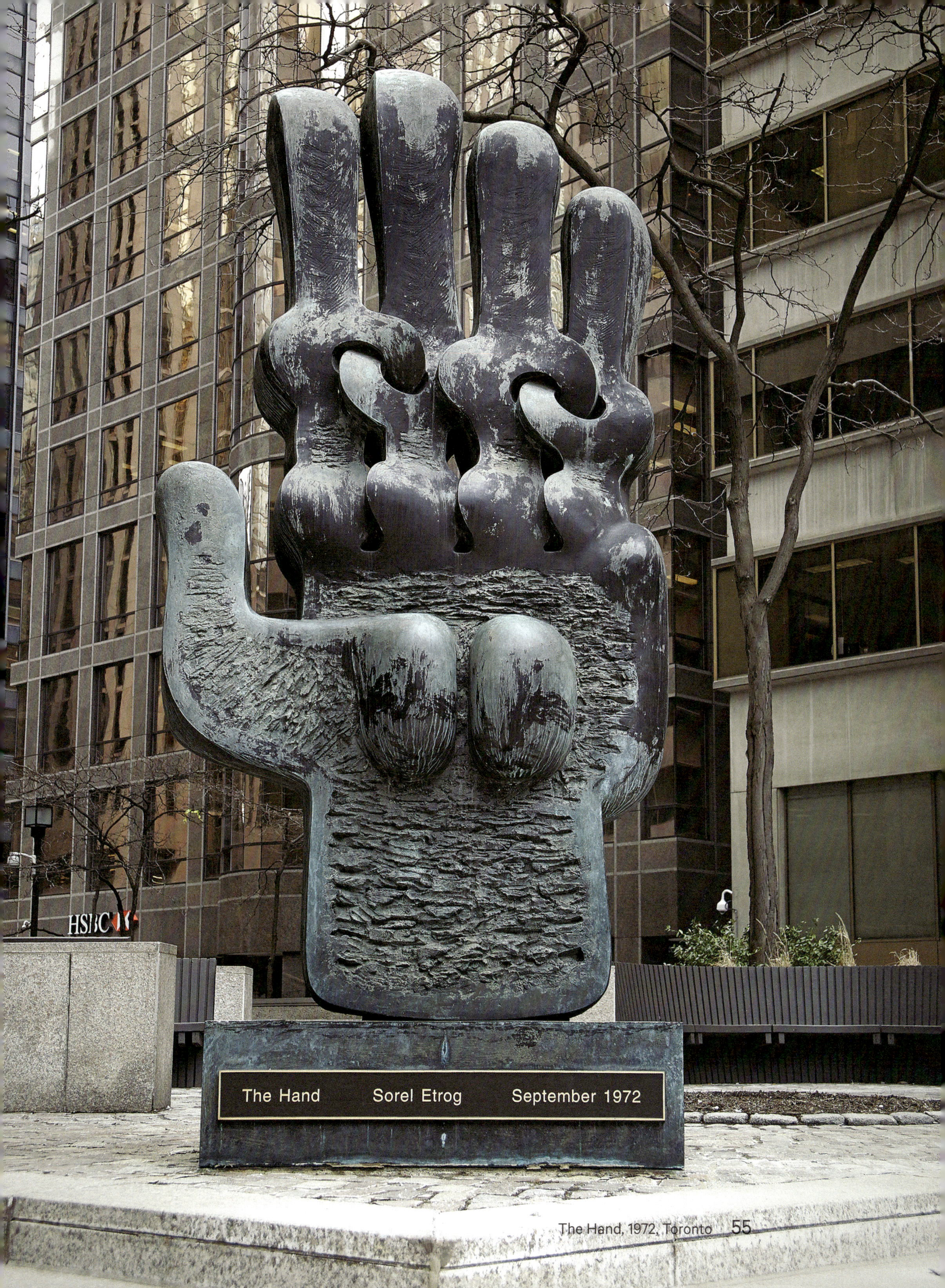

The Hand, 1972, Toronto

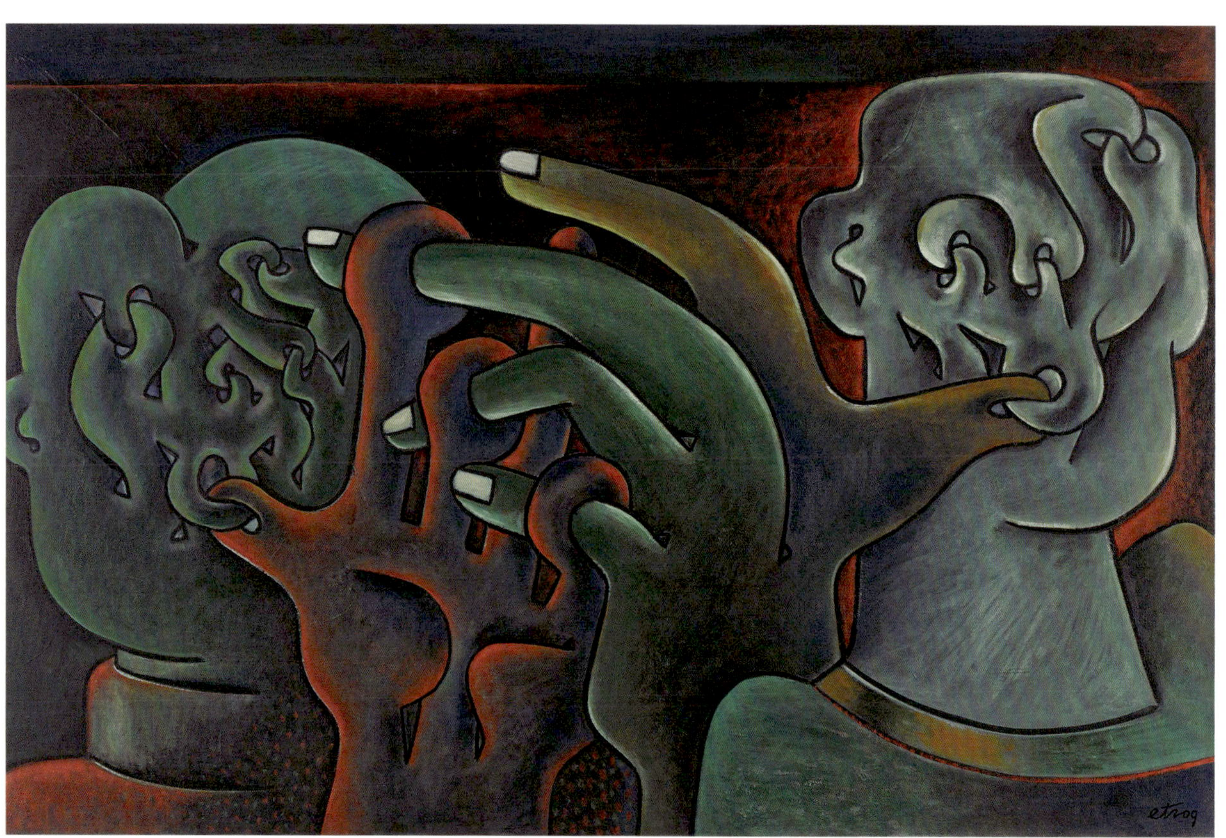

56 Vladimir and Estragon (Waiting for Godot), 1967

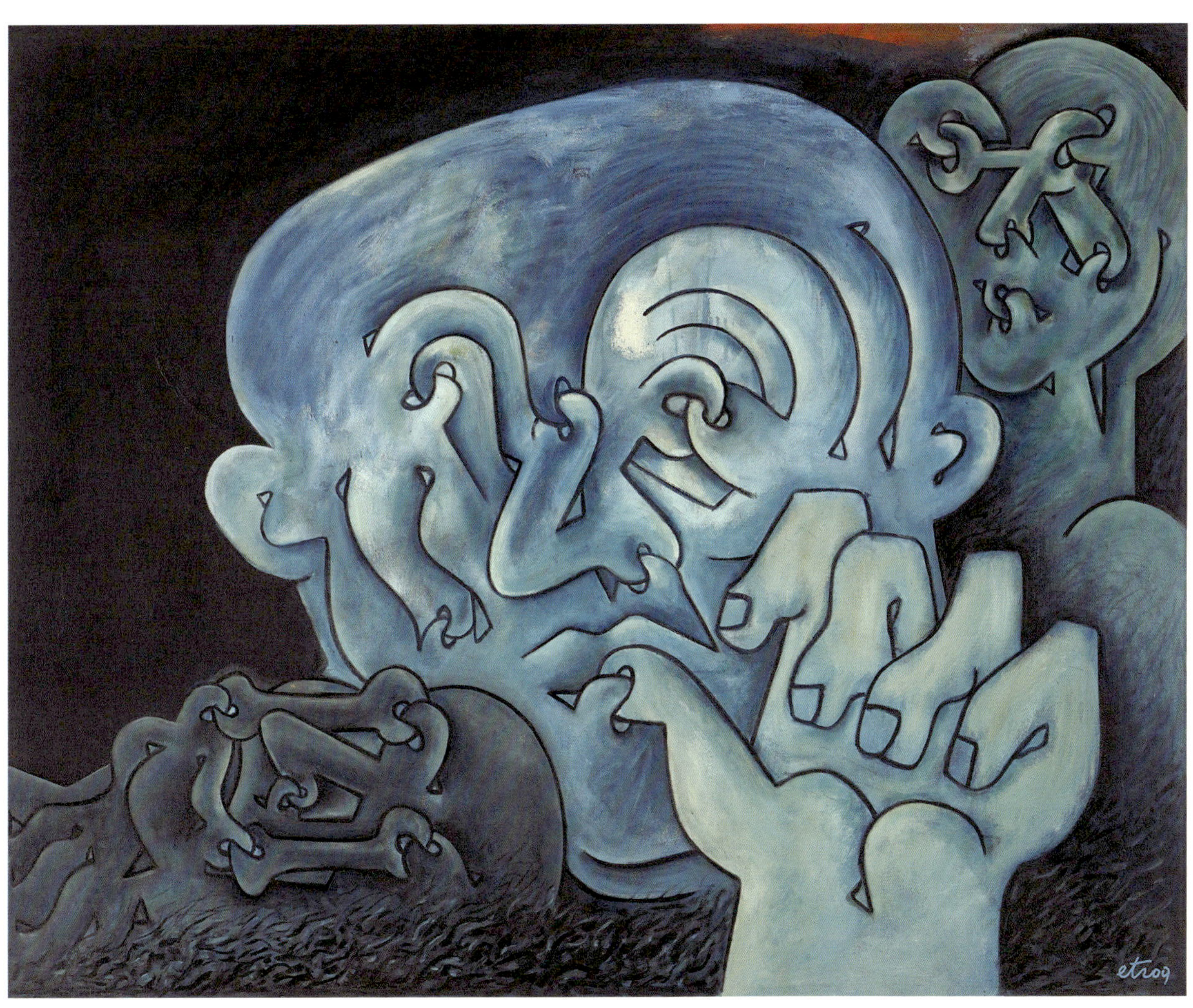

The Patriarch (Sam Zacks), 1969–1970

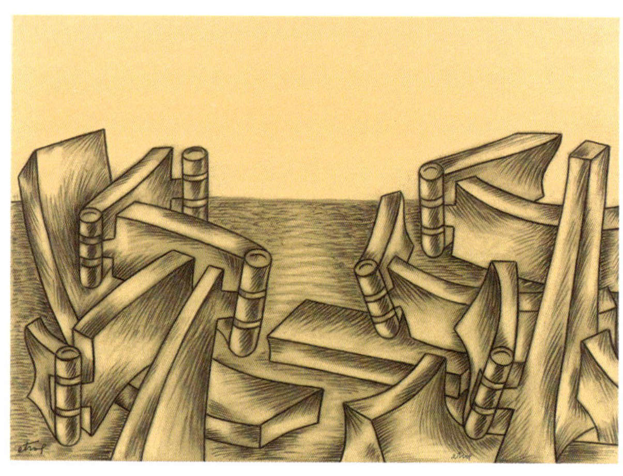

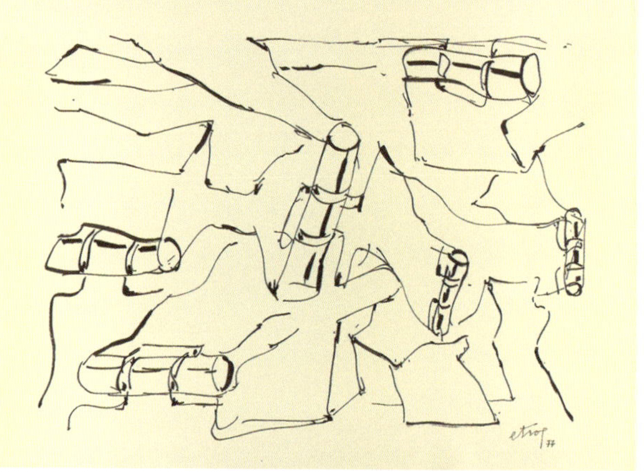

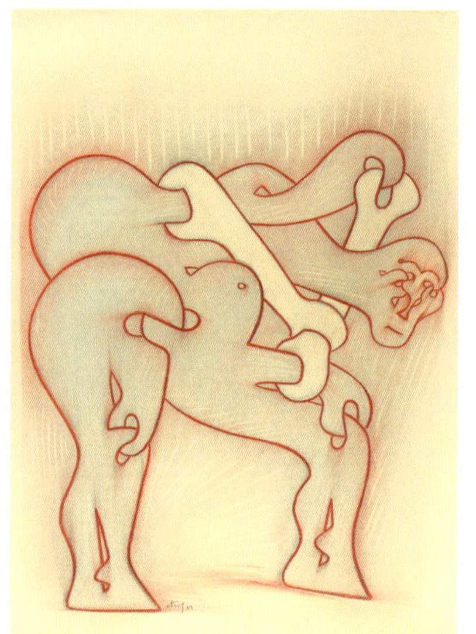

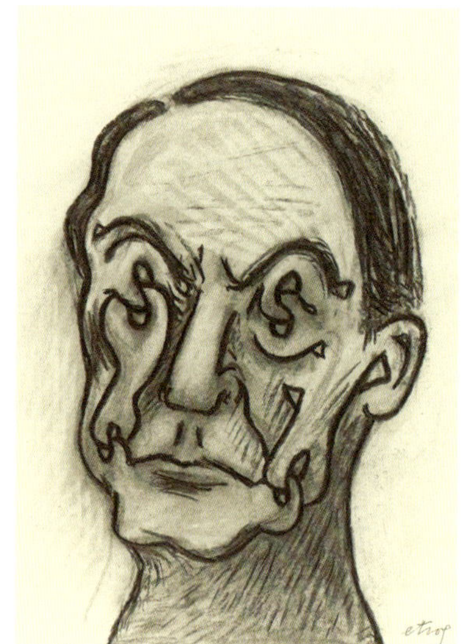

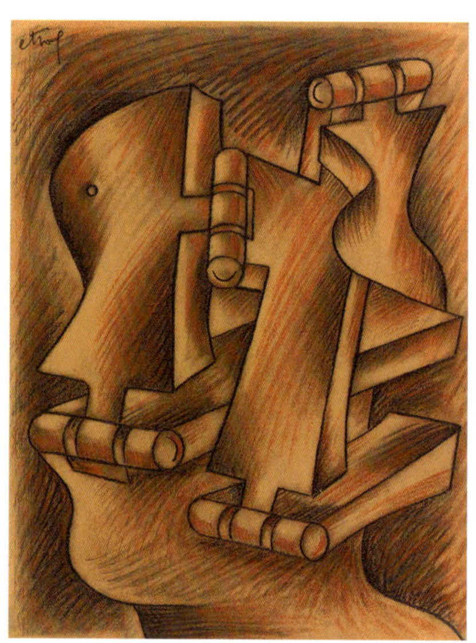

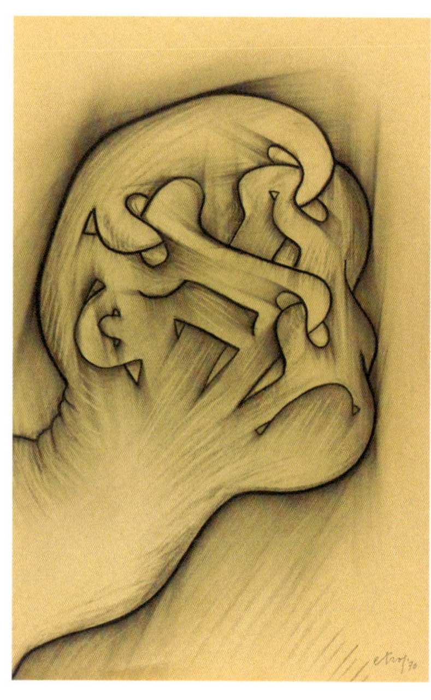

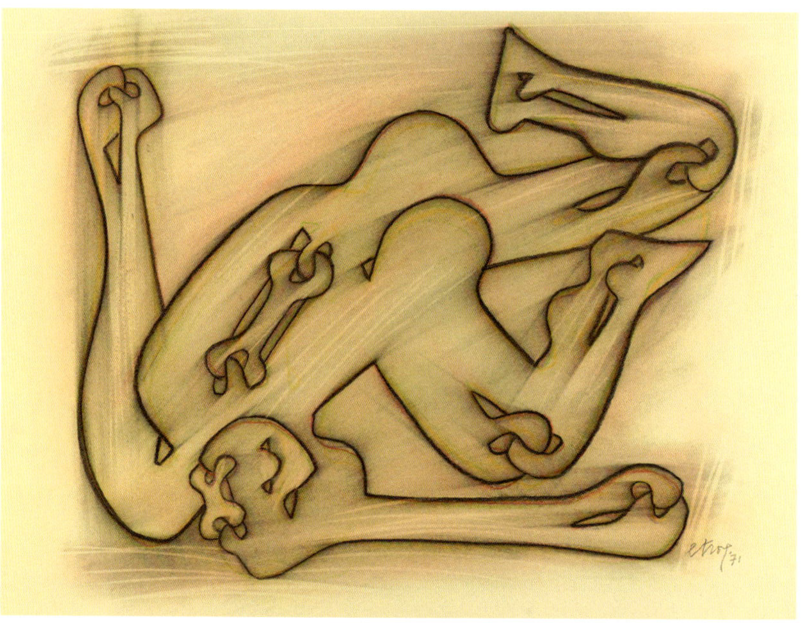

Harbour, 1974–1975; Calligraphic Hinges, 1977
Yoga, 1969; Henry Moore, 1974; Hinge Head with Figure, 1974–1975
Boxer, 1968–1970; Fallen Man, 1971

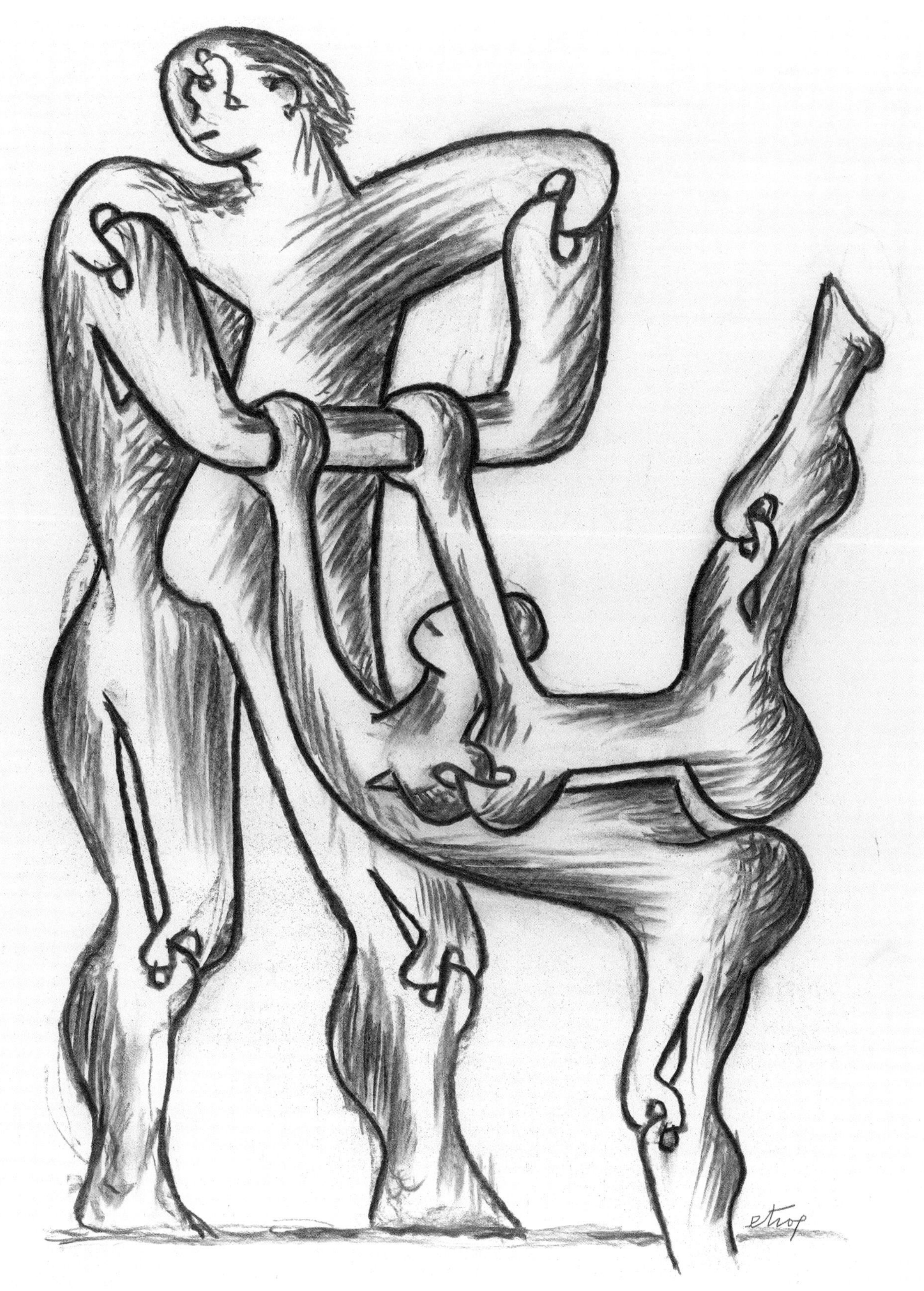

Two Dancers, 1969

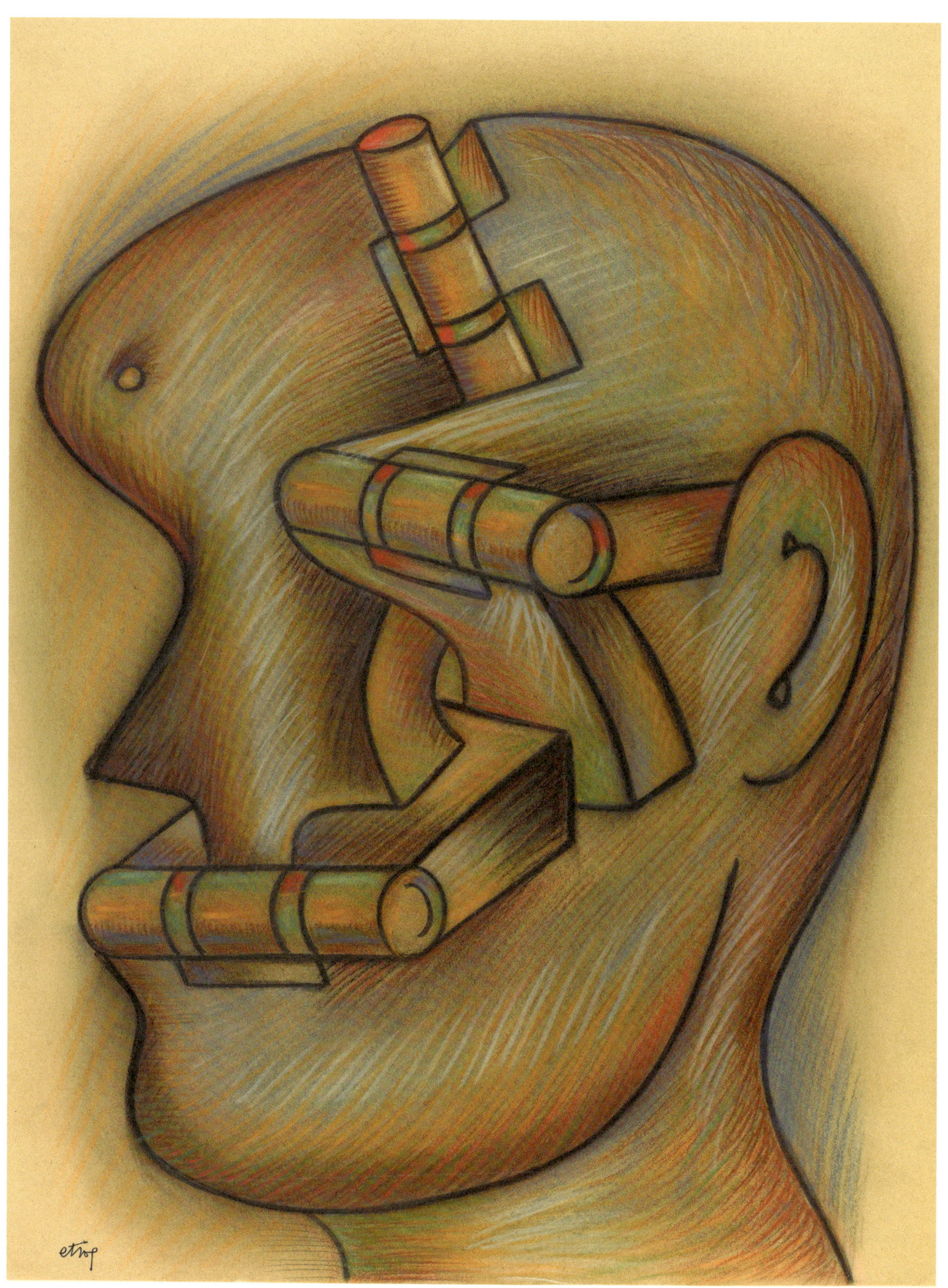

60 Mytho Head, 1974–1975

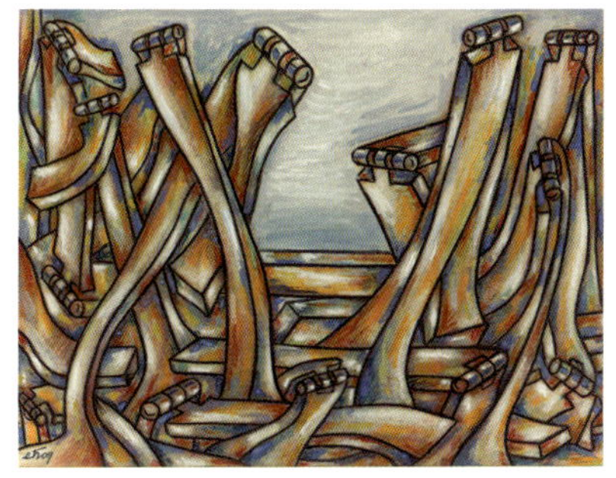

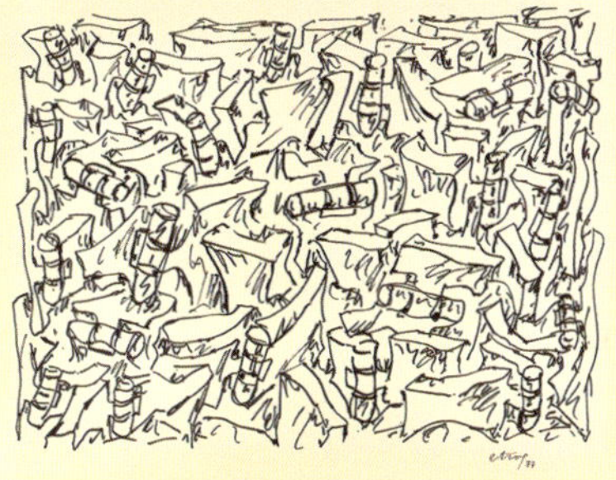

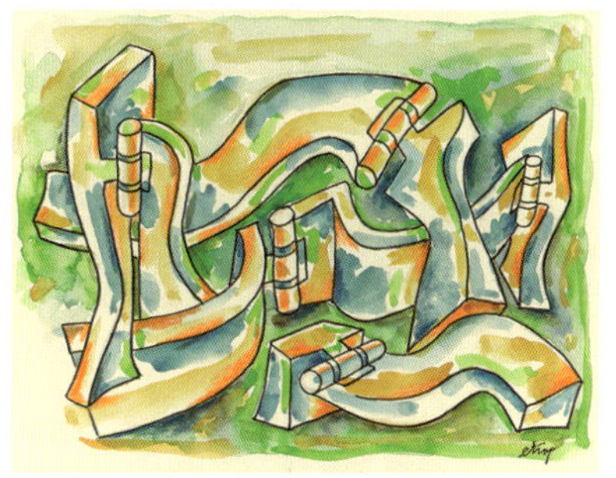

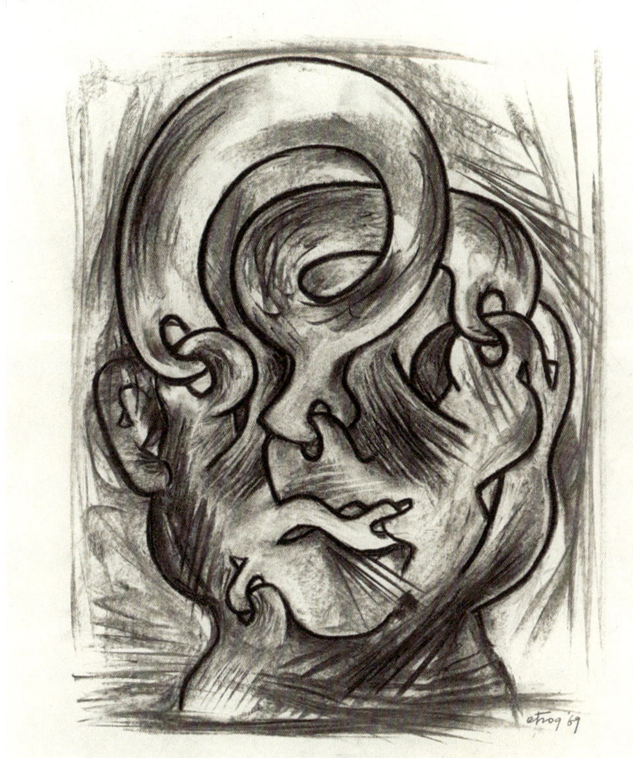

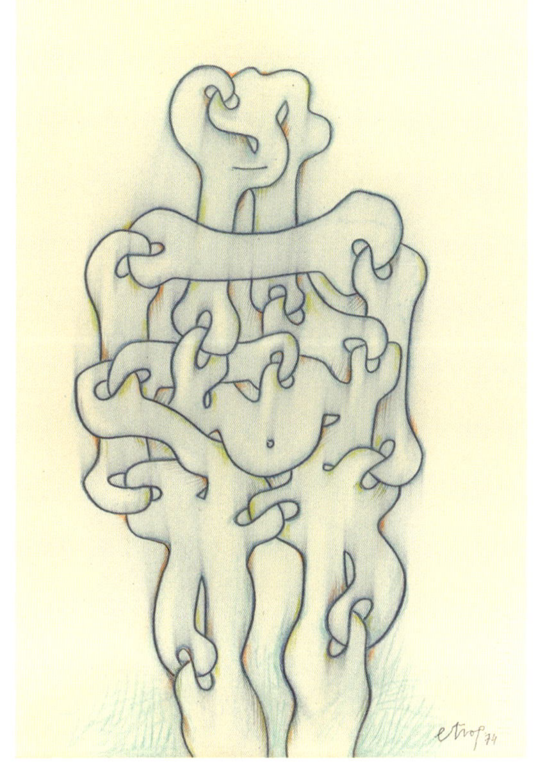

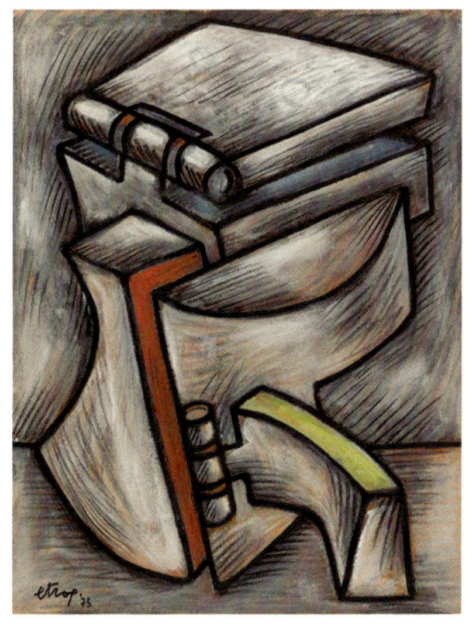

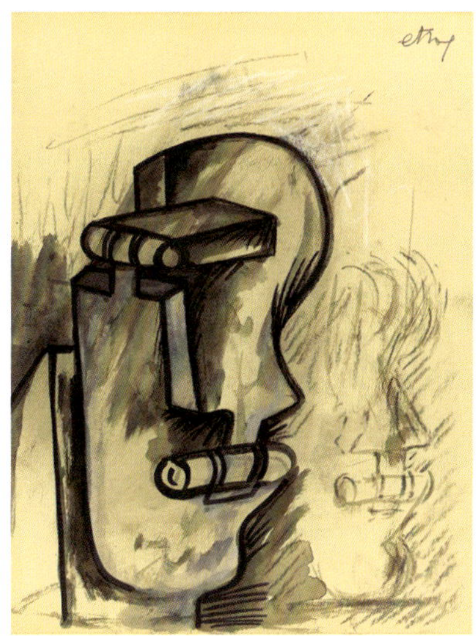

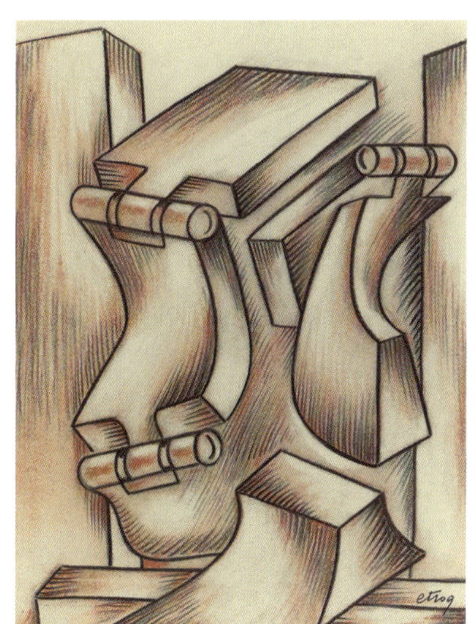

Law of the Jungle, 1975; Busy Town, 1977; Weeds, 1977
Anguish, 1975; Figure, 1974
Parade, 1974–1975; Aviator, 1975; Structural Man, 1974–1975

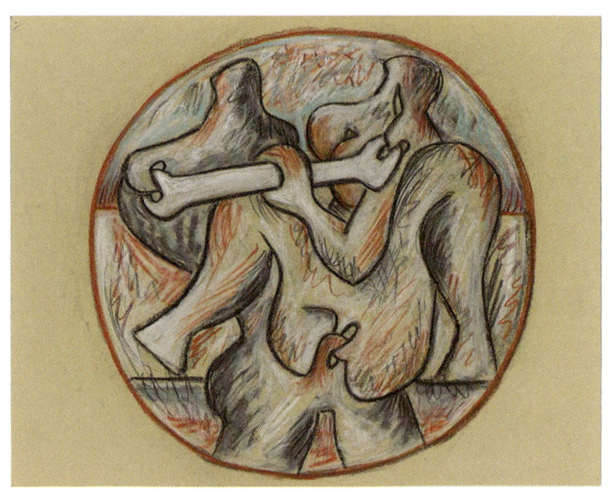
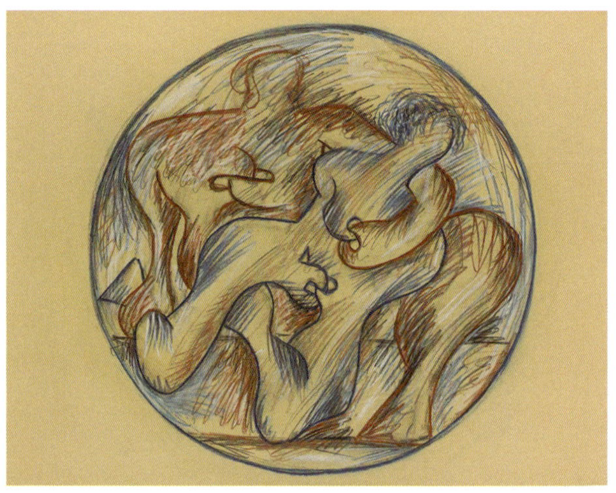
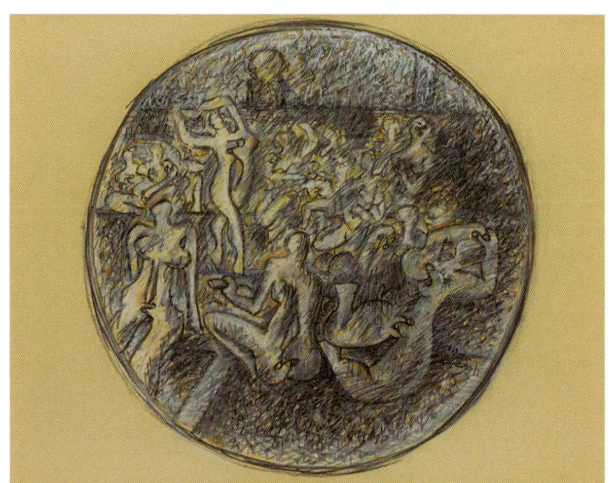
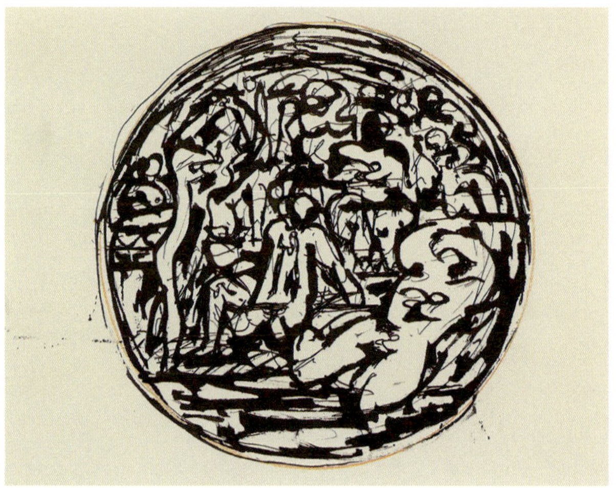

Turkish Bath Study: Two Figures, 1969; Turkish Bath Study: Relaxing Figure, 1969
Turkish Bath Study: Full View 2, 1969; Turkish Bath Study, 1969

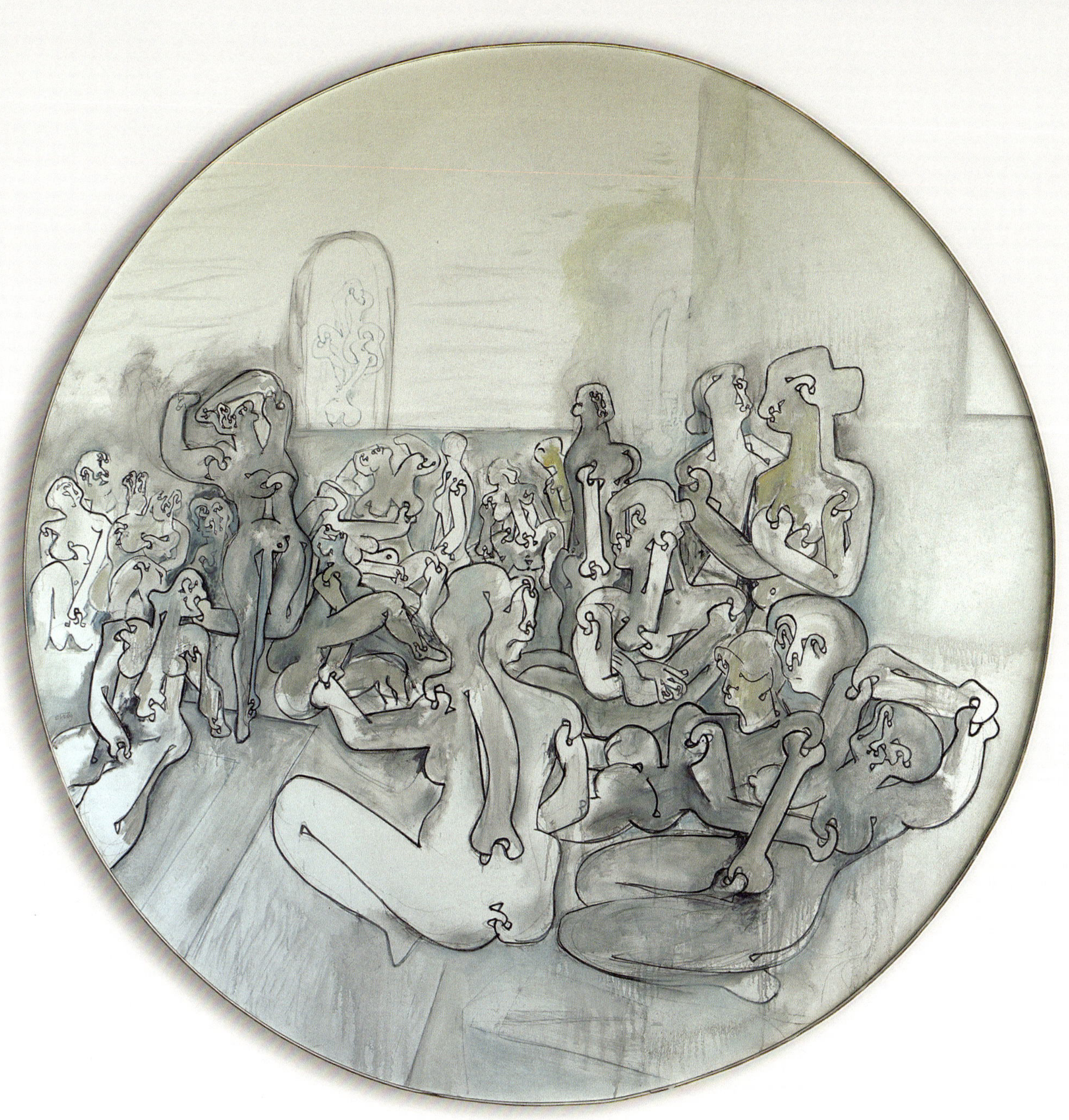

Turkish Bath (Study after Ingres), 1969

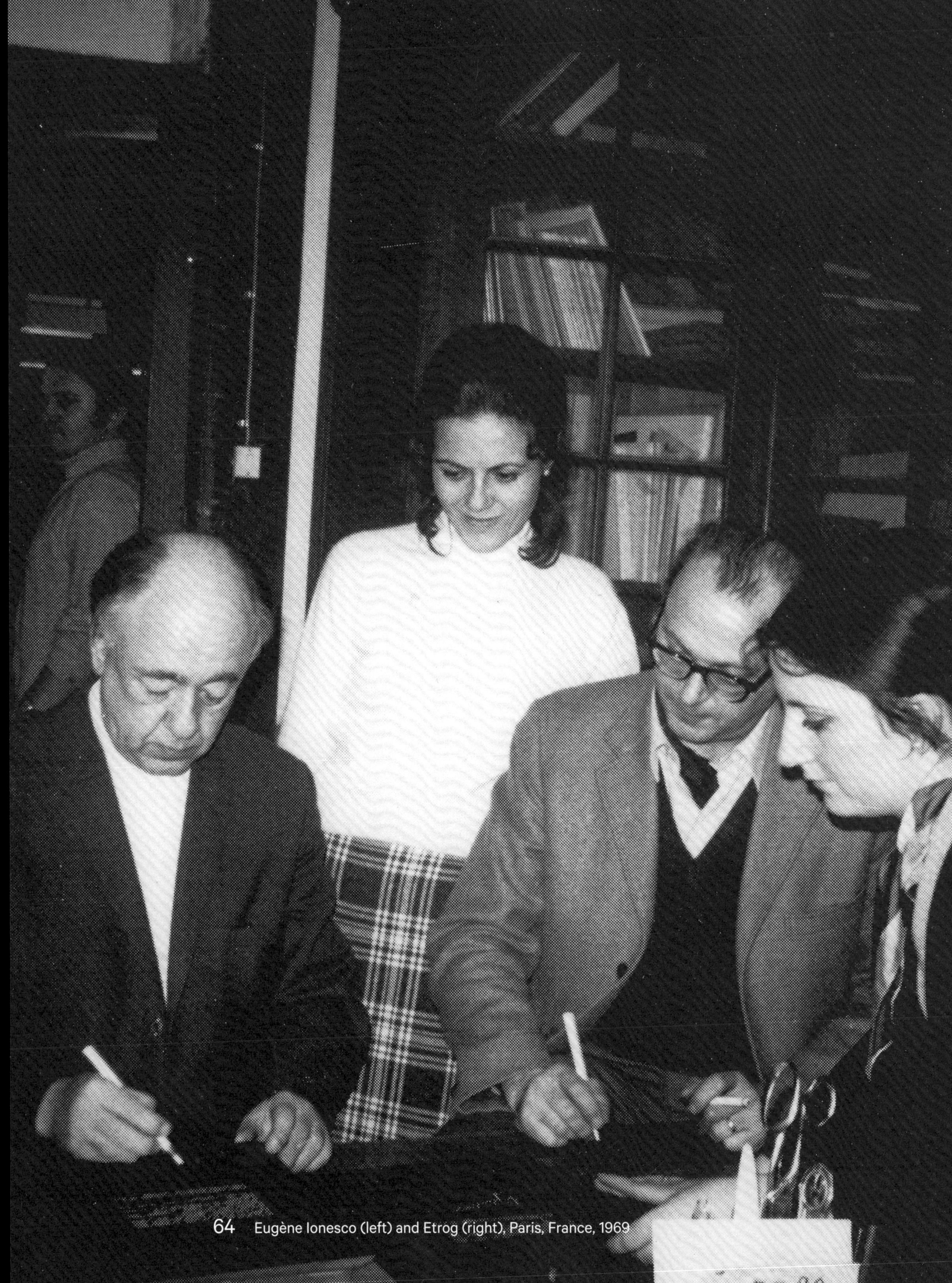

64 Eugène Ionesco (left) and Etrog (right), Paris, France, 1969

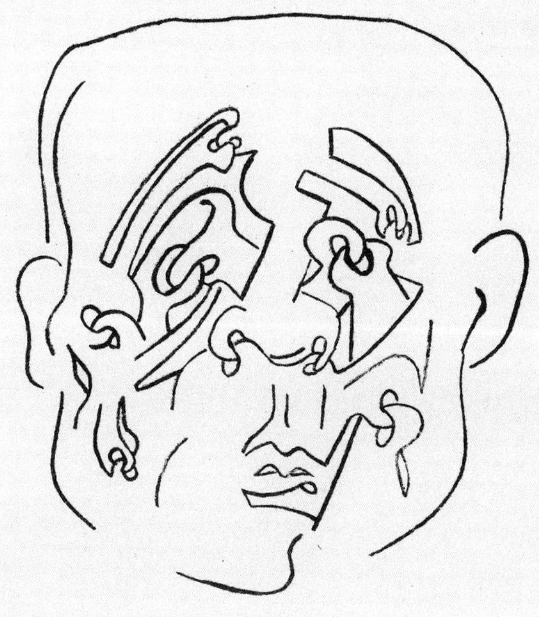

Portrait of Ionesco, 1969

Puis ce fut

le

douzième.

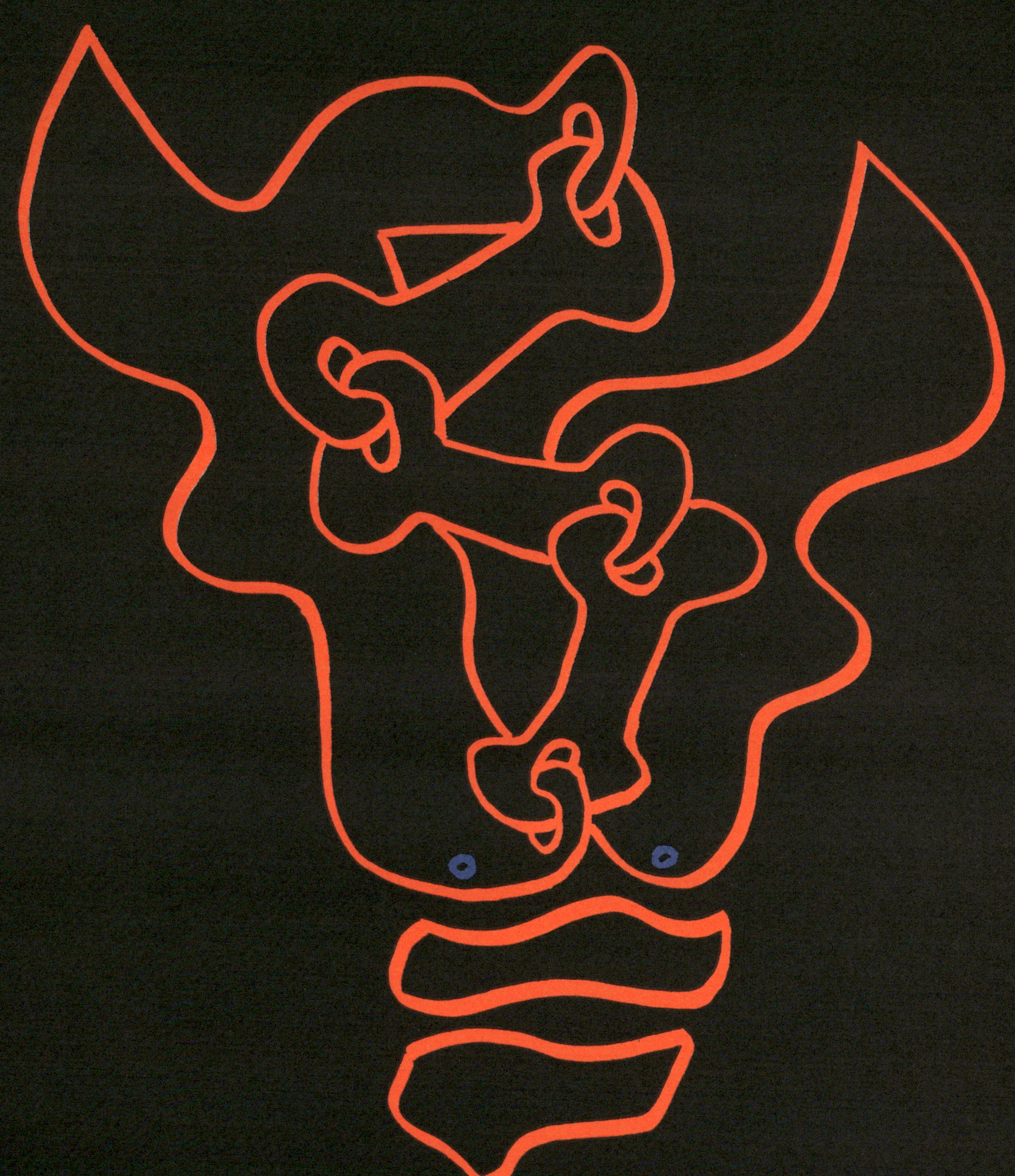

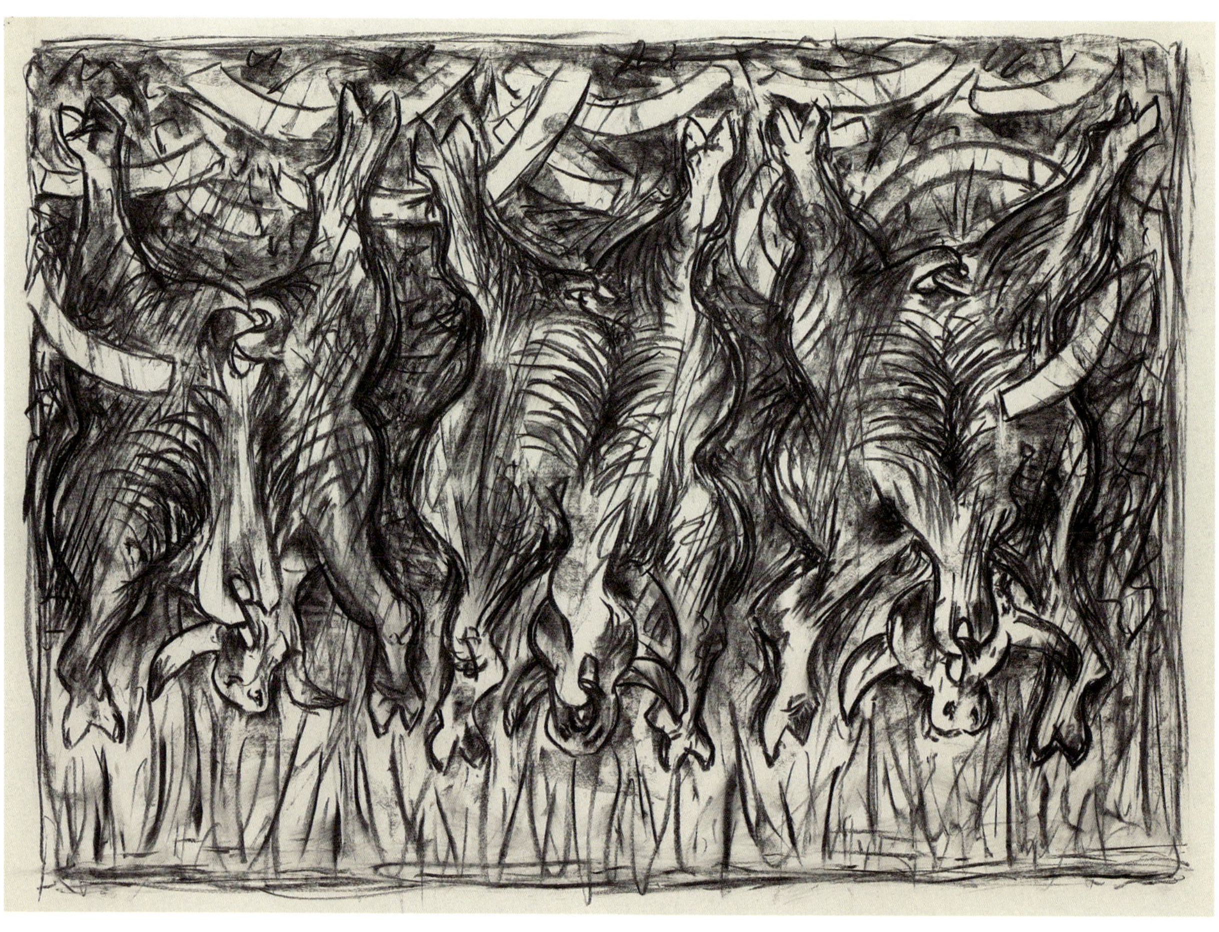

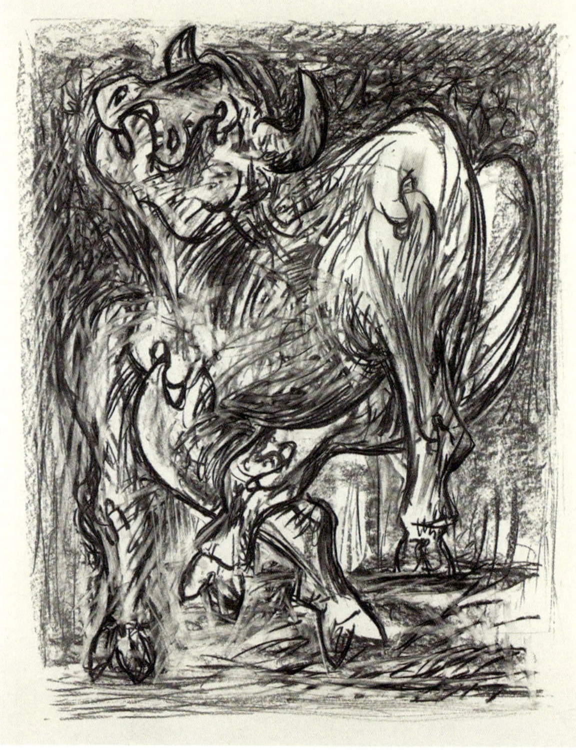

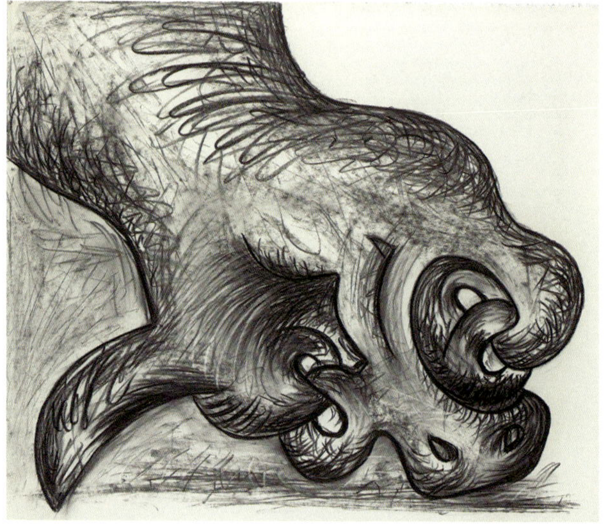

Study for Targets: Three Carcasses, 1969

 Study for Targets: Dancing Bull, 1969; Study for Targets: Fallen Head, 1969

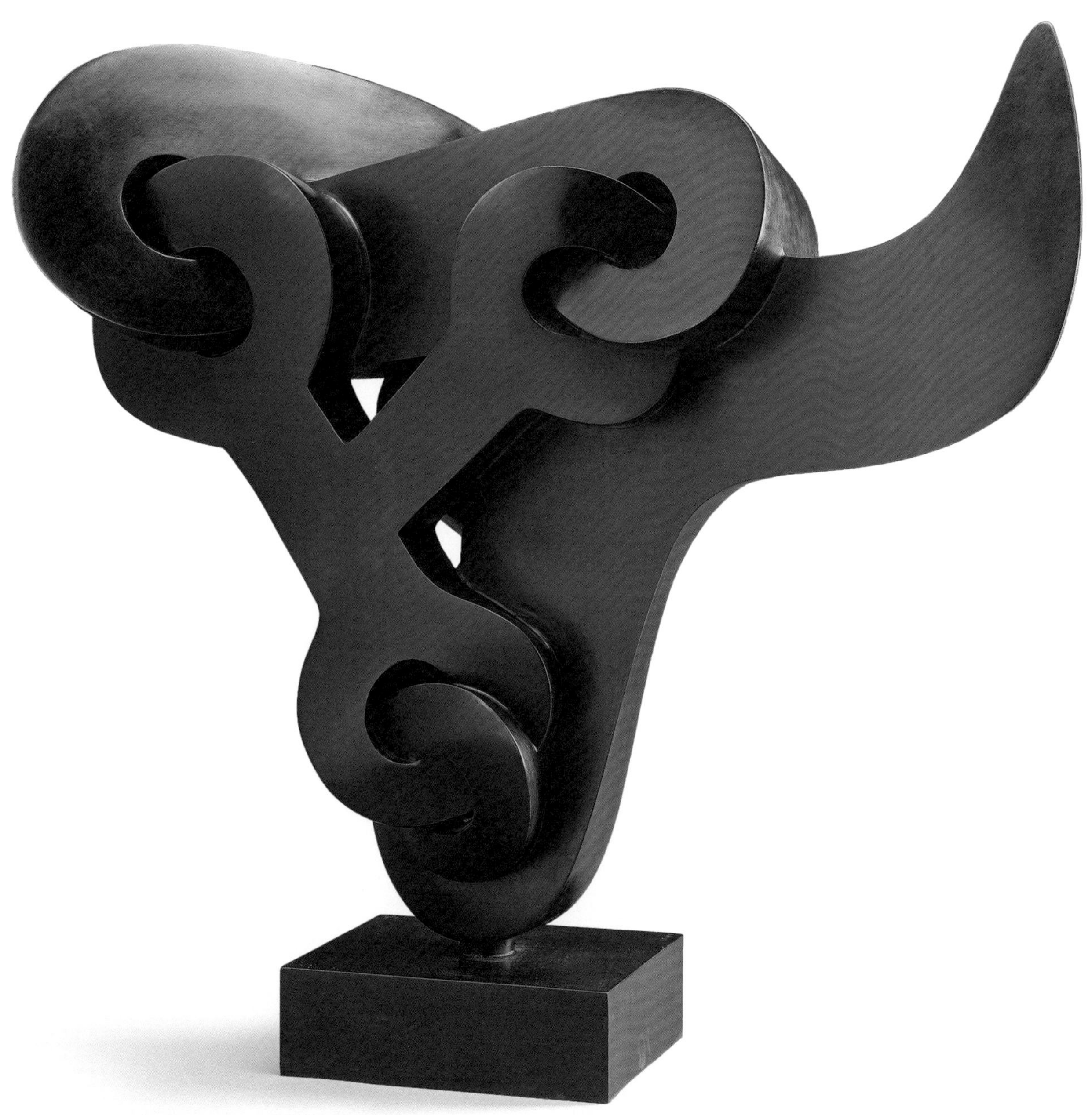

Bull Unicorn, 1969

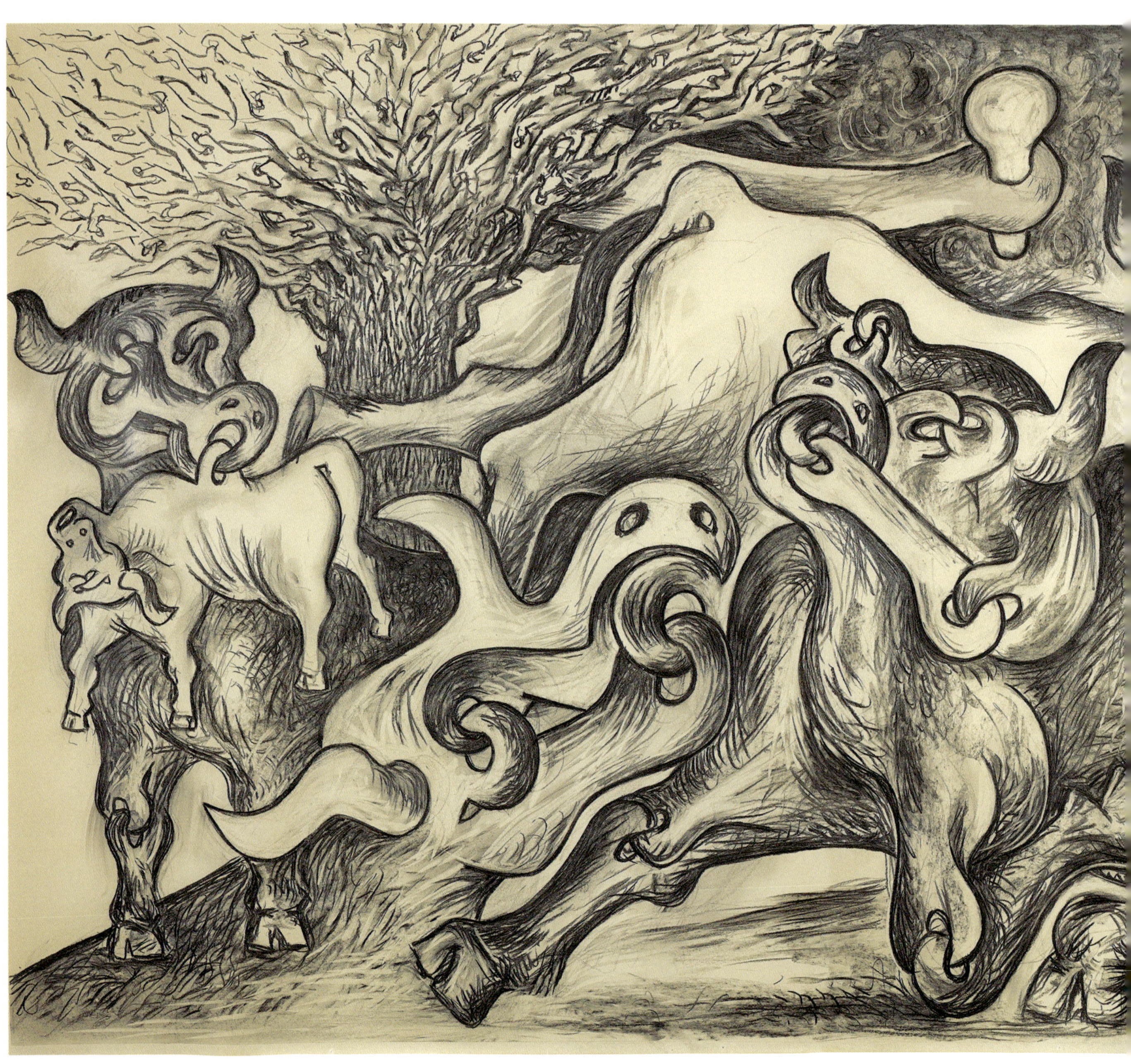

 Targets (Study after Guernica), 1969

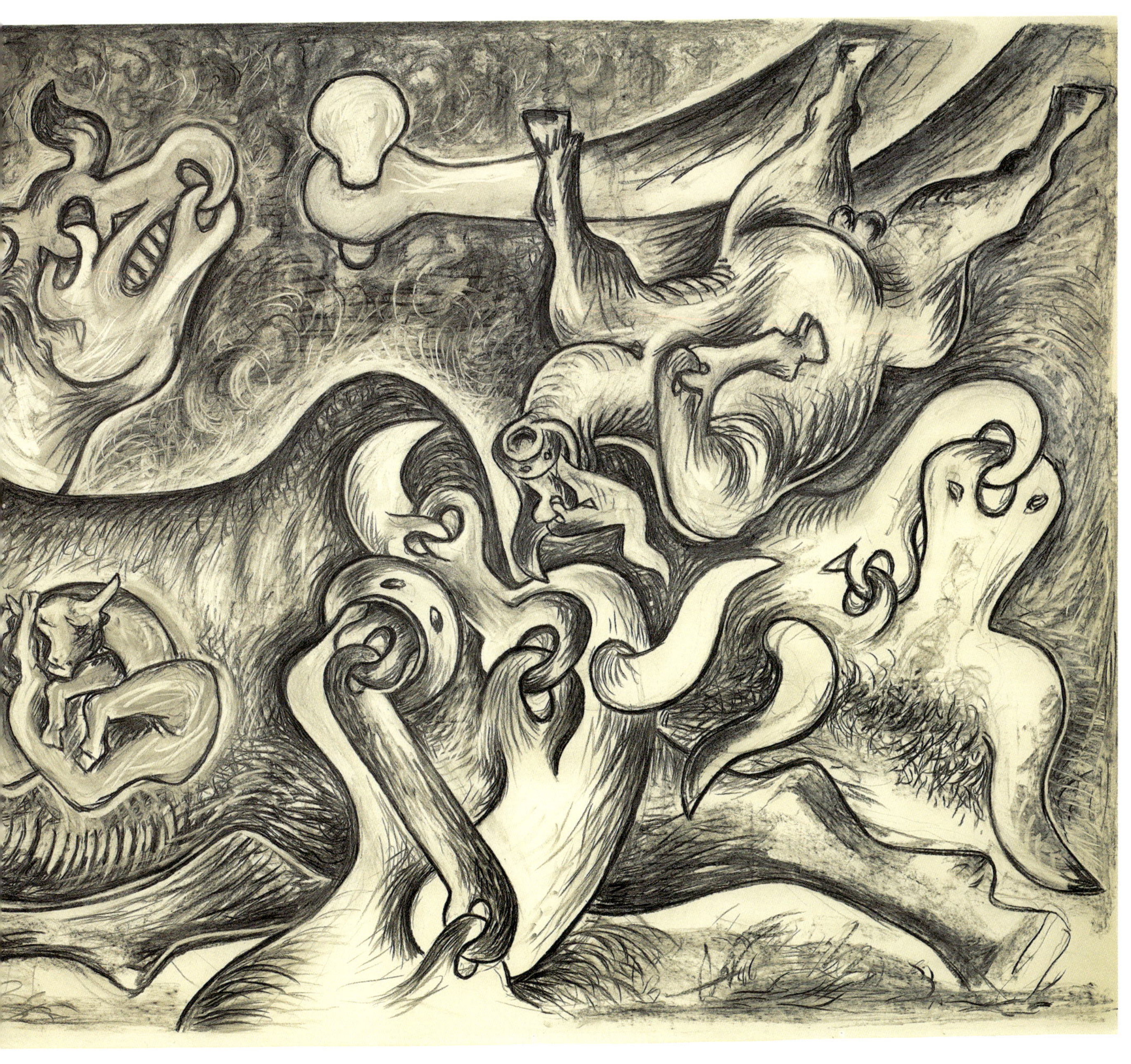

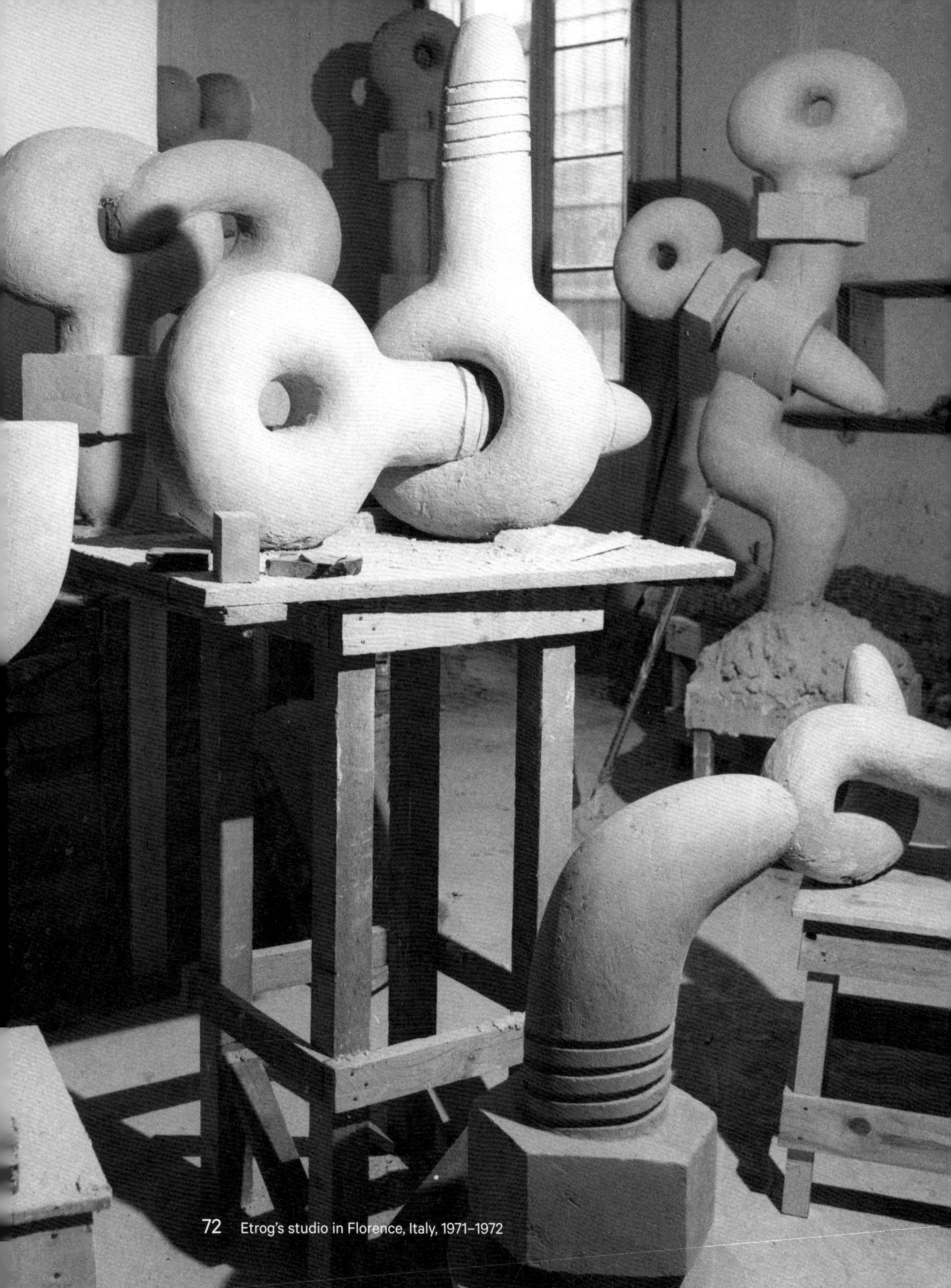

 Etrog's studio in Florence, Italy, 1971–1972

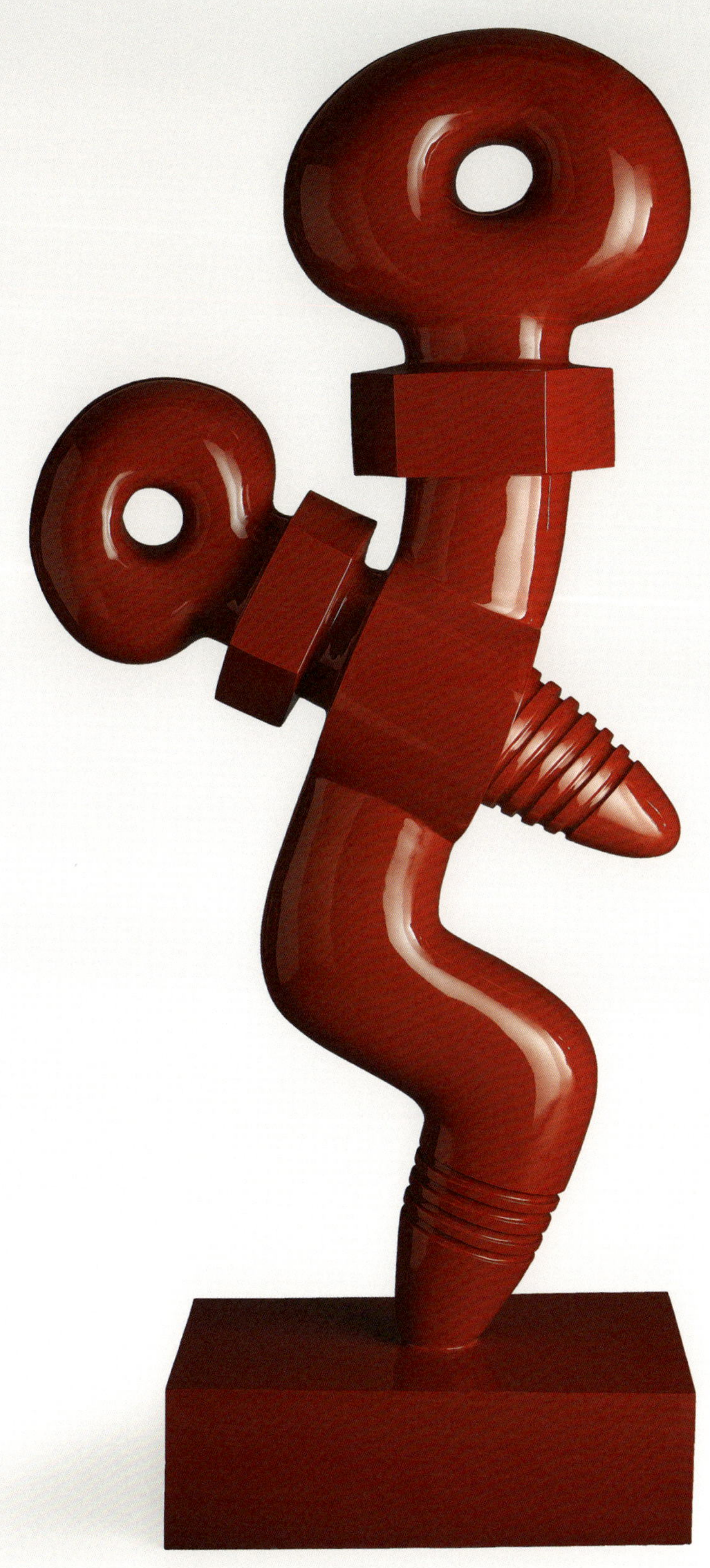

Samburu, 1972

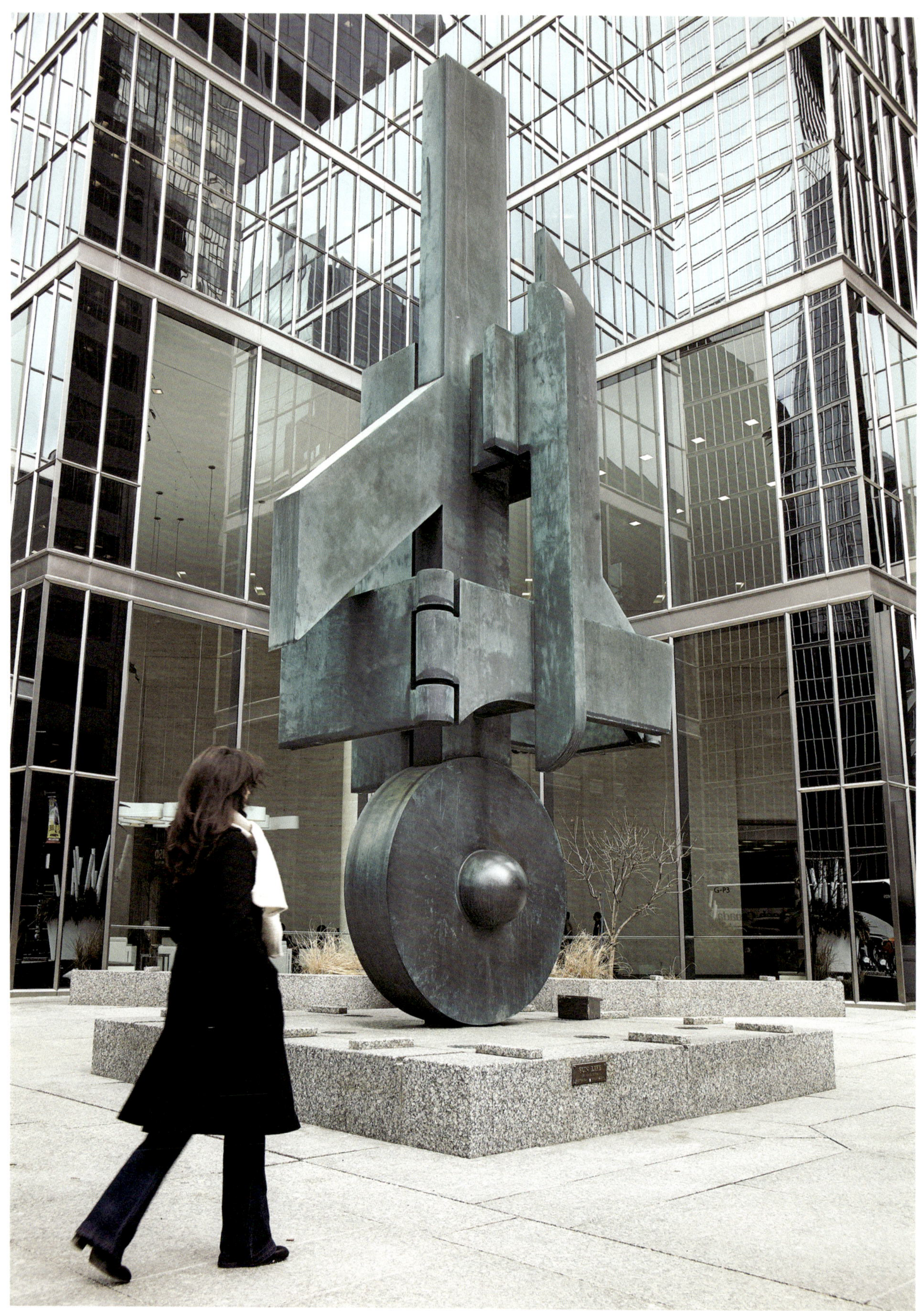

 Sunlife, 1984, Toronto

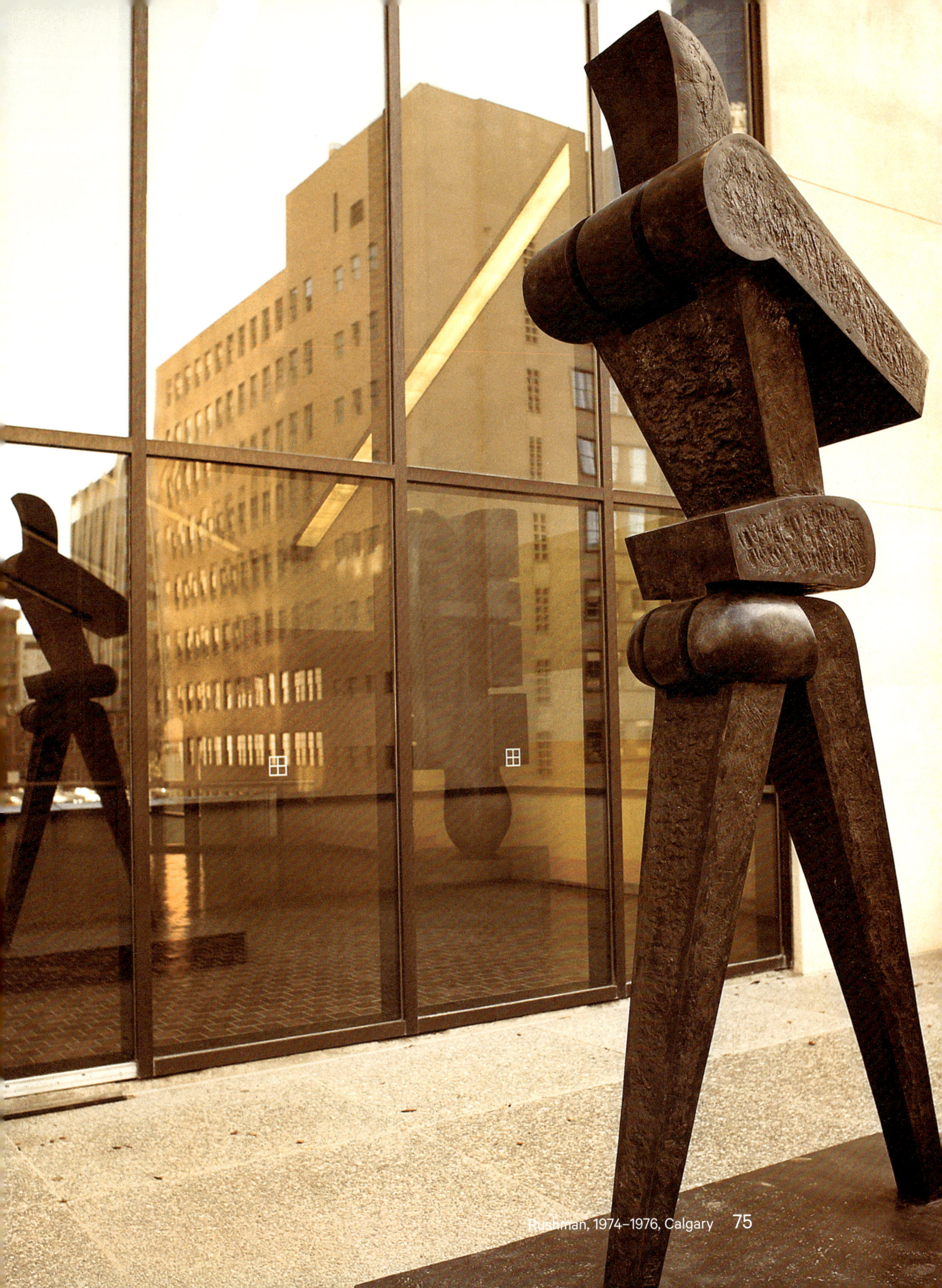

Rushman, 1974–1976, Calgary

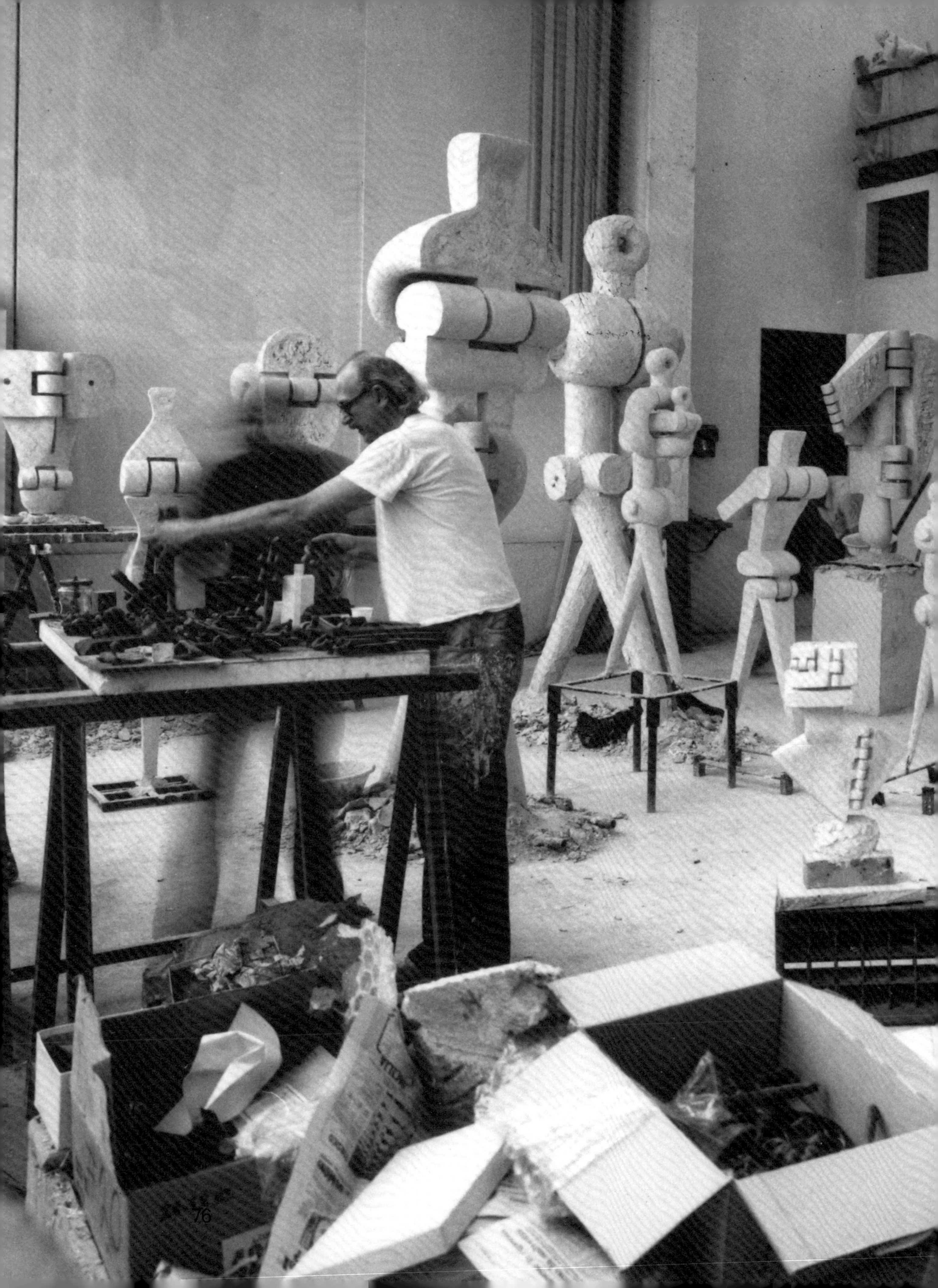

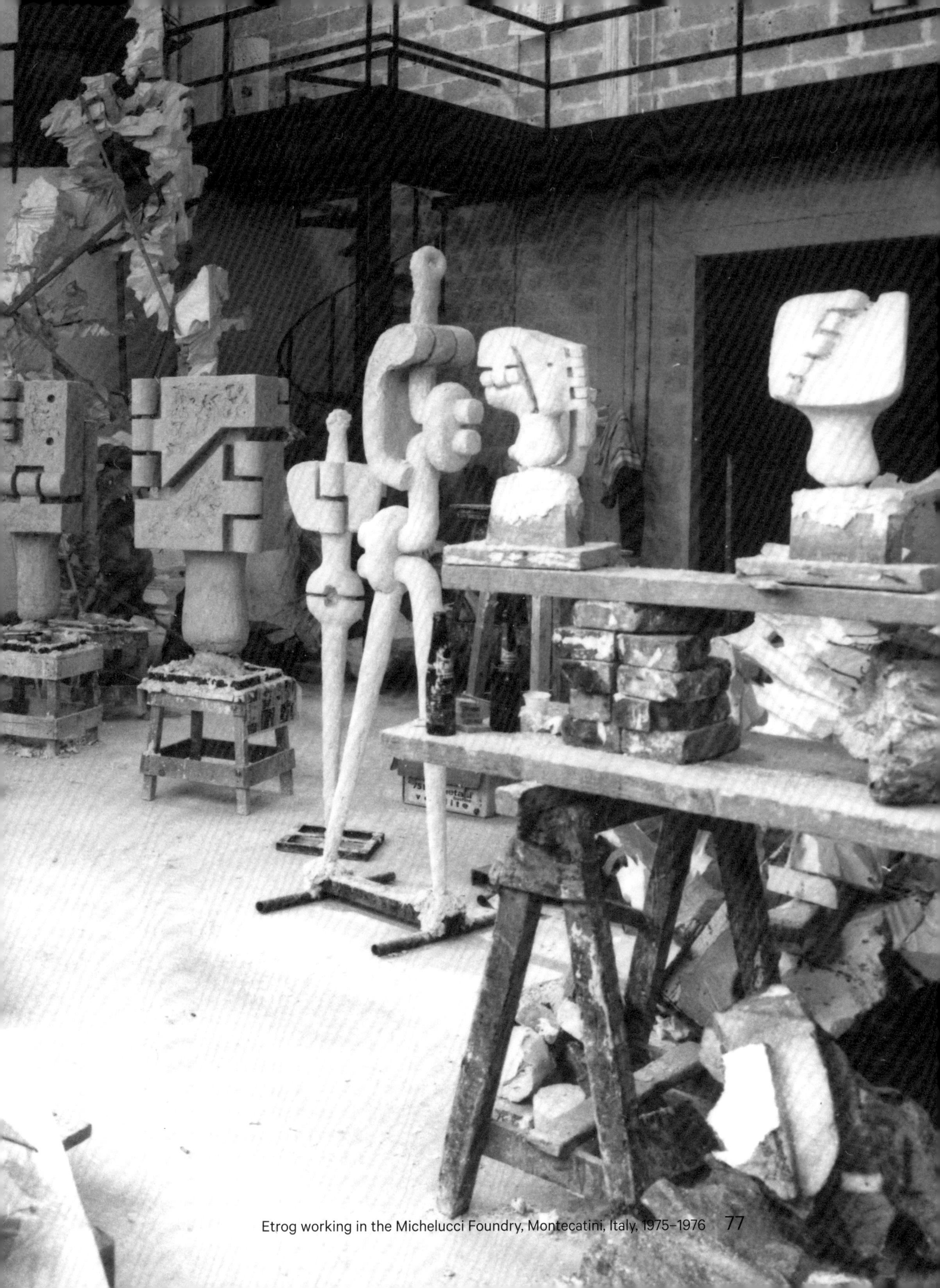

Etrog working in the Michelucci Foundry, Montecatini, Italy, 1975–1976

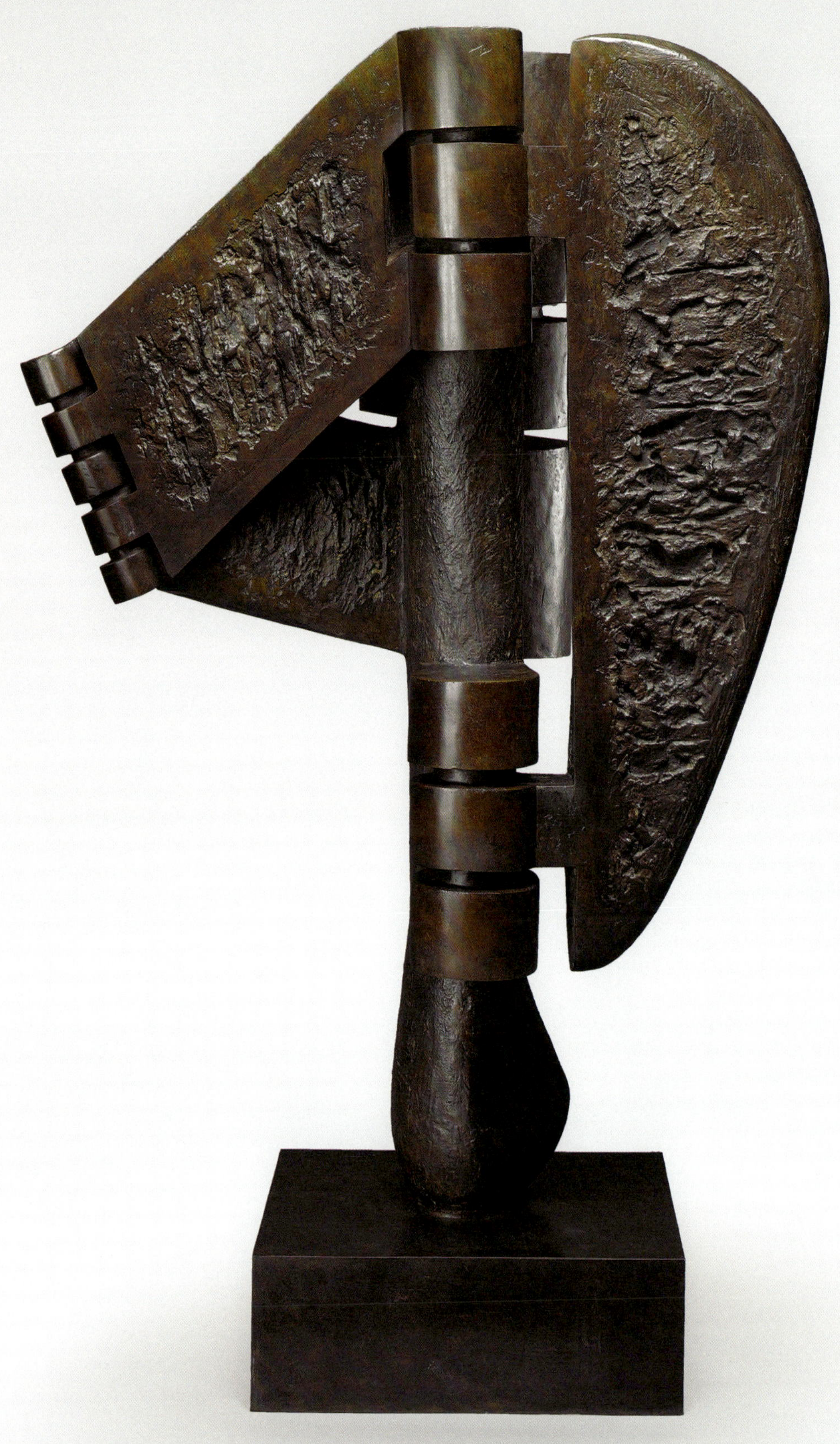

 Ritual Head, 1976

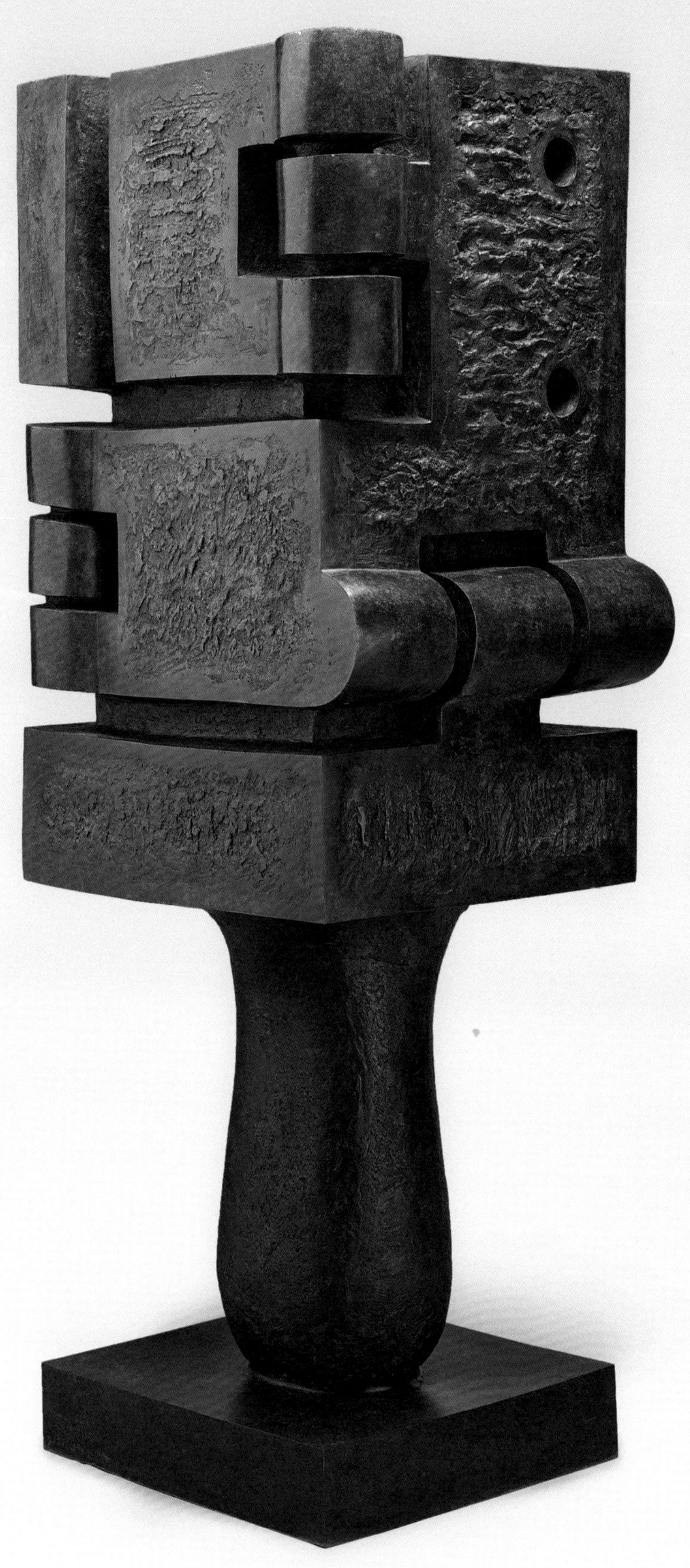

Headoors, 1976

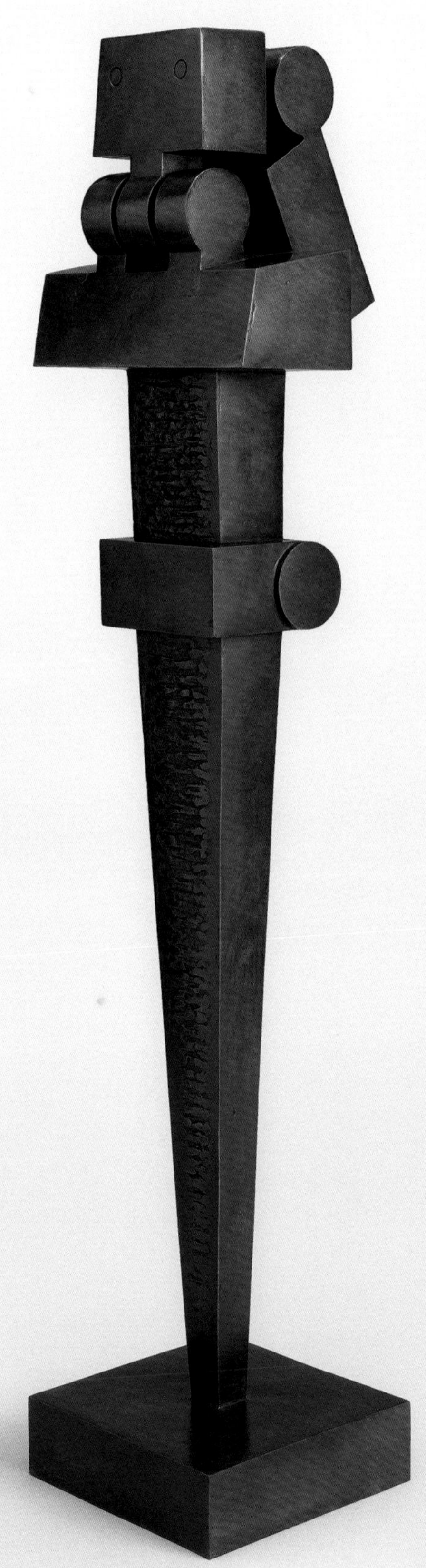

80 Hingo, 1976

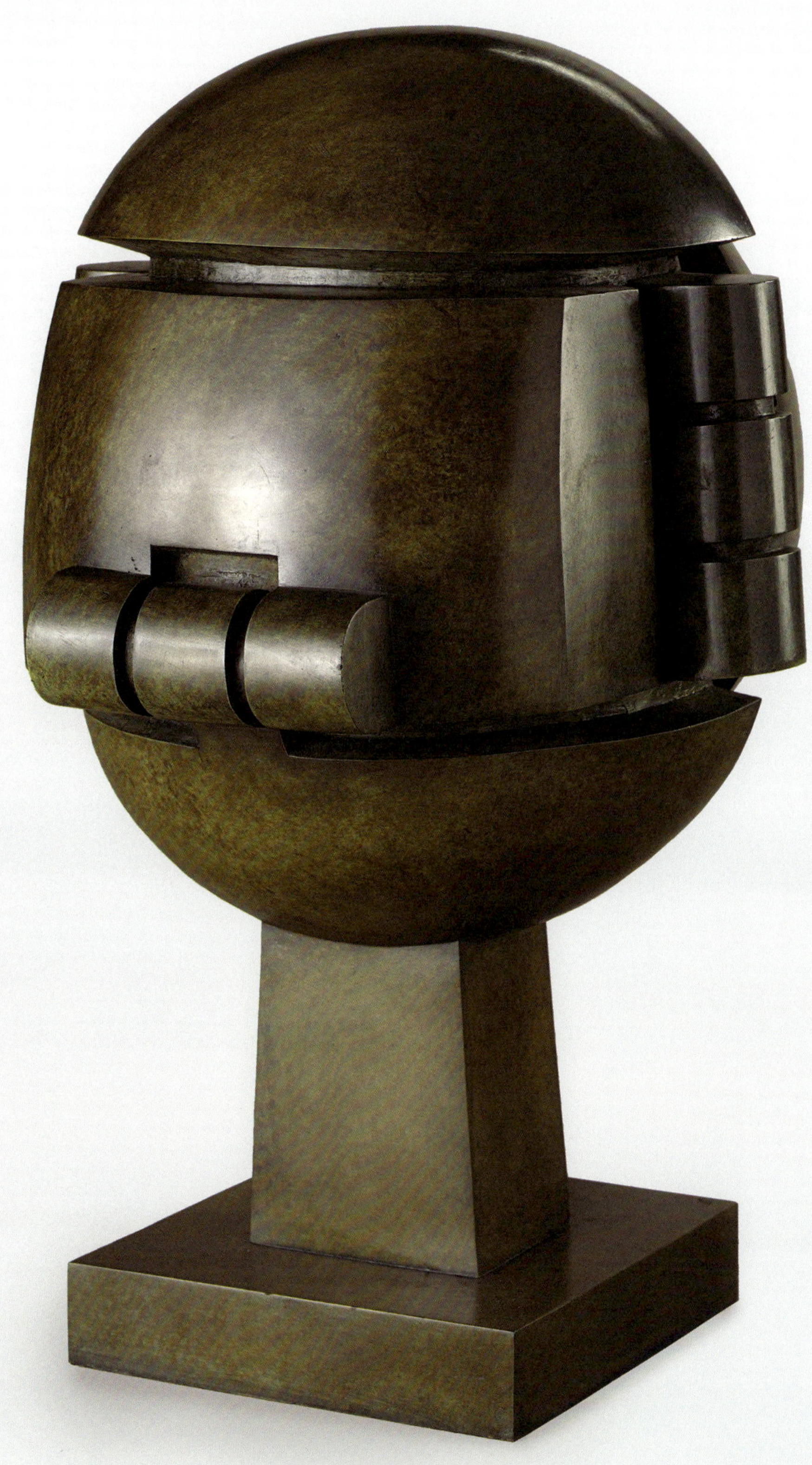

Magic Barrel, 1976

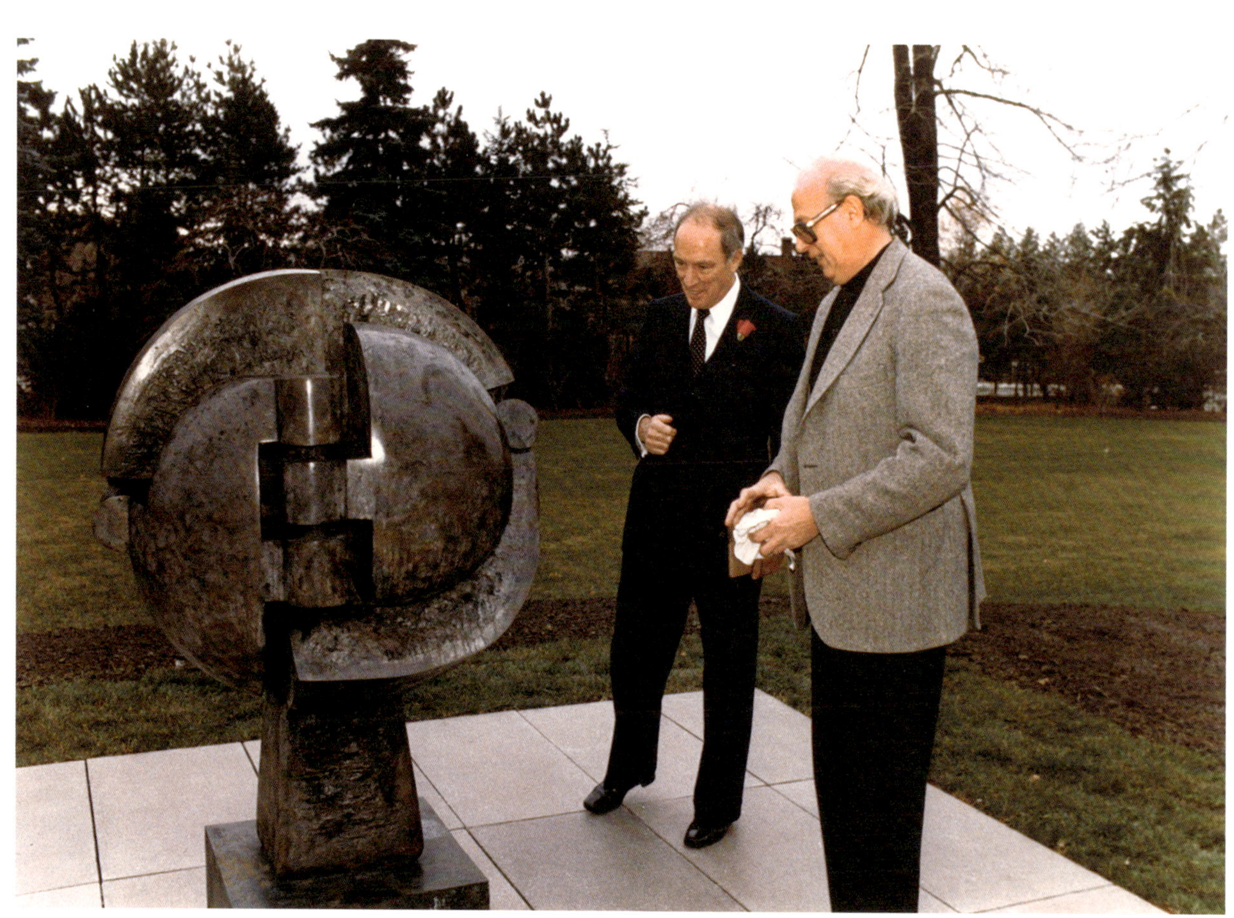

82 Pierre Elliott Trudeau and Etrog with Dream Chamber, 24 Sussex Drive, Ottawa, 1983

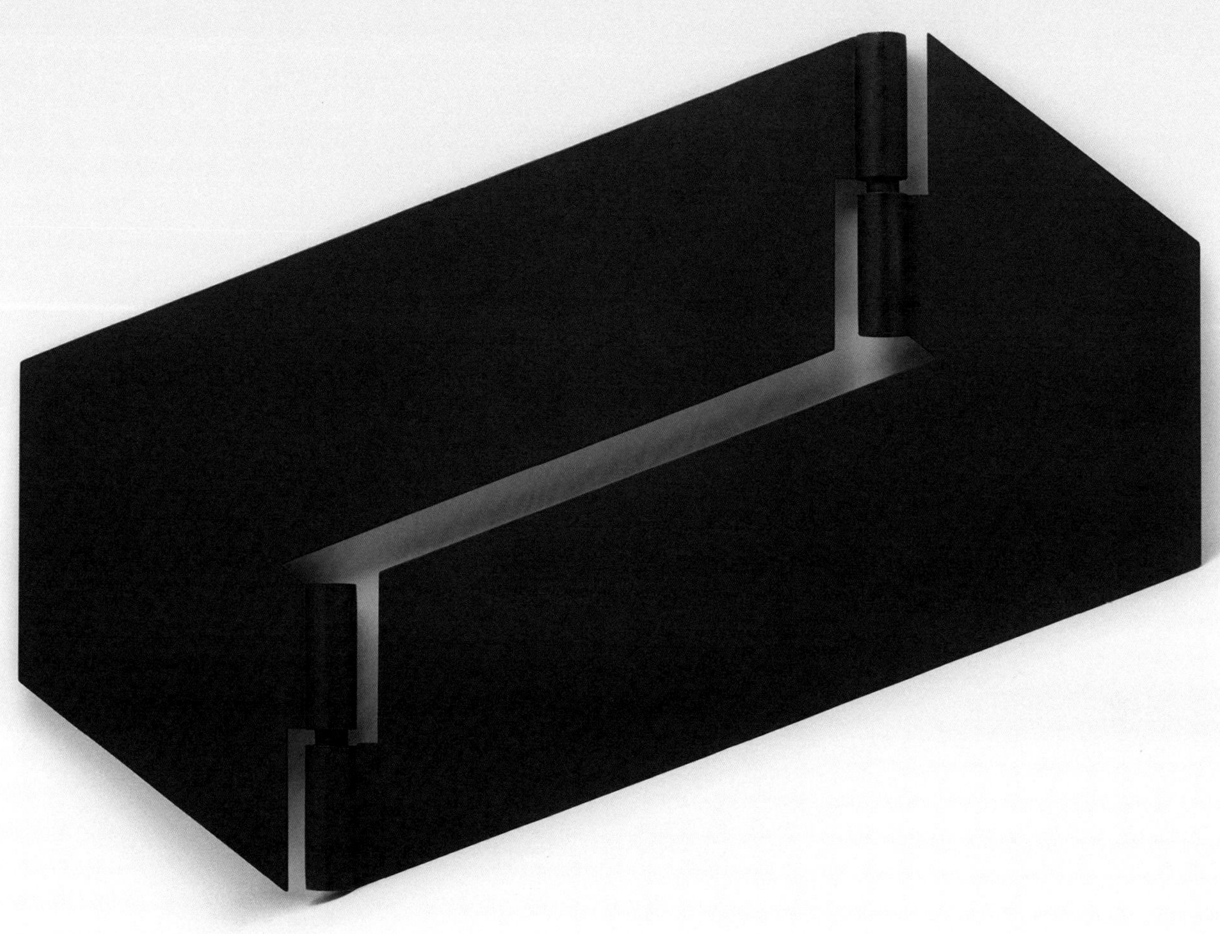

Magic Box, 1980

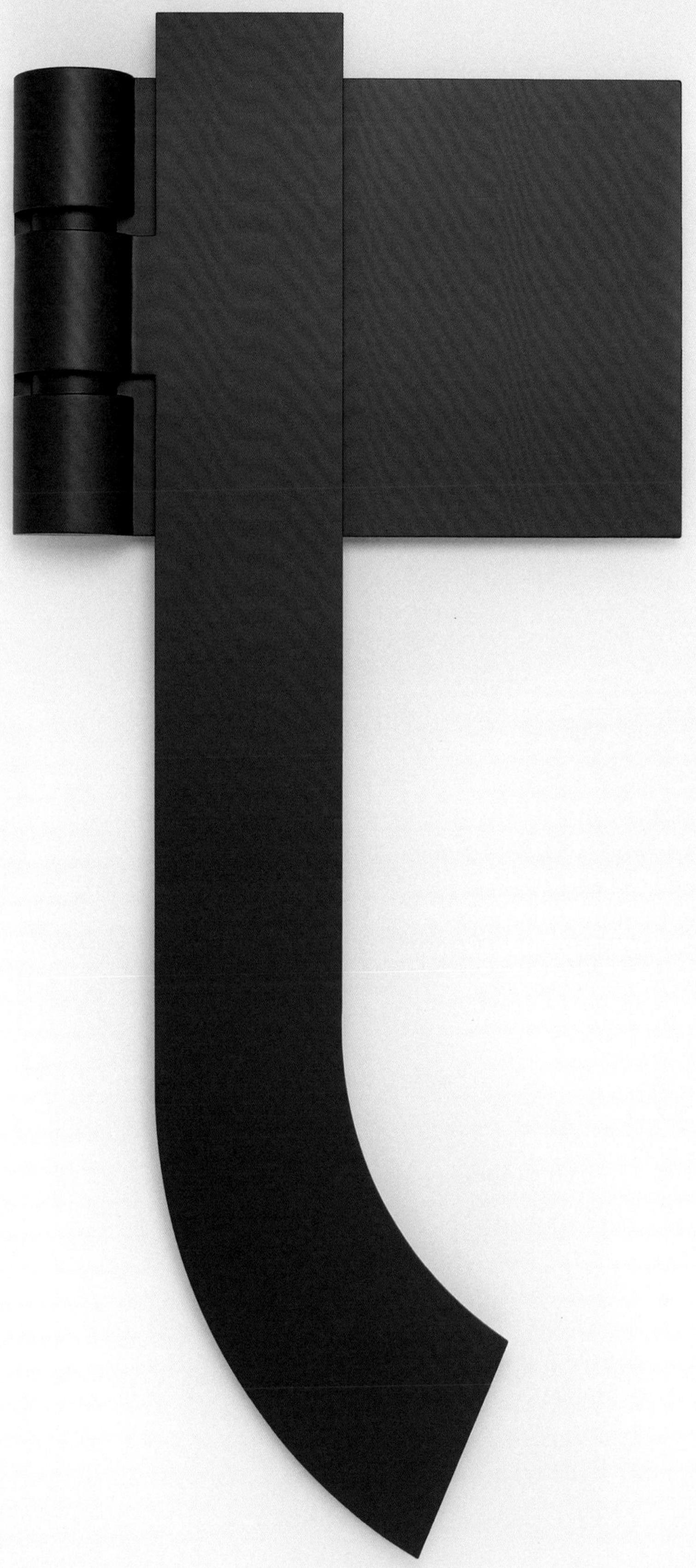

84 Homage to Kurosawa, 1980

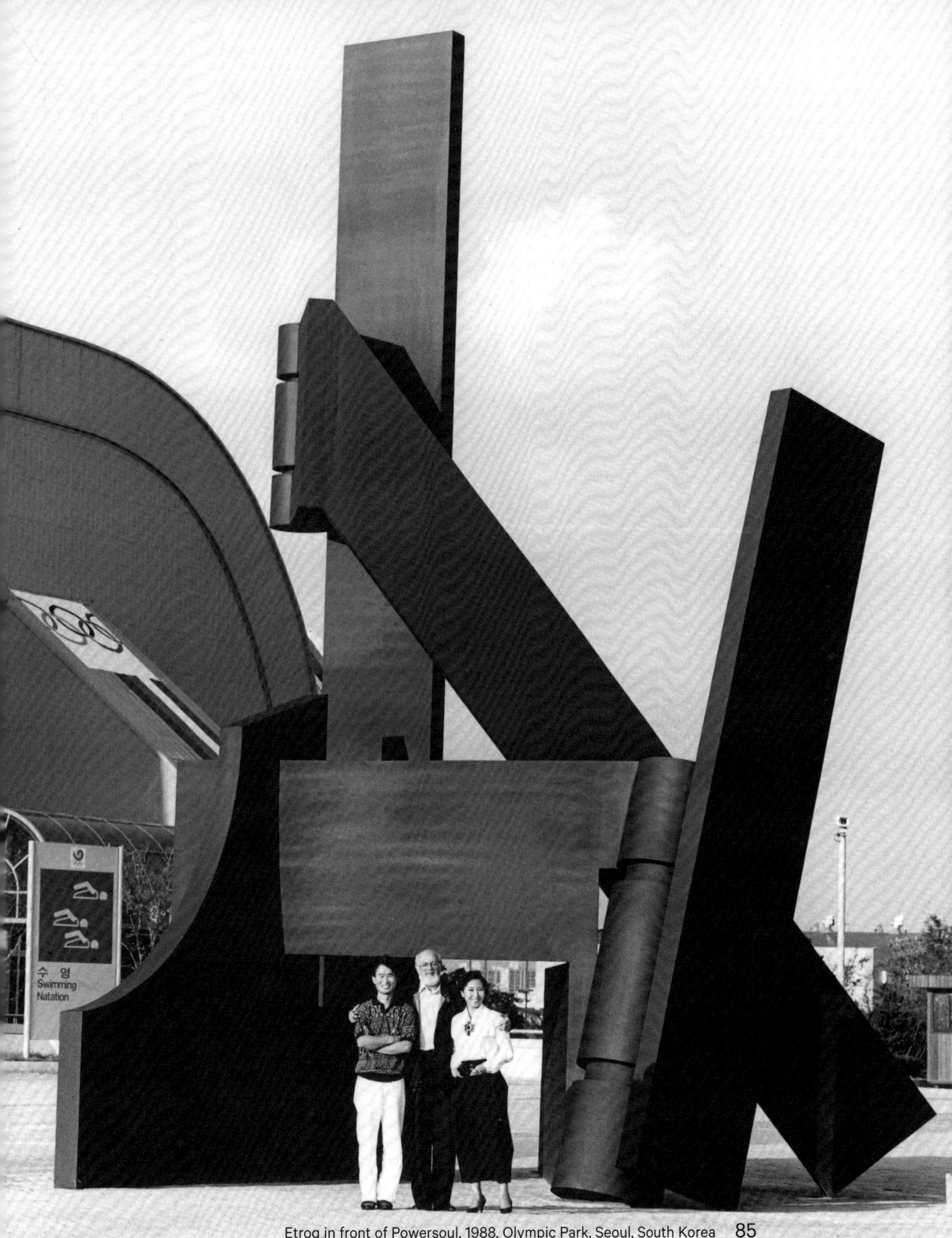

Etrog in front of Powersoul, 1988, Olympic Park, Seoul, South Korea

86 Détente, 1980

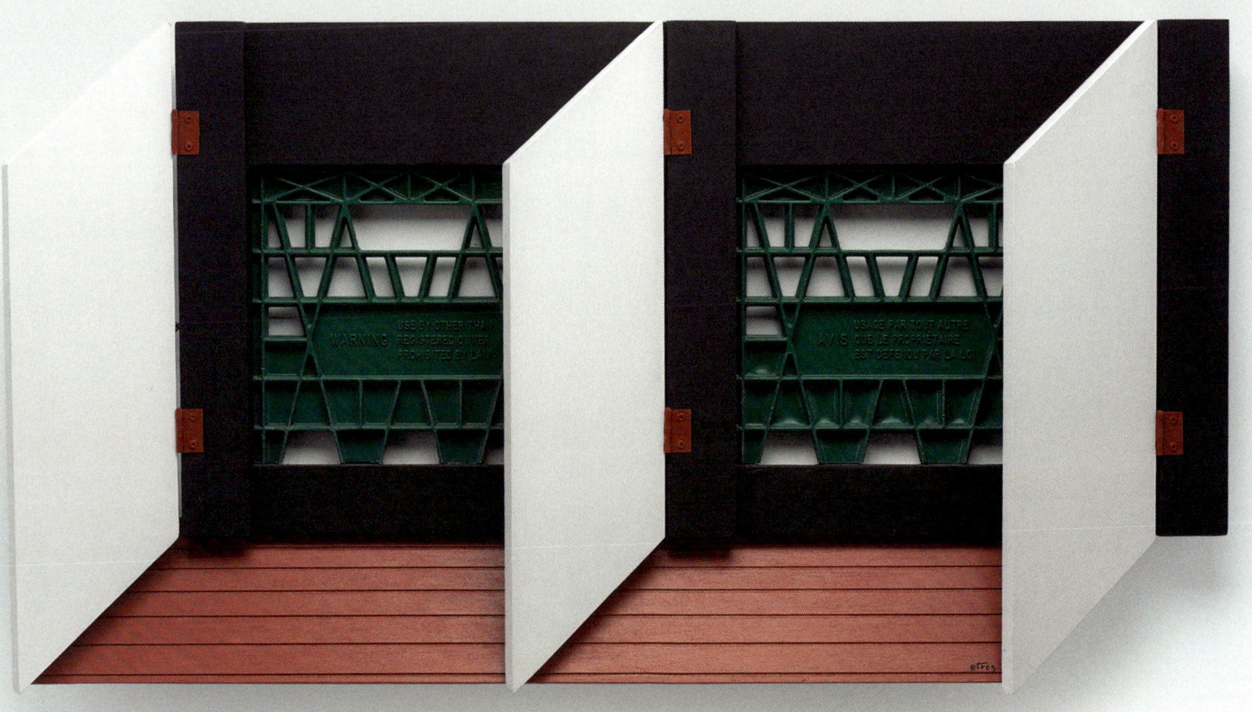

 Composite 11, 1996–1997

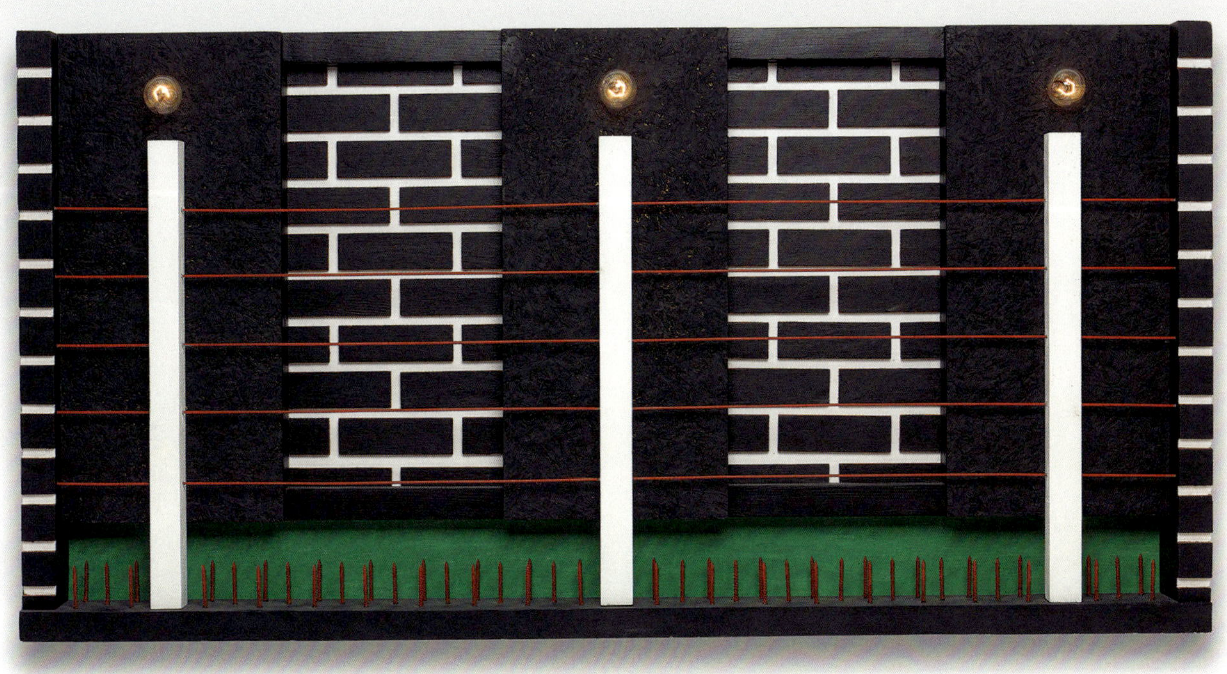

Composite 14, 1996–1997

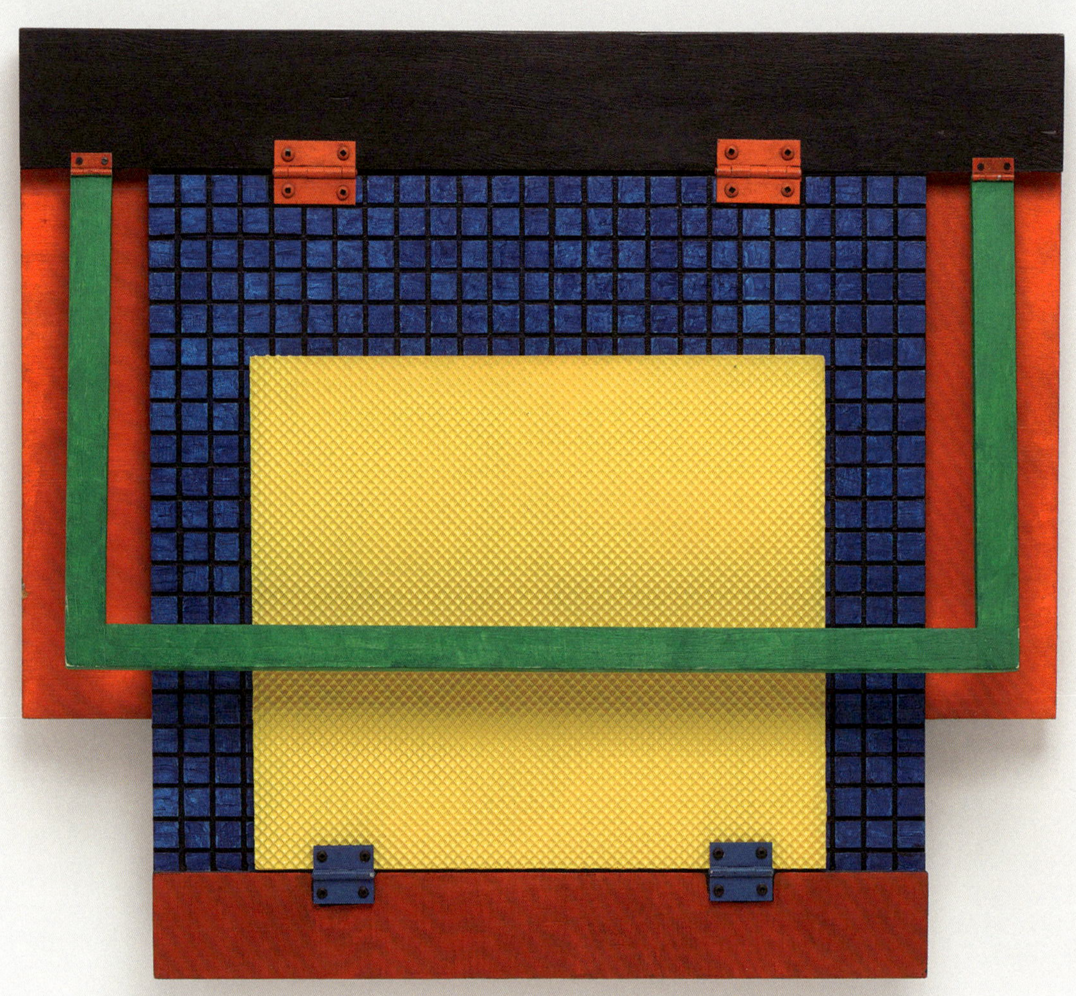

 Composite 3, 1996–1997

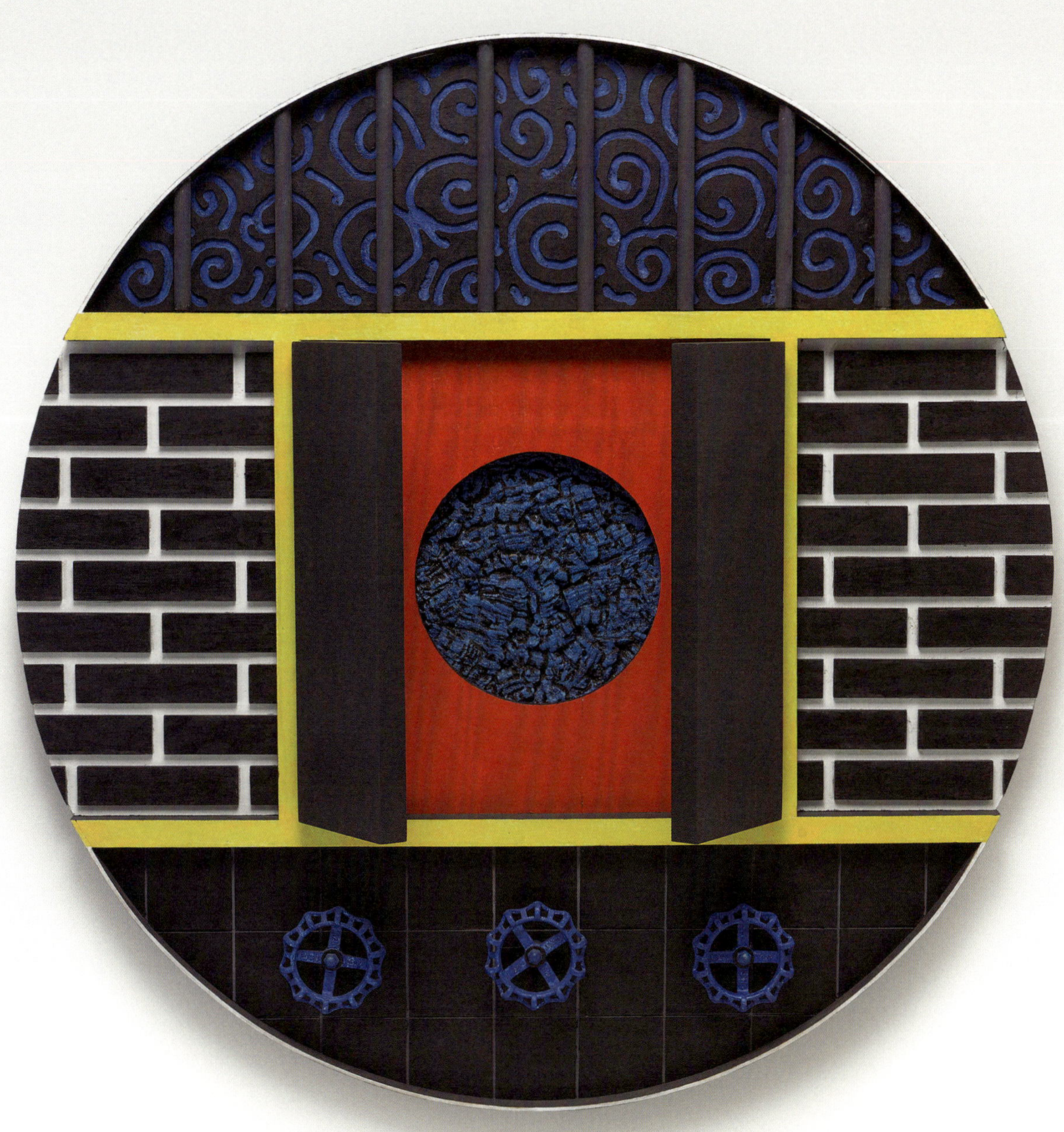

Composite 18, 1996–1997

Selected Excerpts

Over the years, there have been innumerable reviews, articles, books and catalogues published on the work of Sorel Etrog. A selection of texts from this voluminous body of written work has been reproduced here.

Sir Philip Hendy

Preface to *Sorel Etrog*, 1967

In this text, written shortly after Sorel Etrog was selected to represent Canadian sculpture at the Venice Biennale in 1966, Sir Philip Hendy reveals how the artist imbues his sculptures with his energetic spirit.

Sorel Etrog has only to take two metal bars and twist them together to produce independent life: he twists in with them his own energetic spirit and the principle of growth. His art is as fundamental as that but it is also infinitely complex.

He does not in fact twist bars of metal, but only seems to. Being very much a sculptor, and in an age when crude and slapdash effects are apt to alternate with the overly mechanical, he is one of the superb technicians. Of the many spirits which live in his bronzes, the most obvious perhaps is the spirit of metal itself. At first sight one thinks: "Here is metal! Why don't more sculptors make metal speak like this?" For Etrog it sings, because he understands its substance, its tensions and its surfaces—above all, its tensions. Remaining ever his servant, the forms which he moulds or carves and finally casts in it are completely under his control. They split apart and are joined again; knot and unknot, wriggle or roll, showing now one face, now another—then soar or dive, or spread their wings. But they come back always to the point of departure to start their movement again, and prove his dynamism. Because of him they have an indestructible strength.

In the work I have seen he has used metal and the same kind of form. But this only makes more remarkable the variety of his invention. This has developed continuously, becoming both more intricate and more spacious. Etrog now creates not only form but space, and space not only within his forms but around them. And no two forms of Etrog's have quite the same expression.

Sir Philip Hendy (1900–1980) was director of the National Gallery in London from 1946 to 1967.

Theodore Allen Heinrich

The painted constructions, 1968

Sorel Etrog's painted constructions were featured in three solo exhibitions from 1959 to 1961. Here, Theodore Allen Heinrich revisits this early stage of Etrog's career and examines the close relationship between these works and the artist's sculptures.

It is difficult for a secure westerner to have any true concept of such a life as Sorel Etrog's although the experience has been shared by millions elsewhere, among whom have been other articulate artists and writers. It is this combination of human experience and the ability both to convey something of its quality and meaning and to rise above it that gives importance to Etrog's work.

He is a man who has been three times uprooted, only once by deliberate choice, who has had to learn one or more new languages with each change of continent, who has seen, smelled, heard and felt things that most of us are lucky enough to know only as remote events from which we are insulated by newsprint or the cold television screen.

Sorel Etrog was born in 1933 at Jassy, the old and colourful capital of Moldavia in northern Roumania. The city was prosperous and cultivated, rich in churches of the 15th and 17th centuries, with several museums, a university, but somewhat isolated and living in close relation with the traditional peasantry of the surrounding countryside. It was also for centuries the home of a Jewish community unusually large for the Balkans. To this the Etrogs belonged and the boy was not to enjoy many of the advantages Jassy offered. He was six when the Germans came and the nightmare began. Children were not molested and even of this time there are occasional happy memories mixed with those of hunger, penury, the constant threat of house-raids at night, and from 1941 air-raids. The climax came in a pogrom when ten thousand men and boys over seventeen, nearly all the adult Jewish males, were herded into a compound and machine-gunned. Etrog's father was one of the half-dozen who escaped under harrowing circumstances but so badly wounded that it was two and a half years before he could walk again. One of his own playmates when Etrog was nine was shot before his eyes when they were engaged in a boyish effort to earn a few pennies by manufacturing cigarettes for soldiers out of dried sunflower leaves. When the Germans left the Russians came and things were not much better, particularly for Jews. The sudden terrors that even today rise unbidden out of the past were still very frequent haunts in the years of the work to be considered in detail and are often enough their direct source as well as of obsessive details that constantly recur in other, apparently unrelated, contexts.

During the Russian occupation Etrog had his first art instruction at school and for the first time, in his mid-teens, started to draw and to paint. The instruction seems to have been reasonably good, if heavily guided in the direction of socialist realism. He recalls devoting energy and enthusiasm to the execution of a blatantly political collage that covered a whole classroom wall because the activity was fun, but it did not occur to him that he might become an artist. During that final year in Jassy, he had instruction in painting from a well-known artist, Lobëll.

After an abortive, costly and frightening effort to escape from Roumania via Hungary, the family succeeded in reaching Israel by way of Istanbul in 1950. They settled at first under refugee conditions at Rishon le Zion. One of his earliest (1950–1951) surviving paintings, of a gaunt young woman holding a child in a refugee tent, shows her with a hole in place of a stomach: the central void is a fairly constant motif to this day.

He got a job working in a medical supply house and was encouraged to think of preparing for a modest career in business. In January 1953, he began his thirty months of army service and did a second period of active duty during the Suez Crisis in 1956. In the first period he was stationed in Tel Aviv and was fortunate in having a highly cultivated sergeant, Yahin Hirsch, who encouraged him to apply for an Army scholarship to the new art school just established there in 1953. Another influential friend was Rafi Lavi, then starting to be a painter. A combination of army service and the school fortunately proved possible to manage.

At the art school he, too, thought he might be a painter, alternately encouraged by Janco with whom he studied drawing and urged to give it up by his watercolour instructor, Streichman. He also had a stage-design class with the painter Mokady. Meanwhile, he had made his first tentative construction, *Prayer for a New Moon*—actually a normal painting of eccentric shape—a year before either the army or the Institute. Others followed quickly, but in secret, for he dared show them to neither instructors nor fellow-students. He recalls hiding them under his bed. The Institute and its ambience provided a number of benefits. He found congenial friends among the students and sympathetic help among his elders. He particularly remembers the class-hero, Schlomo Schwartz, a virtuoso who could do everything, and a non-productive but vital character known as "Doctor" who was full of music and innovations and could draw with both hands. Through the new friends he started frequenting the lively Millo Club (speciality: half-hamburgers for poor students after panel discussions) and attending Saturday evening concerts at the Museum: The majority of the constructions of this time, after the initial group relating to walks along the harbour, have musical experience, both classical and jazz, as their source.

On finishing both course and military service in 1955 he moved on the introduction and with the strong encouragement of Janco to the small artist's colony of Ein Hod, where he started to work in earnest and openly on his painted constructions. One important piece of technical help he would have been unable to get at the Institute was how to make the applied reliefs and the contour *cloisons* of thin strips of wood stick to the basic structure and to do so without breaking in the process. This he was taught by his father, a man with capable hands and an untraditionally sympathetic attitude toward a gifted son. The grandfather in Roumania had been a carpenter and had forbidden that any of the grandsons enter his workshop or touch the tools. He was much loved by the boys, but for this reason Sorel had grown up with no real experience in working with his hands; the longing one day to have his own tools was naturally exacerbated by the prohibition, and the situation now in Israel with the constructions represented a victory.

In 1956 he was included in his first group exhibition and began attending lectures in art history, a new world to him, being given by the late Dr. Eugene Kolb, then Director of the Tel Aviv Museum, and was given the run of the Museum library by another perceptive new friend, Dr. Friedman, who was in charge of it. These friendships were very important. From or through them he became familiar with Klee, Miro, Picasso and met Chagall, the latter providing not a stylistic model but inspiration as a successful artist whose life and sense of humour, akin to Etrog's own, had raised him far above circumstance.

Dr. Koln in 1956 hung the *Ladder of Surprises* in his office and a little later bought it for the Museum. He then acquired *Requiem in Blue* for himself and early in 1958 bought the elegant *Boom-Boom* for the Museum. During these two years Etrog participated in four more group shows, the last of them appropriately called "Art of Tomorrow". Most of the critics disliked his novel work but one, Ascher Nahor, was consistently favourable and carried his encouragement to the point of being the first purchaser of an Etrog construction, *The Petrol Lamp* of 1954.

These circumstances cumulatively produced the invitation for a one-man show at the Z.O.A. House in Tel Aviv in 1958, a show of some impact. He exhibited twenty-four constructions, sixteen watercolours, ten drawings and a collage which had already entered the collection of the Museum of Modern Art in Haifa. In his introduction to the catalogue Marcel Janco had described the constructions as "oil paintings in relief". Janco remarked a romantic tendency in the young artist and emphasized the relations existing between his "constructivist creations" and both architecture and society—he was struck by their plastic qualities and their humanity.

The success of the show had an unexpected consequence. Etrog was awarded a scholarship for advanced students at the Brooklyn Museum. This meant another major uprooting, but of course he accepted. On the way to America he managed on the most minuscule of travelling allowances to visit the Louvre and the Brussels Fair and to ship to New York many of the unsold pieces from the Tel Aviv exhibition. The paramount experience of the trip was the sight of his first Rembrandts. No other painter but Monet, first seen in New York, had so direct an effect on his technique of painting.

The year in Brooklyn was lonely and discouraging but in many ways useful. His meagre English left him verbally inarticulate and forced him in on himself. In the classes he did life-drawing and some painting of set-up still-lifes. One of the surviving oils in the latter category shows him nostalgically avoiding most of the set problem, which he translated into the terms of an Etrogian construction. Its palette is almost identical with that of *Halleluiah* and there is an overlying simulated scaffolding of the by now well-established *cloisons* and disk-ended drumsticks. He did a good deal of independent drawing in the museum, where he made an excited and influential discovery of primitive, particularly African, art. During the latter part of the year he joined a sculpture class, but did not, curiously, attach any significance to it then or now.

Meanwhile the realities of the American cost of living had become painfully apparent. What in Israel had looked a munificent bursary proved to be a good deal less than sufficient. Nonetheless he declined the offer of a job with a Manhattan advertising agency and took a less time-consuming evening job at a Hebrew Home for the Aged in Brooklyn where he gave art therapy classes, supervised the bingo games and got free meals, some compensation for the low salary. He lived in an abandoned, heatless fish-shop on Underhill Avenue where the water had been turned off. Under these circumstances serious work was extremely difficult. He did many watercolours, some of which were developed as constructions the next summer in Canada, and started only two constructions but they, too, were finished at Southampton, Ontario.

Like all young hopefuls coming to New York he started confidently to make the rounds of the dealers, carrying constructions of the scaffolding series from Tel Aviv wrapped in newspaper. He began of course with the most famous and was startled to meet with reactions ranging from indifference to rudeness. One of the most celebrated contemporary dealers threw him out almost bodily after asking him scornfully, "Young man, don't you realize we live in an age of abstract expressionism?"

A crucial episode occurred by chance in March 1959. He had called uninvited on Rose Fried to try to interest her in his work. She was sympathetic but had no opening in her schedule. While the pieces were still standing against a wall the perceptive Canadian collector Samuel J. Zacks (currently Board Chairman of Toronto's Art Gallery of Ontario) walked in, saw them and instantly bought *White Scaffolding*. Before flying home that night, he visited the fish-shop "studio" and was sufficiently impressed with both the work and the evident need of the artist that, on impulse he invited Etrog to visit him in Toronto. During his stay Mr. and Mrs. Zacks together decided to extend the invitation in a most practical and helpful way: They offered him facilities for working and living at Southampton on Lake Huron where Mr. Zacks then owned a large woodworkshop.

Etrog arrived in Toronto on a hot morning in mid-June and shortly thereafter the very tall, very thin, very shy young artist was installed at Southampton where he worked until late October. There he had for the first time in his life an abundance of free high-quality wood and his first opportunity to use powered band-saws. In the solitude of that summer, with proper tools and materials, and a little later, the possibility of a one-man show with Walter Moos in Toronto, he embarked on a season of prodigious activity. In four months he produced twenty-five constructions, though the painting of some of these was only finished during the next winter in New York; he developed new themes and an altered style; he did many drawings in heavy India ink and a fat bundle of watercolour studies for constructions; and he made seven sculptures. Of these he destroyed two, but a pair in wood, a pair in terracotta and one plaster survive.

In October 1959 he held his first one-man show in North America at the Gallery Moos. It contained twenty-six new and old painted constructions and some drawings. The following year he was given a show of constructions and small sculptures at the Lewis Gallery in Waterbury, Connecticut, and in 1961 Walter Moos gave him a second exhibition in Toronto, in which the constructions were eclipsed by the bronzes. The last of them had already been executed.

Etrog had meanwhile returned to New York in the autumn of 1959. Here continuing an interest in primitive art, first aroused in the Brooklyn Museum, and enormously stimulated by exposure to superb works in the Zacks collection, he widened his knowledge of Oceanic carving, Pre-Columbian clay figures and Peruvian textiles.

It seems to have been the careful scrutiny of a Dogon mask sometime late in 1960 and seeing that the eye-sockets were not "holes" but positive elements in an entily[sic] that "reconciled" him, as he now puts it, to the full three-dimensionality of sculpture. The circular openings appearing in even the earliest constructions and drawings had always been stopped in some way until the penultimate and splendid *Barcarolle*. He did only one more, and then abruptly turning his entire energy and attention to sculpture. That story, so far and so brilliantly as it has developed, had been recorded elsewhere, in William J. Withrow's book and in numerous exhibition forewords. At the same time he moved to Canada, where he has since become a citizen.

The painted constructions have a continuing importance in themselves as well as for their germinal relation to so much of the sculpture. The language of form which developed in the constructions over a decade was already very clearly stated in the very beautiful early drawing (1950 or 1951) reproduced as the tailpiece to this introduction: It has subject, the spread fingers in the ancient Hebrew gesture expressing sanctity, and further reference to story in the abstract symbol of the teeth; it is supported on a palette-like substructure broken into fused planes in very shallow relief; it has a stopped opening; some of the principal decorative elements are indicated as raised above the surface or recessed within it; and it has a minor but active accent of the kind Etrog refers to as soloists.

If the period of the constructions can in one sense be seen as an unconscious avoidance of coming to grips with solid forms, it can far more importantly be understood as a time of maturing reconciliation of a passion for visually and tactilely sensuous surfaces in colour with a deeply buried but ineradicable sense of pure form, the painterly and the sculptural. If the constructions began as a painter's rebellion against confining rectilinear frames, they were equally strongly *for* relationships in space.

His art of the decade of the constructions is one of equipoised tensions built out of polarities on every level of formal structure and meaning, and on interpenetrations and fusions of form and colour. These principles continue into and inform his sculpture with great vitality. The essential difference between the painted constructions and the bronzes and marbles of later years lies less in the fact that reliefs have become implacably three-dimensional in their space-displacing and space-enhancing function of activated solids and voids than in the fact that in them light replaces colour.

Those familiar with his working methods know that it is normal for him to work on a single piece for very extended times and to have a number of works in simultaneous progress. The apparently lengthy gestations of many of the bronzes will now seem to have been even longer, for many of the germinal ideas had their origins in the painted constructions of the years before Sorel Etrog knew that he was a sculptor.

Theodore Allen Heinrich (1910–1981) was professor of art history at York University and former director of the Royal Ontario Museum.

William J. Withrow
Introduction to *Sorel Etrog*, 1967

William J. Withrow explores how Sorel Etrog has been inspired by the art of ancient civilizations, and how a preoccupation with the human condition pervades his work.

Sorel Etrog has consistently remained loyal to the traditional wood, marble and bronze of the sculptor. In terms of media his most experimental work was done first as a student in 1954 and again in 1959 when he created painted wood constructions. But even then the aim was not to invent a novel technique but to find a personal visual language. In the latter half of 1965 Etrog made some unusual embossed graphics but the same single-minded search for a means of expression motivated this work as well.

From his first wood constructions to his monumental bronzes, this search clearly presents the linear development of his career. His style has grown like a plant and in retrospect one can see the pattern evolving with almost no diversive essays. If there were any dead-end sideroads they were explored in the artist's mind only, for his extensive sketch books filled with hundreds of drawings—enough to keep him working for several lifetimes—yield no evidence except reinforcing parallels to the mainstream. What is the ultimate goal? Like the late Giacometti, whom he admired greatly for his intense dedication to the search for perfection, Etrog will always be seeking.

One naturally wonders why Etrog's personal vision must see the world in terms of the tension-dominated combination of opposing forces pervading his work: linear and volumetric, geometric and organic, restful and dynamic, sensual and spiritual.

This polarity was early recognized in an exhibition catalogue of Etrog's paintings in Tel Aviv in 1958 when Marcel Janco, one of his instructors at the Art Institute wrote, "Art is an expression of emotion and rationality working like a pendulum; now it swings towards the functional-rational form; at other times towards the nebulous romantic creation." Etrog continues to combine the poles of this and other opposites to create sculpture which vibrates with the tensions of life. His style is not only the result of an intellectual position taken over the years, but stems also from the circumstances of his life. The influences which have shaped his work are rich and varied, for Etrog has read deeply and travelled widely. But two major influences have made an indelible impact. The first is his own work in the form of the early constructions and the second is the art of ancient civilizations.

Ever since his four years of study at the Brooklyn Museum with its magnificent collection of primitive art, especially Near-Eastern, African and Pre-Columbian, Etrog has been moved by the art of ancient civilizations.

What attracts him to primitive art is its rich simplicity. Its better examples, such as cycladic terracotta votive figures or African fertility goddesses say so much with so little. In the examples of primitive art Etrog admires, all of life's mysteries appear to be distilled. These artists many thousands of years ago captured the quintessence of life itself. It is this ability that Etrog strives for and is the reason for his continuing study of primitive art. His timely introduction to the collection of Mr. and Mrs. S.J. Zacks has strengthened and nourished this student interest, though it is only recently that their collection has taken this direction. So primitive art is for him a source of direct stylistic inspiration and also a source of spiritual power. Etrog's empathy for the artistic efforts of ancient cultures seems to permit him some kind of mystic communication with these long-dead artists. This may explain the timeless and often immutable quality of certain sculptures by Etrog such as *Sunbird* and *Moses*.

In spite of the somewhat esoteric quality emanating from Etrog's interest in primitive art, his work is at the same time contemporary in its mechanical references. His 1965 work particularly presents many suggestions of the uneasy alliance between man and machine. In fact some of his work could be read as a vision of man becoming machine. Regardless of the interpretation, none can deny the obvious connotation of wheels, cogs and armatures which form the upper anatomical parts of such a work as *Moses*.

An analysis of the subject matter with which Etrog has concerned himself over the years reveals that he has been preoccupied with one theme: the human condition. His concern is with the fundamental aspects of existence: the urge to survive which is expressed in our drive to defend, nourish and reproduce ourselves. In procreation Death is most effectively vanquished.

One quality which pervades all Etrog's work, and is both subject matter and form, is growth. Though most evident in a piece like *Blossom*, it could be argued that all his work speaks of organic growth. Etrog's work is not organized on an addictive basis but rather expands from within as though it was the inevitable and almost pre-ordained outcome of a planted seed.

Etrog has turned out an incredible volume of work. The almost unnatural drive which enables him to work a non-stop ten-to-twelve-hour day in the studio, seven days a week and then draw and paint into the early hours of the morning stems from more than the usual desire to succeed. Does it stem from a lack of roots; a lack of identity with any community? Only recently has he begun to identify himself with his country of adoption, Canada. This process of accepting and being accepted has quite naturally been aided by recent large commissions such as those at Expo 67 and at the new railway station in Ottawa. Most significant of all was his commission to represent Canadian Sculpture at the 1966 Venice Biennale. Etrog, like the majority of successful young artists in this and other countries, believes that the ideal of a distinctly national art is outdated. But he is happy to be called a Canadian artist. He has found a home.

William J. Withrow (born 1926) was director of the Art Gallery of Ontario from 1961 to 1990.

Florian Rodari
Secret Paths, 1999–2000

In this previously unpublished text, Florian Rodari discusses a decade-long period of Sorel Etrog's career in which the artist focused almost entirely on a series of large-format drawings of bulls. Some of the works in this series are reproduced on page 68 while Etrog's reinterpretation of Pablo Picasso's *Guernica* is on pages 70–71.

Between the spring of 1979 and the fall of 1989, Etrog concentrated almost exclusively on drawing. Though he had always drawn, this medium had never previously taken on such importance in his work. But, due to his assiduity, the means he brought into play, his attempt to push the theme to its limit, the large format and complexity of the undertaking, this series was different. Beyond any thematic reference, it was a new and unusual test for the instrument, and it expressed a will to affirm something fresh through the medium of drawing. It was doubtless also an attempt to take a break from sculpture and painting while pursuing perennial obsessions. Perhaps it was an escape, a respite? On every type of support, in every size, using every technique, Etrog realized hundreds of sketches, studies, fragments and meticulously-completed works on a single theme: *Bulls*. As is so often the case with this artist, the image came in series, born under the pressure of a vital, almost blind, need; and, with them, the artist sought to exhaust the resources of the theme in every possible way. The sculptor, who has an absolute need for space to express himself and develop his volumes in three dimensions with an acute awareness of the interactions between light and texture, imposed upon himself the stringent limits of surface and line. The animal's figure and movements were now shackled to the strict action of black and white.

This series of drawings is distinguished first by their awesome scale: they are as sizable as large paintings, if not murals. The version that comes closest to the point of departure from which Etrog elaborated his innumerable variations, Picasso's *Guernica*, is almost as big as the Spanish painter's famous picture. Many other sheets in the series, which focus on a single figure or develop a detail, are of substantial size. Most of them are executed in charcoal and give one the impression that they were executed very rapidly. They look like they have been flung onto paper, with no attempt to polish them. There are frequent eraser marks, like negative replications of the rough scrawls in black chalk that convulse the volumes, inflame the surfaces. One observes a remarkable unity in the format, theme, treatment and technique of these large compositions, yet they were preceded, and are commented on, by a myriad of smaller pen-and-ink or pencil drawings—intermediate versions that ceaselessly modulate, suggest new departures, or seek to escape from triteness—only to be discarded in the end.

The approach of the sculptor that Etrog was initially is felt in his choice of medium—the charcoal stick, with its thick husky accents. It is perceptible, too, in his constant striving to reach a focal point, to bend back the pointed extremities of his figures to their center of gravity.

And the result is that, especially in this series' large charcoal drawings, the cognitive resources of drawing tend to give way to an exceptional plasticity. Pencil and eraser carve out sweeping, curving lines in the mass of powerful, heavy figures. Etrog works by adding and removing, exactly as if he were shaping a lump of clay, leaving tool traces like luminous scars, animating the surface with the ruggedness of a fleshy body quivering with vitality. The contrasts between black and white displace space in hard masses that defy common sense. Yet space regains its stability through the artist's sharp perception of points of rest, which suggests the kind of knowledge of levers and tensions one would expect from someone who is accustomed to handling tremendous weights.

Whether working in two or three dimensions, Etrog strives invariably for the same effect: to sustain a tension of ordinary moments on the surface of the canvas or in space, to speed up every rhythm, accentuate every peak, dynamize to the utmost the relationships between colours, shapes, volumes, shadows, degrees of light. In sculpture, for instance, he opts for the slowest, heaviest of materials, and labours over it until it takes on an expression of soaring. In drawing, he labours over lines until they translate an impression of volume and their blackness produces colour.

In the late 1960s, Etrog painted a number of pictures inspired by great compositions of nineteenth- and twentieth-century masters—paintings of grouped figures, bathers or dancers, essentially nudes. Very faithfully repeating the composition of Jean-Dominique Ingres's *Turkish Bath*, for example, he elaborated (like a composer inventing variations) an impressive number of visual musings that celebrate dynamic relationships which distinguish figures from each other or, in the secrecy of their anatomy, structure them. At nerve centres on the back, stomach, nape and head of languid bathers, Sorel looped a stitch that not only reinforced the effect of an articulation between different parts of their bodies and those of the painting, but also arrested the eye of the viewer accustomed by the unusual, suggestive theme to more gracefulness. Indeed, the bodies concealed behind the nakedness of flesh by the French painter's meticulous brushwork are brutally revealed in Etrog's work as mechanisms.

Inasmuch as they are points of maximum energy, these nerve centers where the body's hinges and joins do their work are by nature painful; they are nodes of increased vulnerability. Cavities, pivots, knots where feeling concentrates and is raw, they are essentially the hands, eyes, mouth, chest and genitals. Highly symbolic zones of extreme excitability, they compose a sensual anatomy defined by pleasure and pain rather than logic. Junctions, intersections where energy flows are reversed, where meaning and movement pivot, they are often invisible, and our awareness of them is frequently unconscious. The painter's task is to reveal them, to pinpoint them, to intensify them. For the existence of such "knots" also means that there are relationships, transitions, exchanges between one point and another; there is life, growth, motion; there are reversals—all of which can translate as expression.

Formally, this work contains a complete vocabulary of signs that at times denote a joining together, at other times a transmission, and at still other times exclusion. More often than not, in fact, these three contradictory motions occur simultaneously. Bolts join two elements together but keep them separate as well. Wheels

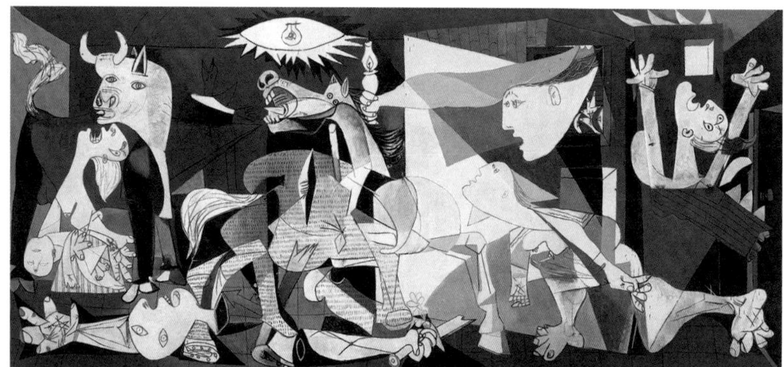

Pablo Picasso (born Malaga, Spain, 1881; died Mougins, France, 1973), *Guernica*, 1937, oil on canvas, 349.3 × 776.6 cm. Museo Nacional Centro de Arte Reina Sofía (Madrid, Spain). © Picasso Estate/SODRAC (2013).

revolving around an axle are liable at any moment to reverse their directions. Hinges close as well as open. Elbows, wrists, knees, ankles, collarbones, hips determine within the human skeleton, much as universal joints, connecting rods and pistons determine within a machine, a combinatory system of complex articulations, the tensions of which are various, mobile, never permanently fixed. All of them favour interlockings, penetrations, couplings that cease only with death. But these multiple linkages do not simply insure the reproduction and perpetuation of a vital relation; they also designate a mode of creating and loving that naturally defines the activity of the being endowed with existence. To act in this manner is to forgo relinquishing oneself; it is endlessly to attempt the union of opposites. Etrog's most moving works are held together by bolts. Yet, in spite of everything, their relentless hardness expresses the closeness of the bond between mother and child.

Etrog chose an unusual theme for this series of drawings entitled *Bulls*, not only because of the depth of the obsession that dwelt for several months on the artist's retina, but also because of its multiple treatment. There is nothing innocent about it. Very early, in the first, wholly abstract works that he executed in Tel Aviv, bullheads appear behind the dense handling of the artist's formal structures. From then on, the bovine theme, sometimes expressed in full and sometimes reduced to a single horn, was never to vanish from his works, doubtless due to its symbolic and formal power. It cropped up in drawings and prints; it combined its bestial characteristics—cavernous nostrils, massive muzzle, uplifted horn—with the powerful faces the sculptor modelled in the 1960s.

In the numerous sketches that Etrog devotes to the theme of bulls, horror and tenderness intertwine by virtue of that ambiguous presence of evil within us, consisting of a morbid attraction as well as repulsion and sometimes, in very sensitive persons, a more discerning approach to the being's truth. The body and its articulations, from the formal modes of which the artist's expressive vocabulary is likewise drawn, inspire the visual ponderings of Sorel Etrog, who, as we have observed more than once, possesses an extreme sensitivity. The artist constantly emphasizes nerve centres, those nodes through which life's energy surges and withdraws. Every orifice, especially the vagina and mouth, allows feeling to flow through it and provides an outlet—an expression—for pleasure and pain.

The encounter between Etrog and Picasso seemed necessary, not so much because of the boost it provided (for it was at least as much of a boon as a hindrance) as because it invited the artist to surpass himself. It would be naive to assume that an artist of Etrog's caliber could dispense with memory.

Sorel Etrog's response to the emotion that *Guernica* arouses (and, earlier, to the one provoked by his discovery of Goya's etchings) was to isolate the articulation of those images, the points of tension which in his eyes constituted most of their meaning; and then to pursue at his own pace, after his own fashion, that which had perhaps escaped the notice of those artists and which seemed to him not only timelessly universal, but also indispensable to his own art.

In the same way that Picasso looked to African Art not as a model but as a confirmation of his own reading of the world, Etrog interprets—or rather, appropriates—*Guernica* like a musician borrowing a folk theme and

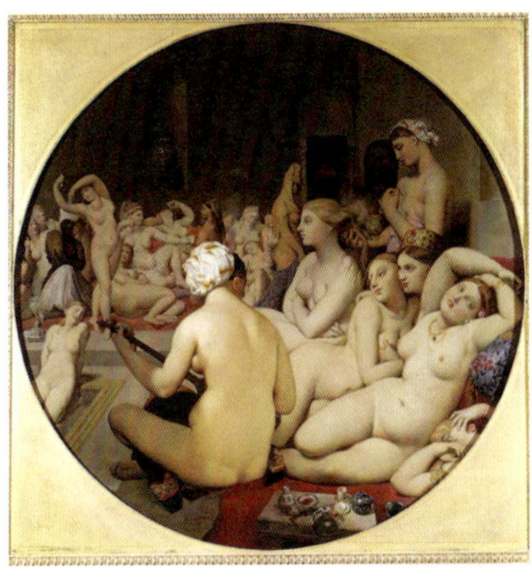

Jean-Auguste-Dominique Ingres (born Montauban, France, 1780; died Paris, France, 1867), *The Turkish Bath*, 1862, oil on wood, 108.0 × 108.0 cm. Musée du Louvre, France.

combining it with his own inner music to reinterpret it, to make it so completely his own that it becomes wholly assimilated to his own language. Artworks are like faces of landscapes: some hold the eye more firmly than others—they constrain the eye to dialogue with them, to question them repeatedly in order to fathom their secret, their riches, but also to respond to their unwavering scrutiny. The familiarity that distinguishes them connects with some as yet unexpressed rhythm, speaks a language that would remain forever undeciphered were it not for the fact that we reach out toward it in a thousand ways. Etrog's relationship to *Guernica* is of this order. The admiration he feels for the painting as an object is not the only reason for his seeking to appropriate it; something else is involved, a kind of injunction, an inner summons. Only by responding to this call can the artist discover his own response.

If one looks closely at the similarities and differences between the two versions—Picasso's and Etrog's—one notices that the latter transposes the bombardment of *Guernica* into a composition in which individual figures (men, women, children, horses, birds) are recast as bulls. Every detail in Picasso's picture that points to the scourge being visited on the scene from outside—expressed by triangular shapes as piercing as arrowheads or blades puncturing flesh—is converted, in Etrog's drawing, into a whirling confusion of bodies, a general madness that is self-destructive as well as blind. This transformation has the effect of replacing the immediate, historical reference to a specific event of the Spanish Civil War with a more universal drama, one that slumbers more deeply in human psychology.

But the violence here is not at all the same violence as in *Guernica*. Picasso rejects, his image clamours of destruction, a specific destruction, a brutal conclusive rupture. With Etrog, it is more a question of distortion, a failure of forms and figures to tear away and separate themselves from each other. Likewise, Etrog's sculpture never divides; it combines, painfully; it compacts; it binds together. Hence the recurring theme of mother and child; hence, too, the couples—lovers, wrestlers, dancers—who are always turning back to each other. All are permanently connected; they can never be separate. Even the assemblages furthest removed from the human figure are bound by articulations. By executing a series of drawings inspired by the theme of bulls Etrog has done more than just question a set of images that express a violent meaning or situation. His obsession has combined with another essential theme in his work—the theme of the link.

The cow and her calf, the passive bullock, and the fighting bull correspond each in its own way to various physical, symbolic and aesthetic criteria. The motif of the horns, that of the body, the mass, the blackness, the power. The skeleton, the bones, the articulations—they join together and keep separate at the same time. A twofold dynamic that is extremely pronounced in Etrog's work. A grammar of oxymorons.

Florian Rodari (born 1949) was director of the Musée de l'Élysée in Lausanne, Switzerland, from 1979 to 1983.

SOREL ETROG

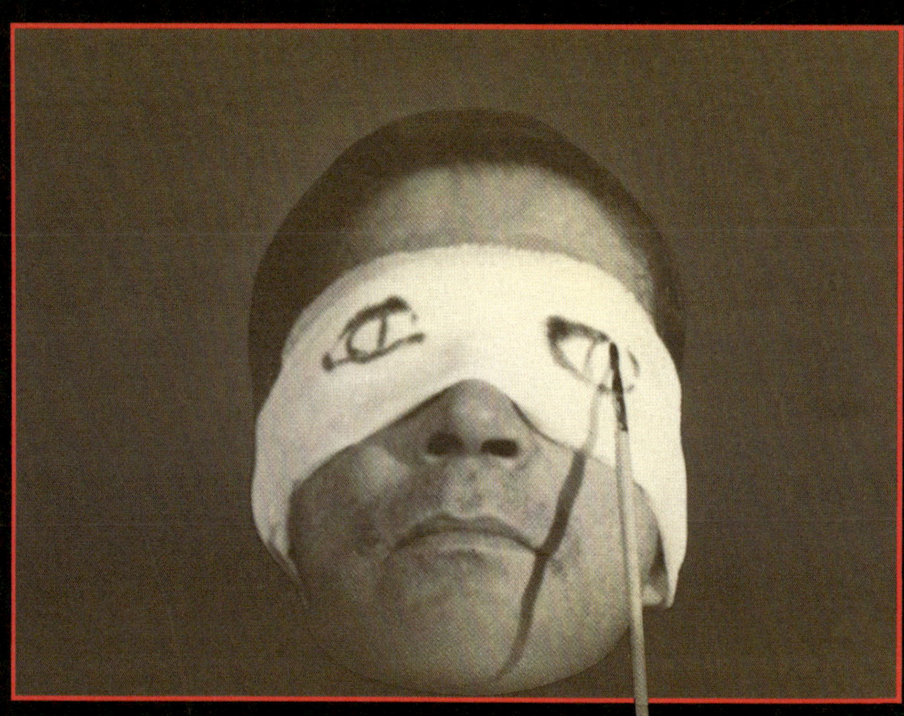

IMAGES FROM THE FILM

SPIRAL

Text by MARSHALL McLUHAN

Marshall McLuhan
Man as the Medium, 1987

In this collaboration between Marshall McLuhan and Sorel Etrog, McLuhan analyzes the multilayered structure of Etrog's film *Spiral* and connects the artist to other prominent modern and avant-garde literary figures of the twentieth century.

Etrog comes from a rich audile-tactile background and tradition of iconic art. He is first and always a sculptor and painter whose "imagery" is one of stark confrontation. His work is always multi-levelled and multi-sensuous in ways that are not easily described in conventional literary terminology. His materials, his "vocabulary", are *symboliste* in the literal sense of mosaic. Nevertheless Etrog is fascinated by the collage structures of many of the eminent "literary" figures of our time, including Beckett, Ionesco, Joyce and Eliot and Yeats. It is a misunderstanding to identify symbolist structures with literature in its older meanings. Symbolist structures, on the other hand, have much in common with film and can be seen in the work and the commentaries of Serge Eisenstein.

The film *Spiral* was not scripted but iconically drafted, image by image. The structural theme of *Spiral* presents the oscillation of two simultaneous and complementary cones or spirals, constituting the synchronique worlds of birth and death. *Spiral* is not a diachronique or lineal structure, but a synchronique and contrapuntal interplay in a resonating structure whose centre is everywhere and whose circumference is nowhere. The opening is a labyrinthine highway and the ambivalent and parallel ambulances set birth and death on wheels. In the interval between time, the preserver, and time, the destroyer, is the creative interval which constitutes both continuity and arrest, both real and imaginary. By grounding his work in the archetype of the spiral, Etrog awakens echoes of the spiral archetype in some of the most celebrated artists of our time. Yeats explained the process of this unending form of experience in his remarks on "The Emotion of Multitude". Whereas classical drama got this emotion by a parallel between the chorus and the actor:

> The Shakespearian drama gets the emotion of multitude out of the sub-plot which copies the main plot, much as a shadow upon the wall copies one's body in the firelight. We think of *King Lear* less as the history of one man and his sorrows than as the history of a whole evil time. Lear's shadow is in Gloucester, who also has ungrateful children, and the mind goes on imagining other shadows, shadow beyond shadow, till it has pictured the world.

T.S. Eliot gives further insight into the process of this archetypal form in his *Dial* reviews of Joyce: "Ulysses, Order and Myth":

> In using the myth, in manipulating a continuous parallel between contemporaneity and antiquity, Mr. Joyce is pursuing a method which others must pursue after him. They will not be imitators, any more than the scientist who uses the discoveries of an Einstein in pursuing his own, independent, further investigations. It is simply a way of controlling, of ordering, of giving a shape and a significance to the immense panorama of futility and anarchy which is contemporary history. It is a method already adumbrated by Mr. Yeats, and of the need for which I believe Mr. Yeats to have been the first contemporary to be conscious. It is, I seriously believe, a step toward making the modern world possible in art.

This principle of a continuous dual structure for achieving order has always been present in the work of Sorel Etrog. In one of his poems he called it "recollecting things to come", which might have been an alternative title for *Finnegans Wake*, itself a dramatic spiral of a single sentence:

> A way a lone a last a love a long the
> (last page)

> riverrun, past Eve and Adam's, from swerve
> of shore to bend of bay, brings us by a
> commodius vicus of recirculation back to
> Howth Castle and Environs.
> (first page)

In the film *Spiral* the ubiquitous and moving centre intensifies awareness of the fragility and transience of existence. In the uncertainty of the interval between the pram and the coffin, between birth and death, *Spiral* presents many labyrinths and portraits of the human cognitive processes. The drama of these two imbalances is portrayed by the action of the two ambulances in the labyrinth of the city streets. The body in the incubator points to a labyrinth (spiral) of respiration in a blind struggle for survival. The open heart surgery reveals the spiral of human circulation in a parallel struggle for blind survival. One of the bizarre conceits of the sequence of the sardine can concerns the obsession of a consumer age with packages, whether books or hi-rise or the nuclear family. This witty observation pervades the film as a continuing metaphor, as do the two ambulances. Where the book and the compressed package are concerned, there is the parallel observation of John Milton about a good book as "the precious life blood of a master spirit embalmed and treasured upon purpose to a life beyond life."

In *Spiral* duration is measured or fragmented. Chronological time yields to time as spaced-out moments of intensity. "Prufrock's" pitiable confession about measuring out his life with coffee spoons points to the quality of the situation: "human kind cannot bear very much reality" (*Burnt Norton*, 1. 42–43).

In *Spiral*, towards the end, we confront the contents of the sardine box as the conqueror worms are spiralling amidst the archetypes of human logic and ingenuity.

The world that Yeats alludes to as "A mound of refuse or the sweepings of a street" is endlessly alluded to as the "midden heap" in *Finnegans Wake*. In Beckett's *Breath* it is the global theatre "littered with miscellaneous and unidentifiable rubbish". Each of these artists handles his "midden heap", his "*Waste Land*", in a unique way. Beckett's world is managed by both narrative and drama. Joyce presents it as "language itself in action." Yeats presents it as the enumeration of old themes, in lyric verse. In *Spiral* Etrog confronts us with the same Waste Land situation on the wired planet in the form of both a visible dialogue of cinema and the action of symbolist drama.

Everywhere in *Spiral* there is visually portrayed the labyrinth of the creative process. The same concern pervades the poetry of Yeats, and nowhere more than in "The Circus Animals' Desertion". Towards the end of a great poetic career he looks back and asks: "What can I but enumerate old themes?" Having traversed the spiral of his own artistic development, he returns in the last stanza to the point where *Spiral* also begins again:

> Those masterful images because complete
> Grew in pure mind, but out of what began?
> A mound of refuse or the sweepings of a street,
> Old kettles, old bottles, and a broken can,
> Old iron, old bones, old rags, that raving slut
> Who keeps the till. Now that my ladder's gone,
> I must lie down where all the ladders start,
> In the foul rag-and-bone shop of the heart.

Marshall McLuhan (1911–1980) taught at the University of Toronto and was one of the most influential media theorists of his day.

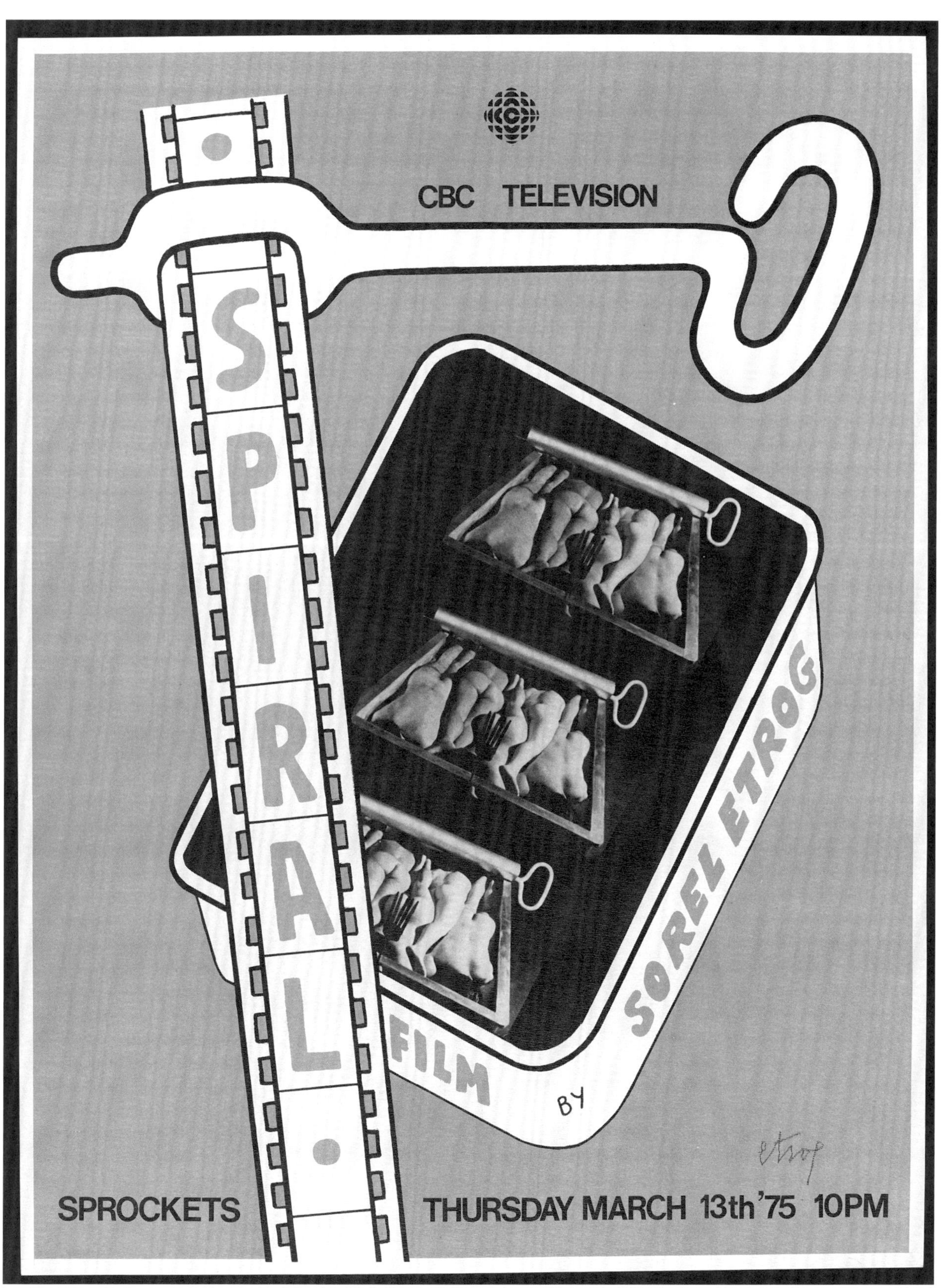
CBC TELEVISION
SPIRAL
FILM
BY
SOREL ETROG
SPROCKETS
THURSDAY MARCH 13th '75 10PM

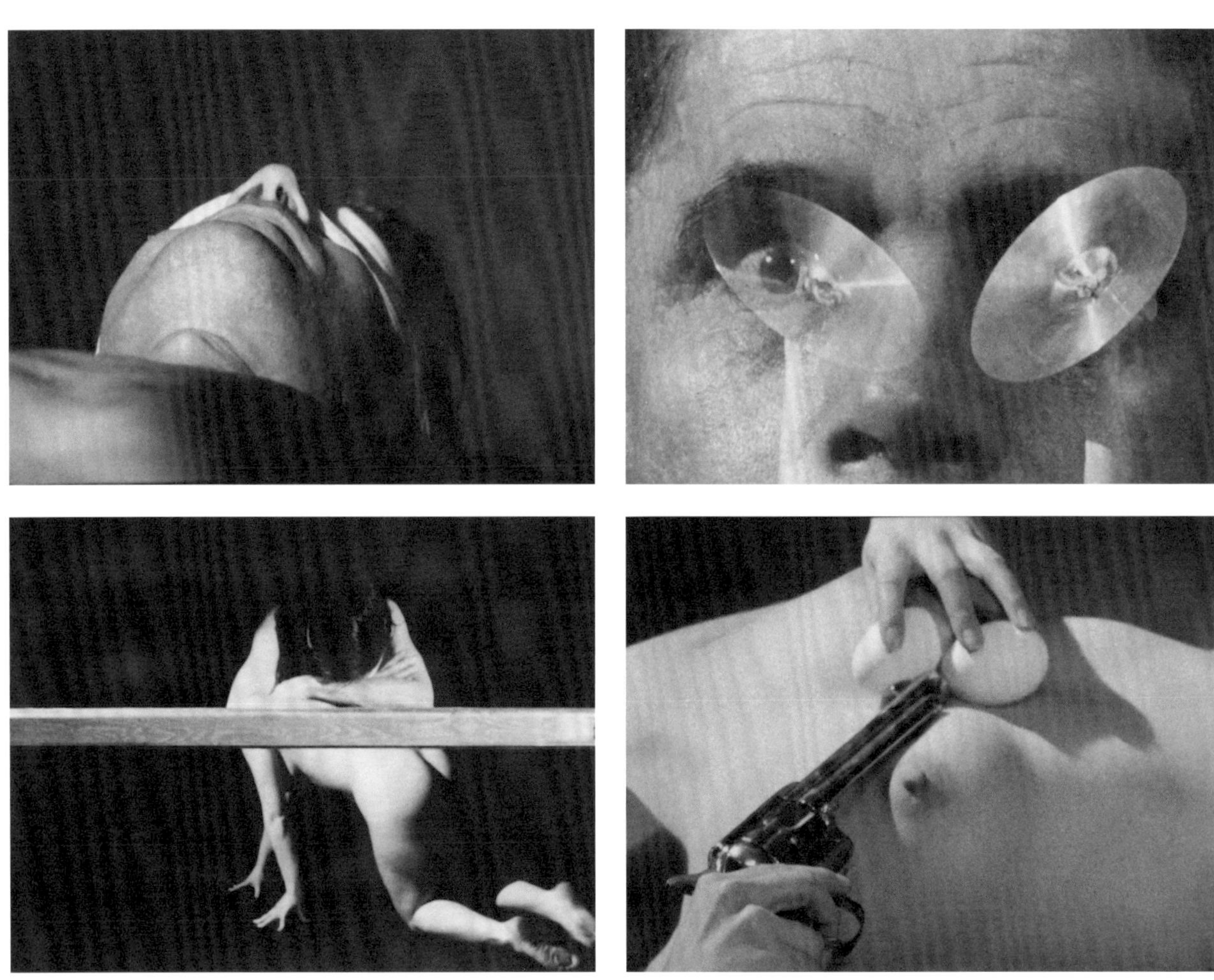

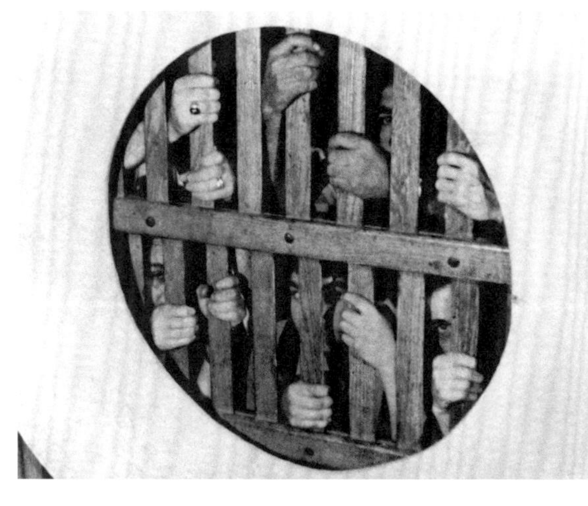

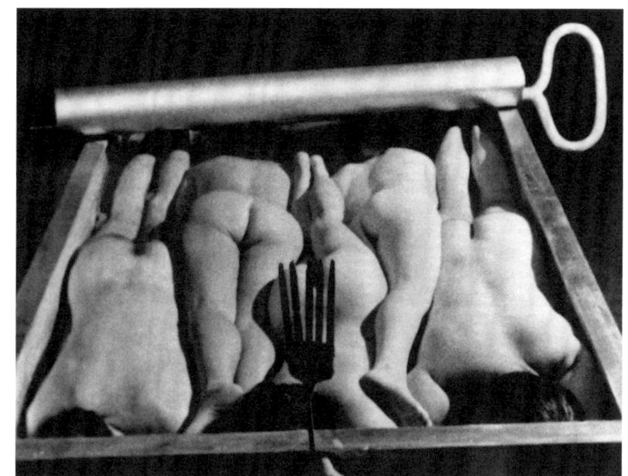

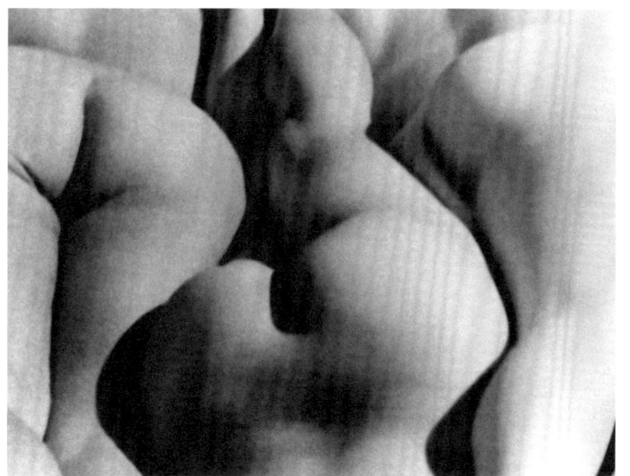

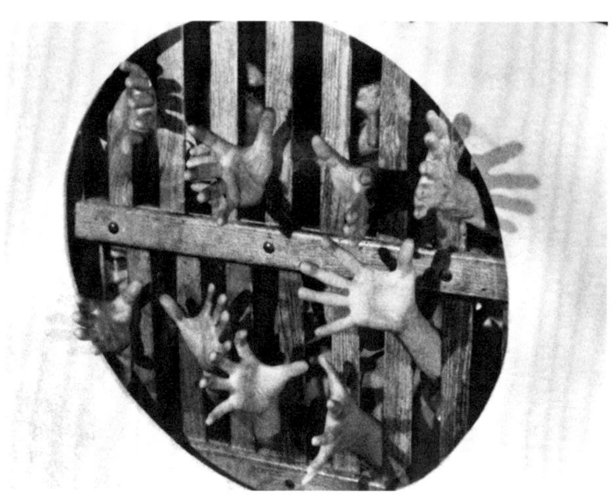

Gary Michael Dault
The Door Opens from the Inside, 2013

The time goes by too swiftly, and you don't want it to, and so you don't notice it. Now, it is a few more years than I meant it to be since I last saw Sorel—and I don't know where those years went.

Our visits used to be regular, usually weekly. I loved boarding the elevator of the downtown Toronto apartment building where he has lived and worked for the past thirty-six years and pushing the button labelled HC—for Health Club. That's where Sorel's vast studio was—at the very top of the building, higher up than the penthouses, right beside the swimming pool. It meant that his studio was always as humid as a jungle.

I was writing a catalogue essay at that time for the Christopher Cutts Gallery in Toronto about the wall-mounted constructions Sorel called *Composites*. But after that was done, we began writing together—spontaneous, almost automatic little ur-poems. He'd write the first line and I'd write the second. Then he'd write a third. And so on and on. And vice versa. We both found this superbly pointless exercise exhilarating. I wish we hadn't stopped. Sorel feels the same way. So why, I wonder, did we? I suppose it was because we assumed (by the cunning use of Magic Thinking) that there would always be time-without-measure in which to fool around with language. There wasn't. Now Sorel is ill and is simply too weary to think about the bracing guilelessness of goalless writing.

During a visit a few weeks ago, I suggested to him—over-briskly, I'm sure—that we try it once again. "Look, I'll write the first line and you write the second!" I told him. "Just as we used to!" He looked at me wanly, a sad smile on his face, and dismissed the idea with a short, exhausted wave of his hand. He can't. Not now. Not anymore.

As securely established as his international reputation is as a sculptor and painter/printmaker—and has been for the past fifty years—it was his being a writer, a man-of-letters, that brought us together as friends. I remember Sorel and I discussing his friendship with absurdist Romanian playwright Eugène Ionesco—whose lithographic portrait he had drawn in 1969 and with whom he collaborated on the poem *Chocs*, published by the Martha Jackson Gallery in New York the same year. For some reason, it occurred to me to ask him what I see now was an almost sublimely irrelevant question: "What language did you and Ionesco speak when you worked together?" The old twinkle came momentarily back into Sorel's eyes. "Romanian," he said, the obviousness of this whole exchange suddenly striking us both as very funny.

I used to love to listen to him talking about Samuel Beckett. He had met Beckett in Paris over a pre-arranged dinner in 1969 and eventually worked with him, producing illustrations for *Imagination Dead Imagine*, published in a splendid limited edition in 1982. All in all, they knew each other for twenty years. On Friday, April 13, 1984, in Toronto, Sorel staged what he called a "bodifestation," a gallery-filling enactment in celebration of Beckett's 78th birthday, called *Kite*—published that same year (as *The Kite*) by John Calder in London. I had always admired the portrait Sorel had drawn of Beckett. I asked him about it again during our last visit. He was too weary to go into much detail. "It was during that introductory dinner," he told me. "I'd listen while he talked, and I doodled the portrait while I listened." It was published as a lithograph by Atelier Arte Paris in 1969.

I admire the sculpture, especially the vigorous *Painted Constructions* (1952–60), the *Links* (1963–71)—in particular, the tempestuous, mythological *Bulls* from 1969—the *Hinges* (1972–79) and the extraordinary *Steel Constructions* from the 1980s (I was never big on the *Screws* and *Bolts* from the early 1970s, though I admit that *Nagas* from 1971–72 exudes a smooth, post-Arp sculptural authority, and the weird, giant bolt-figures of *Sadko* and *Kabuki* have an exciting haughtiness that carries them beyond the cartoonishness that, for me, bedevils most of the bolt-works).

But it is Sorel Etrog the writer, the man of letters, whom I feel closest to, whom I understand best. The last time I visited him, I was looking again through his well-stocked library, momentarily revisiting the writers I knew he loved and books I knew he had of their works: Nietzsche, Jung, Joyce of course (*Finnegans Wake* is always close by), and books I had forgotten he had or at least had never seen on his shelves before such as Helene Parmelin's *Picasso Plain*, for example, or the poems of Frederick Seidel.

As a matter of fact, I'd forgotten the degree to which Irishness and Celtic culture generally was close to his heart. Noticing me browsing along the shelves, Sorel requested that I pull off the shelf his copy of Robert O'Driscoll's *The Celtic Consciousness* (1982)—he wants to show me photos of the sets and costumes he had designed for a number of plays by W.B. Yeats. They are brilliantly savage and quintessentially theatrical. "Did you ever meet Siobhán McKenna?" I ask him. And of course he had. He costumed her.

Sorel loves words dearly, passionately, and he loves them in about six different languages—including Joycean. It's still as heady an experience as it ever was to browse through Sorel's homage to Joyce, his typographic collage, *Dream Chamber: Joyce and the Dada Circus*, bound together (in corrugated cardboard covers!) with John Cage's *About Roaratorio* (*Finnegans Wake* as performable music), edited by O'Driscoll and published in conjunction with the Joyce Centenary Festival in Toronto, January 28–February 9, 1982.

In his book about Sorel (Prestel, 2001), French critic Pierre Restany quotes him as having said: "I am an egg and inside my restless planet night mysteries are hissing." This is the Sorel Etrog I love. It's brilliant being an egg. It's brilliant to see yourself as a restless planet. And it's brilliant to discern that you contain night mysteries and that they are (the most brilliant thing of all) "hissing."

Near the end of my last visit, after a quiet moment or two, Sorel looked at me and said: "I've done a lot of things." He then confided to me that he felt it was time for him to die. I don't know. Is there ever a time to die? But then he always insisted that "doors open from the inside only." I guess that is what is happening now.

Gary Michael Dault is an art critic and writer for the *Globe and Mail*.

For two friends
Marshall McLuhan
Marcel Janco

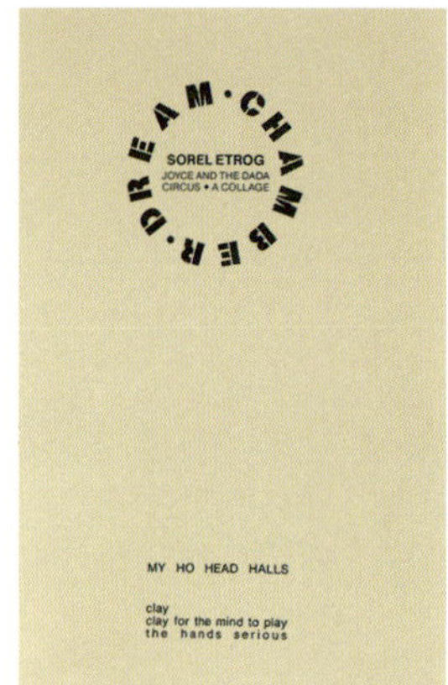

DREAM · CHAMBER ·
SOREL ETROG
JOYCE AND THE DADA
CIRCUS • A COLLAGE

MY HO HEAD HALLS

clay
clay for the mind to play
the hands serious

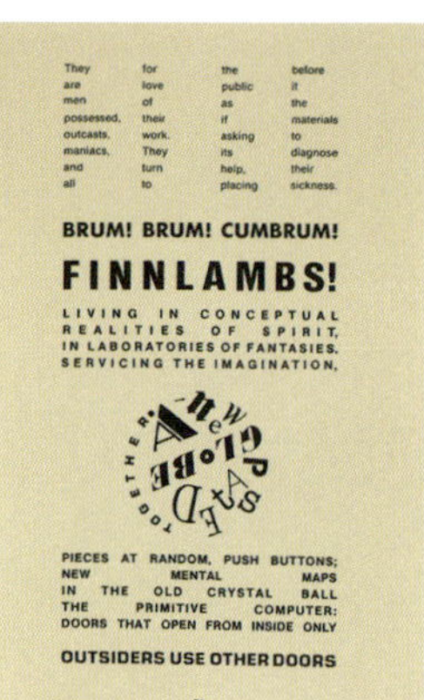

They are men possessed, outcasts, maniacs, and all for love of their work. They turn to the public as if asking its help, placing before it the materials to diagnose their sickness.

BRUM! BRUM! CUMBRUM!

FINNLAMBS!

LIVING IN CONCEPTUAL
REALITIES OF SPIRIT,
IN LABORATORIES OF FANTASIES,
SERVICING THE IMAGINATION,

PIECES AT RANDOM, PUSH BUTTONS;
NEW MENTAL MAPS
IN THE OLD CRYSTAL BALL
THE PRIMITIVE COMPUTER:
DOORS THAT OPEN FROM INSIDE ONLY

OUTSIDERS USE OTHER DOORS

21

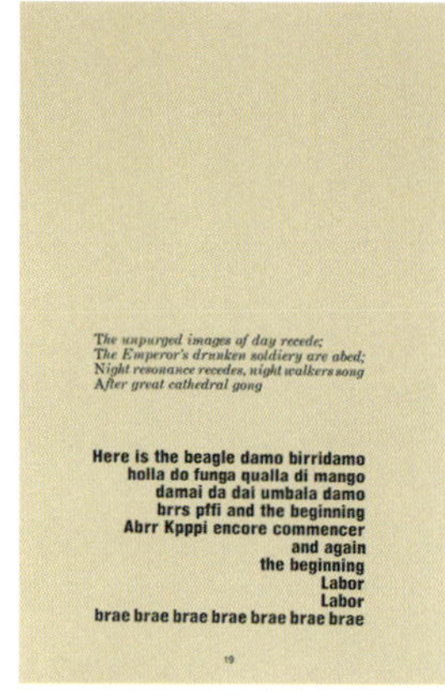

The unpurged images of day recede;
The Emperor's drunken soldiery are abed;
Night resonance recedes, night walkers song
After great cathedral gong

Here is the beagle damo birridamo
holla do funga qualla di mango
damai da dai umbala damo
brrs pffi and the beginning
Abrr Kpppi encore commencer
and again
the beginning
Labor
Labor
brae brae brae brae brae brae brae

19

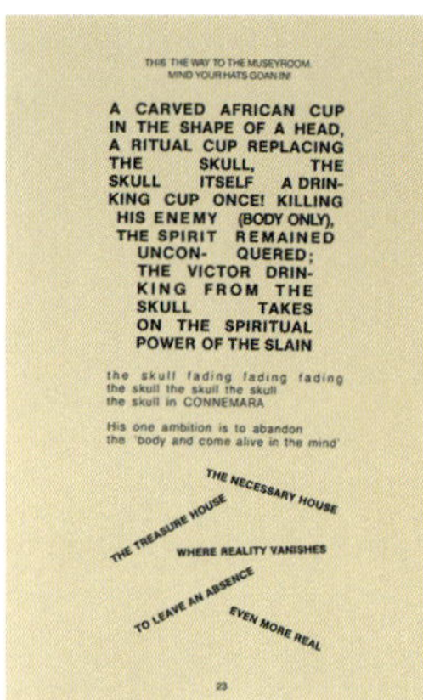

THIS THE WAY TO THE MUSEYROOM.
MIND YOUR HATS GOAN IN!

A CARVED AFRICAN CUP
IN THE SHAPE OF A HEAD,
A RITUAL CUP REPLACING
THE SKULL, THE
SKULL ITSELF A DRIN-
KING CUP ONCE! KILLING
HIS ENEMY (BODY ONLY),
THE SPIRIT REMAINED
UNCON- QUERED;
THE VICTOR DRIN-
KING FROM THE
SKULL TAKES
ON THE SPIRITUAL
POWER OF THE SLAIN

the skull fading fading fading
the skull the skull the skull
the skull in CONNEMARA

His one ambition is to abandon
the 'body and come alive in the mind'

23

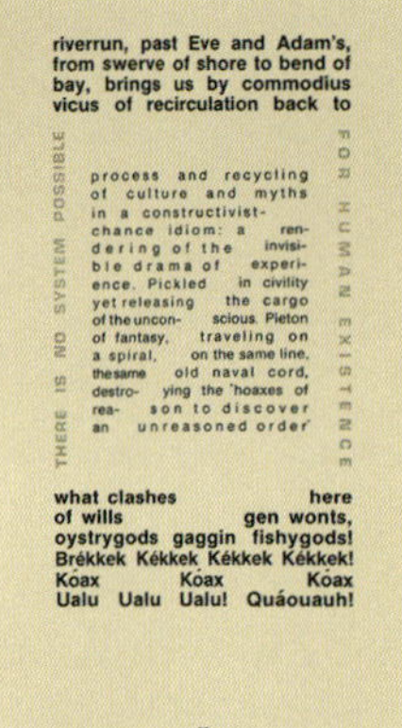

riverrun, past Eve and Adam's,
from swerve of shore to bend of
bay, brings us by commodius
vicus of recirculation back to

THERE IS NO SYSTEM POSSIBLE

process and recycling
of culture and myths
in a constructivist-
chance idiom: a ren-
dering of the invisi-
ble drama of experi-
ence. Pickled in civility
yet releasing the cargo
of the uncon- scious. Pieton
of fantasy, traveling on
a spiral, on the same line,
the same old naval cord,
destro- ying the 'hoaxes of
rea- son to discover
an unreasoned order'

FOR HUMAN EXISTENCE

what clashes here
of wills gen wonts,
oystrygods gaggin fishygods!
Brékkek Kékkek Kékkek Kékkek!
Kóax Kóax Kóax
Ualu Ualu Ualu! Quáouauh!

25

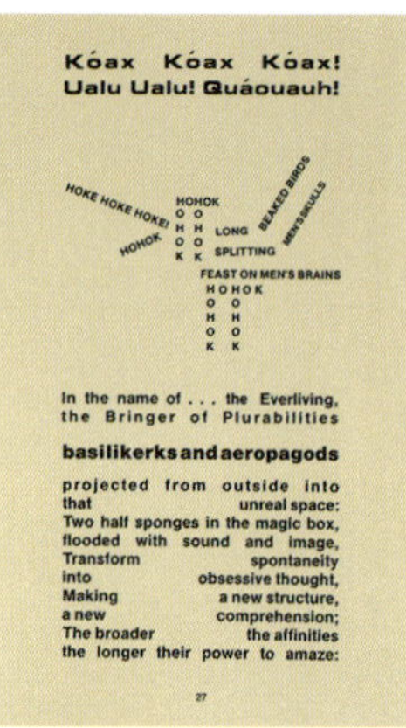

Kóax Kóax Kóax!
Ualu Ualu! Quáouauh!

In the name of . . . the Everliving,
the Bringer of Plurabilities

basilikerksandaeropagods

projected from outside into
that unreal space:
Two half sponges in the magic box,
flooded with sound and image,
Transform spontaneity
into obsessive thought,
Making a new structure,
a new comprehension;
The broader the affinities
the longer their power to amaze:

27

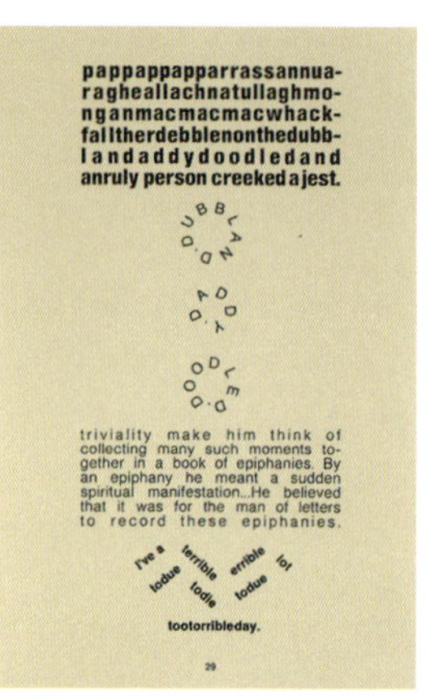

pappappapparrassannua-
ragheallachnatullaghmo-
nganmacmacmacwhack-
fallthebdebblenonthedubb-
landaddydoodledand
anruly person creeked a jest.

triviality make him think of
collecting many such moments together in a book of epiphanies. By
an epiphany he meant a sudden
spiritual manifestation...He believed
that it was for the man of letters
to record these epiphanies.

tootorribleday.

29

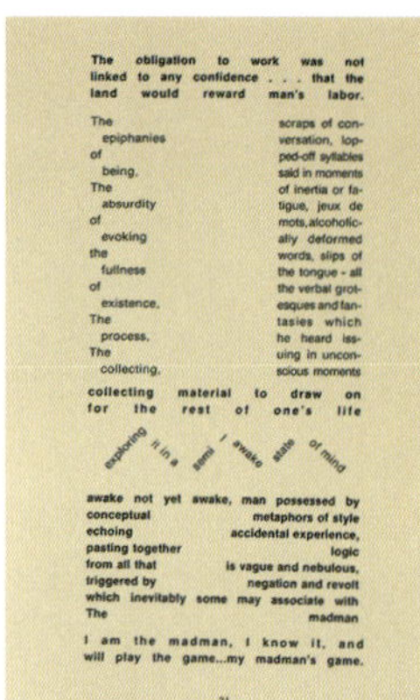

The obligation to work was not
linked to any confidence . . . that the
land would reward man's labor.

The epiphanies of being. The absurdity of evoking the fullness of existence. The process. The collecting.

scraps of conversation, lopped-off syllables said in moments of inertia or fatigue, jeux de mots, alcoholically deformed words, slips of the tongue - all the verbal grotesques and fantasies which he heard issuing in unconscious moments

collecting material to draw on
for the rest of one's life

awake not yet awake, man possessed by conceptual metaphors of style echoing accidental experience, pasting together logic from all that is vague and nebulous, triggered by negation and revolt which inevitably some may associate with The madman

I am the madman, I know it, and
will play the game...my madman's game.

31

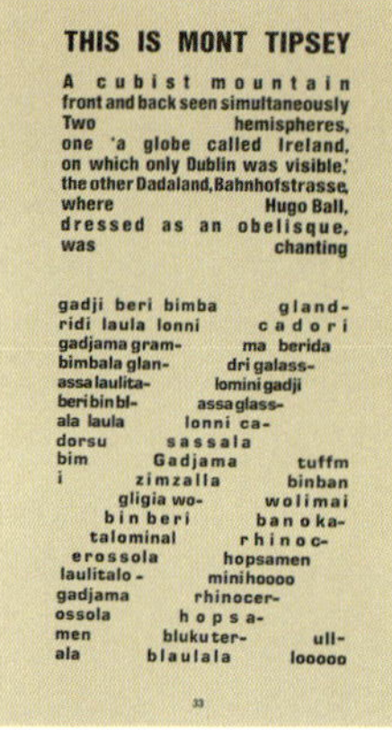

THIS IS MONT TIPSEY

A cubist mountain
front and back seen simultaneously
Two hemispheres,
one 'a globe called Ireland,
on which only Dublin was visible,'
the other Dadaland, Bahnhofstrasse,
where Hugo Ball,
dressed as an obelisque,
was chanting

gadji beri bimba gland-
ridi laula lonni cadori
gadjama gram- ma berida
bimbala glan- dri galass-
assa laulita- lomini gadji
beri bin bl- assa glass-
ala laula lonni ca-
dorsu sassala
bim Gadjama tuffm
i zimzalla binban
gligia wo- wolimai
bin beri ban oka-
talominal rhinoc-
erossola hopsamen
laulitalo - minihoooo
gadjama rhinocer-
ossola hopsa-
men blukuter- ull-
ala blaulala looooo

33

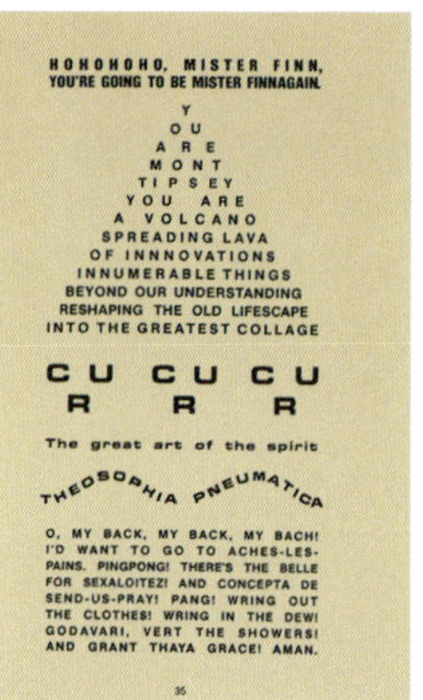

HOHOHOHO, MISTER FINN,
YOU'RE GOING TO BE MISTER FINNAGAIN.

Y
O U
A R E
M O N T
T I P S E Y
Y O U A R E
A V O L C A N O
SPREADING LAVA
OF INNOVATIONS
INNUMERABLE THINGS
BEYOND OUR UNDERSTANDING
RESHAPING THE OLD LIFESCAPE
INTO THE GREATEST COLLAGE

CU CU CU
R R R

The great art of the spirit

THEOSOPHIA PNEUMATICA

O, MY BACK, MY BACK, MY BACH!
I'D WANT TO GO TO ACHES-LES-
PAINS. PINGPONG! THERE'S THE BELLE
FOR SEXALOITEZ! AND CONCEPTA DE
SEND-US-PRAY! PANG! WRING OUT
THE CLOTHES! WRING IN THE DEW!
GODAVARI, VERT THE SHOWERS!
AND GRANT THAYA GRACE! AMAN.

35

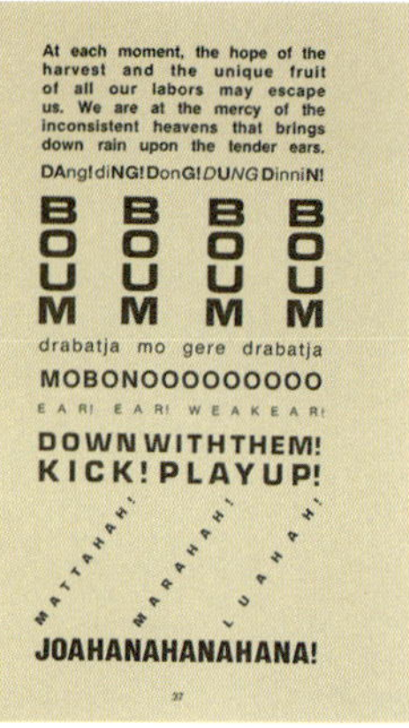

At each moment, the hope of the
harvest and the unique fruit
of all our labors may escape
us. We are at the mercy of the
inconsistent heavens that brings
down rain upon the tender ears.

DAngldiNG! DonG! *DUNG* DinniN!

BOUM BOUM BOUM BOUM

drabatja mo gere drabatja

MOBONOOOOOOOOO

EAR! EAR! WEAKEAR!

DOWN WITH THEM!
KICK! PLAYUP!

JOAHANAHANAHANA!

37

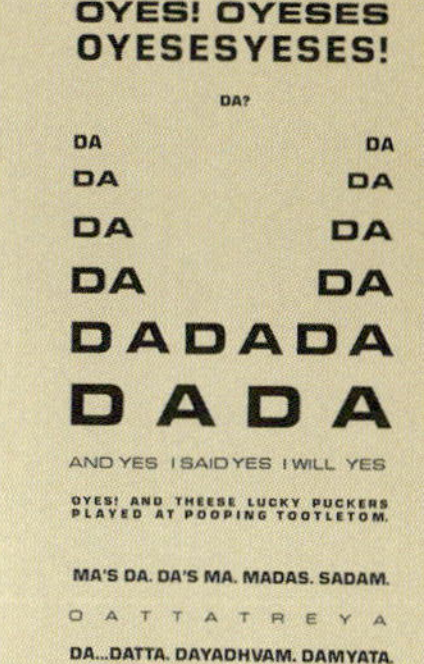

OYES! OYESES
OYESESYESES!

DA?

DA DA
DA DA
DA DA
DA DA
DADADA
DADA

AND YES I SAID YES I WILL YES

OYES! AND THEESE LUCKY PUCKERS PLAYED AT POOPING TOOTLETOM.

MA'S DA. DA'S MA. MADAS. SADAM.

D A T T A T R E Y A

DA...DATTA. DAYADHVAM. DAMYATA.
SHANTIH SHANTIH SHANTIH

39

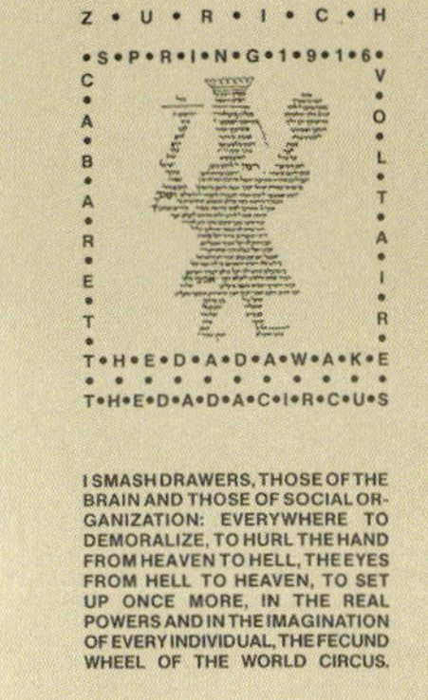

Z • U • R • I • C • H
• S • P • R • I • N • G • 1 • 9 • 1 • 6 •
C • A • B • A • R • E • T
V • O • L • T • A • I • R • E
T • H • E • D • A • D • A • W • A • K • E
T • H • E • D • A • D • A • C • I • R • C • U • S

I SMASH DRAWERS, THOSE OF THE BRAIN AND THOSE OF SOCIAL ORGANIZATION: EVERYWHERE TO DEMORALIZE, TO HURL THE HAND FROM HEAVEN TO HELL, THE EYES FROM HELL TO HEAVEN, TO SET UP ONCE MORE, IN THE REAL POWERS AND IN THE IMAGINATION OF EVERY INDIVIDUAL, THE FECUND WHEEL OF THE WORLD CIRCUS.

41

TIRED AT LAST OF THIS OLD WORLD,

They reacted to the disintegration of the world around them, Calling for a public execution of false morality, Echoing the earlier experimentalists, Duchamp and Picabia, to express 'objectivity of a subjectivity:'

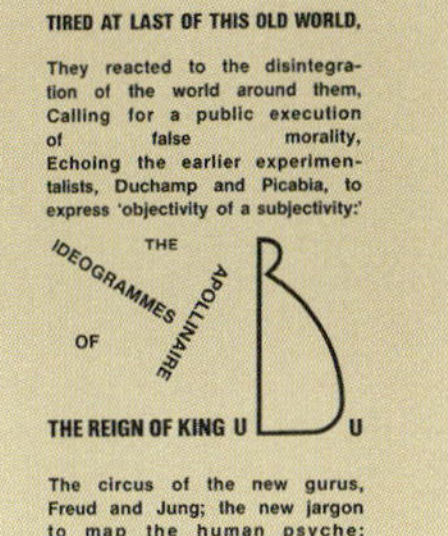

THE REIGN OF KING U U

The circus of the new gurus, Freud and Jung; the new jargon to map the human psyche; The manipulation of the dream machine; The futurist manifesto:

THE WORLD'S BEAUTY IS ENRICHED BY A NEW BEAUTY: THE BEAUTY OF SPEED

43

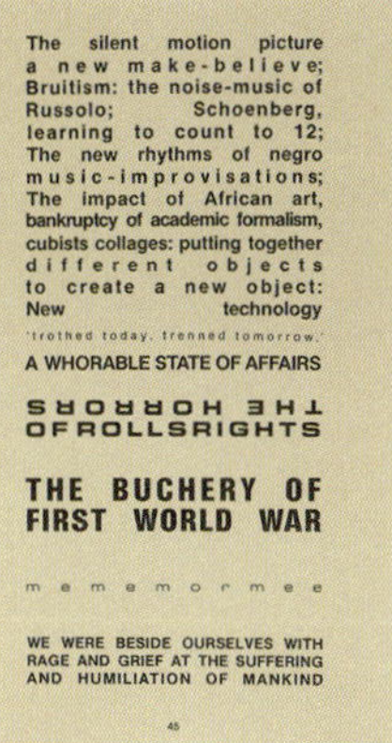

The silent motion picture a new make-believe; Bruitism: the noise-music of Russolo; Schoenberg, learning to count to 12; The new rhythms of negro music-improvisations; The impact of African art, bankruptcy of academic formalism, cubists collages: putting together different objects to create a new object: New technology

'trothed today, trenned tomorrow.'

A WHORABLE STATE OF AFFAIRS

THE HORRORS
OF ROLLSRIGHTS

THE BUCHERY OF FIRST WORLD WAR

m e m e m o r m e e

WE WERE BESIDE OURSELVES WITH RAGE AND GRIEF AT THE SUFFERING AND HUMILIATION OF MANKIND

45

SOD'S BROOD, BE ME FEAR!

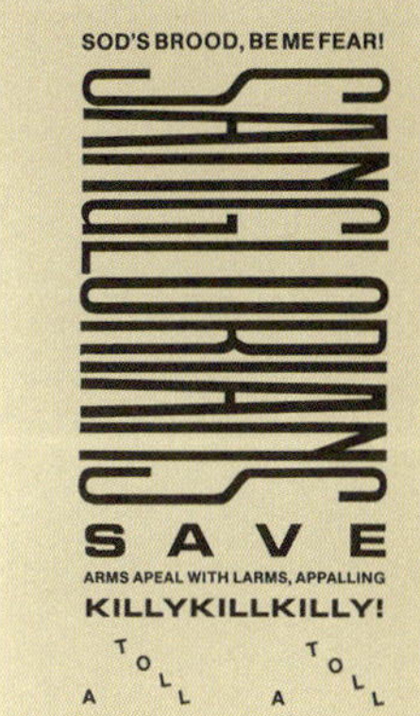

S A V E

ARMS APEAL WITH LARMS, APPALLING
KILLYKILLKILLY!

T O L L A T O L L

who will now carry the burning banner, to play the daily black joke?
thinkinthou gaily?
Lick-Pa-flai-hai-pa-Pa-li-si-lang-lang.

SANGLORIANS

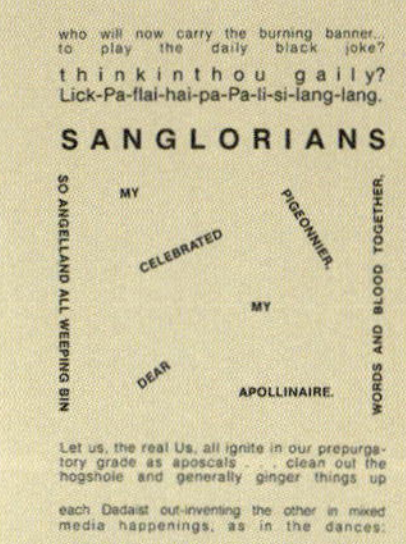

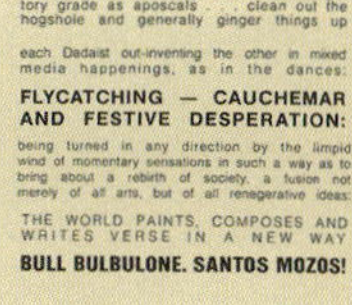

Let us, the real Us, all ignite in our prepurgatory grade as aposcals ... clean out the hogshole and generally ginger things up

each Dadaist out-inventing the other in mixed media happenings, as in the dances:

FLYCATCHING — CAUCHEMAR AND FESTIVE DESPERATION:

being turned in any direction by the limpid wind of momentary sensations in such a way as to bring about a rebirth of society, a fusion not merely of all arts, but of all renagerative ideas:

THE WORLD PAINTS, COMPOSES AND WRITES VERSE IN A NEW WAY

BULL BULBULONE. SANTOS MOZOS!

49

ENDONATIONAL CALAMITIES

GAYLEGS TO RIOT OF US! GALLOCKS TO LAFFT!

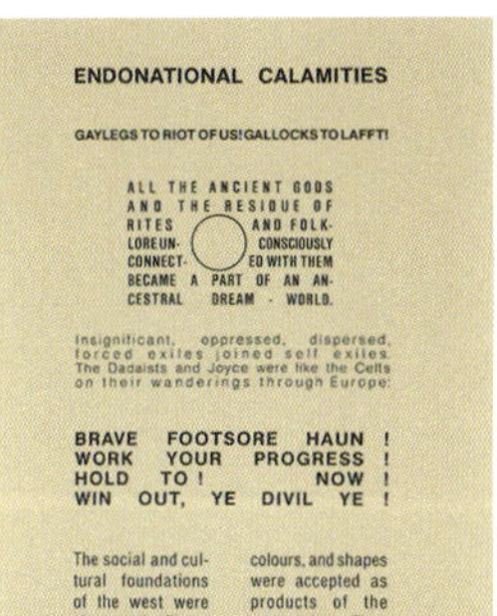

ALL THE ANCIENT GODS AND THE RESIDUE OF RITES AND FOLKLORE UNCONNECTED WITH THEM CONSCIOUSLY BECAME A PART OF AN ANCESTRAL DREAM - WORLD.

Insignificant, oppressed, dispersed, forced exiles joined self exiles. The Dadaists and Joyce were like the Cells on their wanderings through Europe:

BRAVE FOOTSORE HAUN ! WORK YOUR PROGRESS ! HOLD TO ! NOW ! WIN OUT, YE DIVIL YE !

The social and cultural foundations of the west were shattered; Fixed points of established order were destroyed; Radical departures from familiar logic were taken; Words, colours, and shapes were accepted as products of the unconscious. They got rid of the intoxication of the past, put experience into motion, and created 'Anti-art', 'Anticulture'.

51

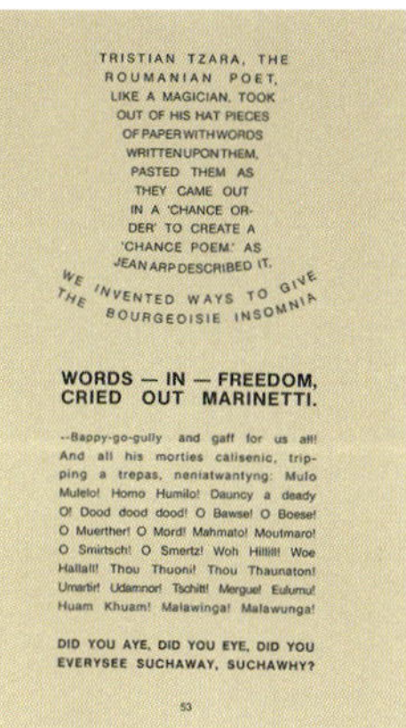

TRISTIAN TZARA, THE ROUMANIAN POET, LIKE A MAGICIAN, TOOK OUT OF HIS HAT PIECES OF PAPER WITH WORDS WRITTEN UPON THEM, PASTED THEM AS THEY CAME OUT IN A 'CHANCE ORDER' TO CREATE A 'CHANCE POEM.' AS JEAN ARP DESCRIBED IT,

WE INVENTED WAYS TO GIVE THE BOURGEOISIE INSOMNIA

WORDS — IN — FREEDOM, CRIED OUT MARINETTI.

--Bappy-go-gully and gaff for us all! And all his morties calisenic, tripping a trepas, neniatwantyng: Mulo Mulelo! Homo Humilo! Dauncy a deady O! Dood dood dood! O Bawse! O Boese! O Muerther! O Mord! Mahmato! Moutmaro! O Smirtsch! O Smertz! Woh Hillill! Woe Hallall! Thou Thuoni! Thou Thaunaton! Umartir! Udamnor! Tschilt! Merguel Eulumu! Huam Khuam! Malawinga! Malawunga!

DID YOU AYE, DID YOU EYE, DID YOU EVERYSEE SUCHAWAY, SUCHAWHY?

53

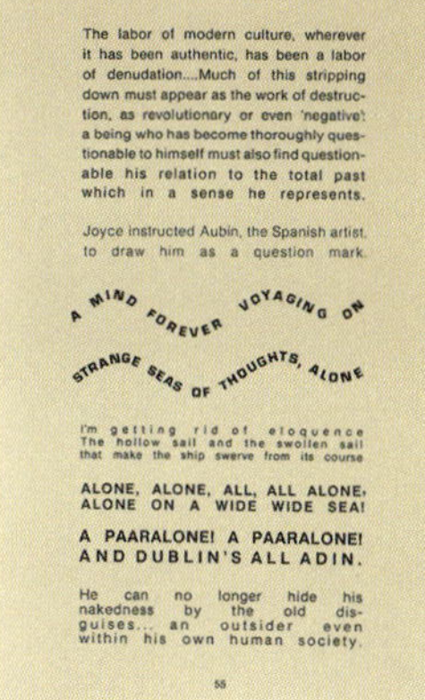

The labor of modern culture, wherever it has been authentic, has been a labor of denudation....Much of this stripping down must appear as the work of destruction, as revolutionary or even 'negative': a being who has become thoroughly questionable to himself must also find questionable his relation to the total past which in a sense he represents.

Joyce instructed Aubin, the Spanish artist, to draw him as a question mark.

A MIND FOREVER VOYAGING ON
STRANGE SEAS OF THOUGHTS, ALONE

I'm getting rid of eloquence
The hollow sail and the swollen sail that make the ship swerve from its course

ALONE, ALONE, ALL, ALL ALONE, ALONE ON A WIDE WIDE SEA!

A PAARALONE! A PAARALONE! AND DUBLIN'S ALL ADIN.

He can no longer hide his nakedness by the old disguises... an outsider even within his own human society.

55

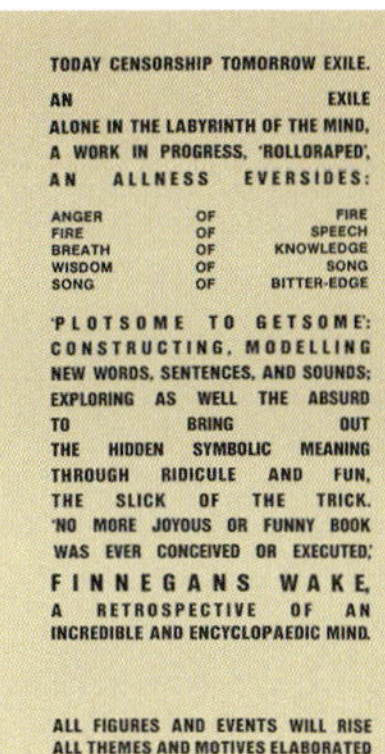

TODAY CENSORSHIP TOMORROW EXILE.

AN EXILE ALONE IN THE LABYRINTH OF THE MIND, A WORK IN PROGRESS, 'ROLLORAPED', AN ALLNESS EVERSIDES:

ANGER	OF	FIRE
FIRE	OF	SPEECH
BREATH	OF	KNOWLEDGE
WISDOM	OF	SONG
SONG	OF	BITTER-EDGE

'PLOTSOME TO GETSOME': CONSTRUCTING, MODELLING NEW WORDS, SENTENCES, AND SOUNDS; EXPLORING AS WELL THE ABSURD TO BRING OUT THE HIDDEN SYMBOLIC MEANING THROUGH RIDICULE AND FUN, THE SLICK OF THE TRICK. 'NO MORE JOYOUS OR FUNNY BOOK WAS EVER CONCEIVED OR EXECUTED,'

FINNEGANS WAKE, A RETROSPECTIVE OF AN INCREDIBLE AND ENCYCLOPAEDIC MIND.

ALL FIGURES AND EVENTS WILL RISE ALL THEMES AND MOTIVES ELABORATED

57

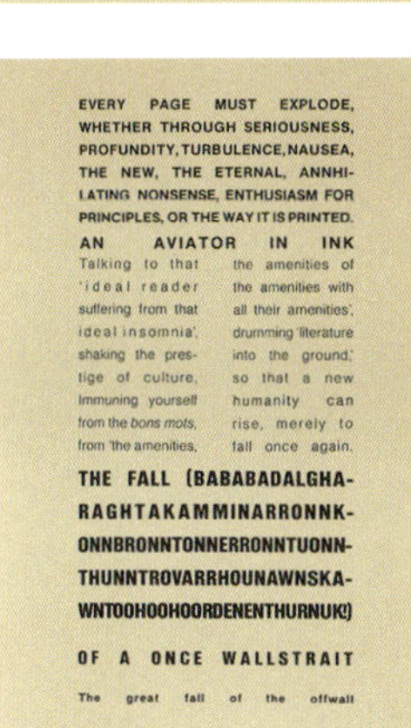

EVERY PAGE MUST EXPLODE, WHETHER THROUGH SERIOUSNESS, PROFUNDITY, TURBULENCE, NAUSEA, THE NEW, THE ETERNAL, ANNIHILATING NONSENSE, ENTHUSIASM FOR PRINCIPLES, OR THE WAY IT IS PRINTED.

AN AVIATOR IN INK

Talking to that 'ideal reader suffering from that ideal insomnia', shaking the prestige of culture, immuning yourself from the bons mots, from 'the amenities, the amenities of the amenities with all their amenities', drumming literature into the ground, so that a new humanity can rise, merely to fall once again.

THE FALL (BABABADALGHARAGHTAKAMMINARRONNKONNBRONNTONNERRONNTUONNTHUNNTROVARRHOUNAWNSKAWNTOOHOOHOORDENENTHURNUK!)

OF A ONCE WALLSTRAIT

The great fall of the offwall

59

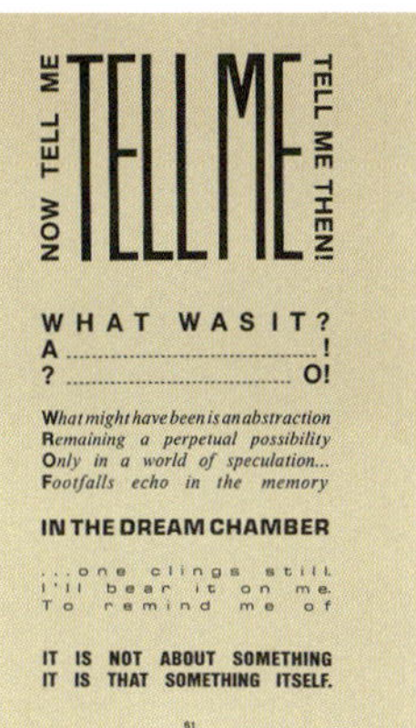

WHAT WAS IT?
A ....!
? .... O!

*What might have been is an abstraction
Remaining a perpetual possibility
Only in a world of speculation...
Footfalls echo in the memory*

IN THE DREAM CHAMBER

...one clings still
I'll bear it on me.
To remind me of

IT IS NOT ABOUT SOMETHING
IT IS THAT SOMETHING ITSELF.

61

List of Works

Works in the Exhibition

Society of Triangles
1954–1955
oil-painted wood relief
71.4 × 65.5 cm
Gift of Walter Carsen, Toronto, 1995
96/32
Page 16

String Quartet (Bartok)
1955
oil on wood
58.4 × 73.0 cm
Gift of Sam and Ayala Zacks, 1970
71/152
Page 17

White Scaffolding
1956–1958
oil on wood
77.5 × 40.6 cm
Gift of Sam and Ayala Zacks, 1970
71/156
Page 18

Barbarian Head
1959
bronze
25.0 × 17.0 cm
On loan from Sorel Etrog
Page 26

Corinth
1959
bronze
16.3 × 6.7 × 9.2 cm
On loan from Sorel Etrog
2008/27
Page 26

The Golem
1959
wood
40.6 × 33.0 × 15.2 cm
Gift of Sam and Ayala Zacks, 1970
71/145
Page 29

Haielet
1959
bronze
38.0 × 11.0 cm
On loan from Sorel Etrog
Page 27

War Remembrance
1959
bronze
14.7 × 21.5 cm
On loan from Sorel Etrog
Page 27

Blossom
1960–1961
bronze
height: 111.0 cm
On loan from Sorel Etrog
Page 34

Ritual Dancer
1960–1962
bronze (edition 6 of 7)
height: 147.3 cm
Gift of Mrs. O.D. Vaughan, 1980
80/100
Page 31

Waterbury
1961
carved wood
height: 305.0 cm
On loan from Sorel Etrog
Page 8

Capriccio
1961–1964
bronze
height: 284.5 cm
On loan from Sorel Etrog
Page 32

The Jester
1962–1964
bronze (edition 5 of 7)
height: 196.0 cm
Gift of Sam and Ayala Zacks, 1970
71/139
Page 30

Sunbird II
1962–1964
bronze (edition 1 of 5)
199.5 × 89.9 × 68.3 cm
Purchase, Corporations'
Subscription Endowment, 1965
64/30
Page 35

Moses
1964
bronze
129.0 × 48.0 cm
Collection of Sorel Etrog
Page 40

Pulcinella
1964–1966
bronze
113.0 × 41.9 × 20.3 cm
Collection of Mrs. Sonja Bata
Page 41

Complexes of a Young Lady
1965
bronze
height: 274.3 cm
Collection of Jay and Barbara Hennick
Page 33

L'oiseau qui n'existe pas
1966
bookwork with embossing
40.8 × 31.8 cm (each sheet)
Anonymous gift, 1980
80/73
Pages 46–47

Giallo di Sienna
1966–1967
marble
21.6 × 27.9 × 11.5 cm
Gift of Sam and Ayala Zacks, 1970
71/144
Page 48

Vladimir and Estragon (Waiting for Godot)
1967
oil on canvas
97.8 × 152.4 cm
Gift of Sorel Etrog, 2011
2011/386
Page 56

Homage to Cimabue
1968
bronze
height: 38.1 cm
On loan from Sorel Etrog
Page 26

Boxer
1968–1970
pastel on paper
59.7 × 45.0 cm
Gift of Sorel Etrog, 2013
108575
Page 58

Beckett
1969
lithograph on paper
66.0 × 50.8 cm
Gift of Sam and Ayala Zacks, 1970
71/140
Page 43

Bull Unicorn
1969
bronze
80.0 × 81.2 × 35.6 cm
On loan from Sorel Etrog
Page 69

Chocs
1969
bookwork with 13 lithographs and acetates: written by Eugène Ionesco; designed and illustrated by Sorel Etrog
Published by Martha Jackson Editions, NY
Courtesy of the E.P. Taylor Research Library & Archives, Art Gallery of Ontario
Pages 66–67

Imagination Dead Imagine
1969–1977
bookwork: 10 original prints designed and illustrated by Sorel Etrog (English translation of Samuel Beckett's *Imagination morte imaginez*, 1965)
First published by Calder & Boyars Ltd, London
Courtesy of the E.P. Taylor Research Library & Archives, Art Gallery of Ontario
Pages 44–45

Portrait of Ionesco
1969
lithograph on paper
49.5 × 37.5 cm
Gift of Sam and Ayala Zacks, 1970
71/147
Page 65

Quartet
1969
painted bronze
137.2 × 127.0 cm
Collection of Esther and Sam Sarick
Page 49

Study for Targets: Dancing Bull
1969
charcoal on paper
102.0 × 81.5 cm
On loan from Sorel Etrog
Page 68

Study for Targets: Fallen Head
1969
charcoal on paper
77.0 × 91.0 cm
On loan from Sorel Etrog
Page 68

Study for Targets: Three Carcasses
1969
charcoal on paper
77.0 × 107.0 cm
On loan from Sorel Etrog
Page 68

Targets (Study after Guernica*)*
1969
graphite on paper
152.0 × 366.0 cm
On loan from Sorel Etrog
Pages 70–71

Turkish Bath (Study after Ingres)
1969
oil on canvas
diameter: 200.6 cm
On loan from Sorel Etrog
Page 63

Two Dancers
1969
charcoal on paper
61.0 × 46.0 cm
On loan from Sorel Etrog
Page 59

Yoga
1969
pastel on paper
65.0 × 50.0 cm
Gift of Sorel Etrog, 2013
108578
Page 58

The Patriarch (Sam Zacks)
1969–1970
oil on canvas
101.6 × 127.0 cm
Gift of Sorel Etrog, 2011
2011/385
Page 57

Fallen Man
1971
pastel on paper
45.9 × 61.2 cm
Gift of Sorel Etrog, 2013
108579
Page 58

Bashota
1972
bronze
31.5 × 7.0 x 8.0 cm
On loan from Sorel Etrog
Page 26

Cybelle
1972
painted bronze
26.5 × 7.5 × 6.0 cm
On loan from Sorel Etrog
Page 27

Quartet
1972
painted bronze
48.3 × 12.7 cm
On loan from Sorel Etrog
Page 27

Samburu
1972
painted bronze
182.0 × 84.0 × 45.0
On loan from Sorel Etrog
Page 73

Buffon
1973
painted bronze
height: 29.2 cm
On loan from Sorel Etrog
Page 27

Figure
1974
pastel and graphite on paper
49.8 × 35.0 cm
Gift of Sorel Etrog, 2013
108581
Page 61

Henry Moore
1974
charcoal on paper
44.0 × 33.4 cm
On loan from Sorel Etrog
Page 58

Spiral
1974
16mm film (black and
white, sound, 30 mins.)
music: *Cello Concerto No. 1*
by Dmitri Shostakovich
On loan from Sorel Etrog
Pages 110–111

Harbour
1974–1975
pastel on paper
33.8 × 47.5 cm
On loan from Sorel Etrog
Page 58

Hinge Head with Figure
1974–1975
pastel on paper
32.3 × 25.0 cm
On loan from Sorel Etrog
Page 58

Mytho Head
1974–1975
pastel on paper
60.8 × 45.5 cm
Gift of Sorel Etrog, 2013
108595
Page 60

Parade
1974–1975
pastel, oil, watercolour, ink and porous pointed pen on paper
32.2 × 25.1 cm
On loan from Sorel Etrog
Page 61

Structural Man
1974–1975
pastel on paper
22.9 × 17.8 cm
On loan from Sorel Etrog
Page 61

Anguish
1975
pastel on paper
39.0 × 30.5 cm
Gift of Sorel Etrog, 2013
108573
Page 61

Aviator
1975
watercolour, ink, porous pointed pen, charcoal and pastel on paper
35.3 × 27.9 cm
Gift of Sorel Etrog, 2013
108574
Page 61

Law of the Jungle
1975
watercolour, pastel and oil on paper
22.9 × 30.4 cm
On loan from Sorel Etrog
Page 61

Antitete
1976
bronze
7.5 × 9.3 × 4.7 cm
On loan from Sorel Etrog
Page 27

Crusader II
1976
bronze
height: 16.5 cm
On loan from Sorel Etrog
Page 26

Dream Chamber
1976
bronze
height: 157.5 cm
Collection of Canadian Apartment Properties Real Estate Investment Trust
Page 82

Headoors
1976
bronze (edition 1 of 5)
129.5 × 45.7 × 40.6 cm
Gift of Sorel Etrog Ltd., 2011
2011/379
Page 79

Hingo
1976
bronze (edition 2 of 7)
123.2 × 26.7 × 22.9 cm
Gift of Sorel Etrog Ltd., 2011
2011/380
Page 80

Magic Barrel
1976
bronze (edition 1 of 7)
61.6 × 40.5 × 41.0 cm
Gift of Sorel Etrog, 2009
2009/245
Page 81

Ritual Head
1976
bronze
137.2 × 46.0 × 87.0 cm
On loan from Sorel Etrog
Page 78

Busy Town
1977
porous pointed pen and ink on paper
56.8 × 76.0 cm
Gift of Sorel Etrog, 2013
108587
Page 61

Calligraphic Hinges
1977
porous pointed pen and ink on paper
75.6 × 56.8 cm
Gift of Sorel Etrog, 2013
108586
Page 58

Weeds
1977
watercolour, pointed porous pen and graphite on paper
21.0 × 27.0 cm
On loan from Sorel Etrog
Page 61

Homage to Kurosawa
1980
painted steel
111.7 × 50.1 cm
On loan from Sorel Etrog
Page 84

Magic Box
1980
painted steel (edition 3 of 6)
48.8 × 102.8 × 5.0 cm
Gift of Sorel Etrog, 2009
2009/246
Page 83

Dream Chamber: Joyce and the Dada Circus. A Collage; About Roaratorio: An Irish Circus on Finnegans Wake
1982
bookwork: illustrated by Sorel Etrog; edited by Robert O'Driscoll
Published by Black Brick Press, Toronto
Courtesy of the E.P. Taylor Research Library & Archives, Art Gallery of Ontario
Pages 114–115

Composite 3
1996–1997
wood, acrylic paint, hardboard, styrene sheet and metal hinges
57.4 × 64.2 × 10.0 cm
Gift of Sorel Etrog, 2011
2011/381
Page 90

Composite 11
1996–1997
wood, acrylic paint, plastic and metal
58.7 × 111.7 × 18.2 cm
Gift of Sorel Etrog, 2001
2001/214
Page 88

Composite 14
1996–1997
wood, acrylic paint, plywood, particleboard, metal rod, screws, incandescent lamps and electrical fixtures
75.0 × 99.0 × 11.4 cm
Gift of Sorel Etrog, 2011
2011/382
Page 89

Composite 18
1996–1997
wood, acrylic paint, plywood, hardboard, foam packing material, metal hinges and valve handles
123.2 × 123.2 × 14.0 cm
Gift of Sorel Etrog, 2011
2011/383
Page 91

Works Not in the Exhibition

Hasidic Head
1959
bronze
122.0 × 122.0 cm
Courtesy of Holy Blossom Temple
Page 37

Mother and Child
1962–1964
bronze (edition 2 of 7)
52.1 × 24.1 × 20.3 cm
Gift of Sam and Ayala Zacks, 1970
71/146
Page 38

Standing Figure (Madonna)
1962–1964
bronze (edition 5 of 7)
116.8 × 17.8 × 15.2 cm
Gift of Sam and Ayala Zacks, 1970
71/151
Page 39

Flight No. 1
1963–1964
bronze (edition 1 of 7)
40.0 × 84.8 × 22.2 cm
Gift of Sam and Ayala Zacks, 1970
71/143
Page 36

Survivors Are Not Heroes
1967
bronze
height: 548.6 cm
Pages 52–53

Hand II
1969
etching on paper
50.8 × 35.6 cm
On loan from Sorel Etrog
Page 54

Hand IV
1969
etching on paper
50.8 × 35.6 cm
On loan from Sorel Etrog
Page 54

Hand VII
1969
etching on paper
50.8 × 35.6 cm
On loan from Sorel Etrog
Page 54

Hand VIII
1969
etching on paper
73.7 × 35.6 cm
On loan from Sorel Etrog
Page 54

Turkish Bath Study
1969
ink on paper with stick
sheet: 28.0 × 35.5 cm
Page 62

Turkish Bath Study: Full View 2
1969
pastel and charcoal on paper
sheet: 49.0 × 67.0 cm
Page 62

Turkish Bath Study: Relaxing Figure
1969
pastel and charcoal on paper
sheet: 49.0 × 69.0 cm
Page 62

Turkish Bath Study: Two Figures
1969
pastel and charcoal on paper
sheet: 25.0 × 32.5 cm
Page 62

Sadko
1971–1972
painted bronze
height: 365.8 cm
Page 25

The Hand
1972
bronze
height: 365.8 cm
Page 55

Rushman
1974–1976
bronze
height: 157.5 cm
Page 75

Détente
1980
painted steel
35.5 × 240.6 cm
On loan from Sorel Etrog
Pages 86–87

Sunlife
1984
bronze
height: 848.6 cm
Page 74

Powersoul
1988
steel
height: 1005.8 cm
Page 85

Public Collections

North America

Agnes Etherington Art Centre, Queen's University, Kingston, Ontario

Art Gallery of Alberta, Edmonton

Art Gallery of Greater Victoria, British Columbia

Art Gallery of Hamilton, Ontario

Art Gallery of Ontario, Toronto

Art Gallery of Windsor, Ontario

Bank of Canada, Ottawa, Ontario

Beaverbrook Art Gallery, Fredericton, New Brunswick

City of Dallas Office of Cultural Affairs Public Art Collection, Dallas, Texas

Confederation Centre Art Gallery, Charlottetown, Prince Edward Island

Fogg Museum, Harvard University, Cambridge, Massachusetts

Franklin D. Murphy Sculpture Garden, Armand Hammer Museum of Art and Culture Center, University of California, Los Angeles

Goucher College, Baltimore, Maryland

Guild Inn, Scarborough, Ontario

Hammerson Corporate Collection, Toronto, Ontario

Hart House, University of Toronto, Ontario

Hirshhorn Museum and Sculpture Garden, Washington, DC

Hopkins Center for the Arts, Dartmouth College, Hanover, New Hampshire

Imperial Oil Collection, Toronto, Ontario

Kitchener-Waterloo Art Gallery, Ontario

Los Angeles County Museum of Art, California

Lynden Sculpture Garden, Milwaukee, Wisconsin

MacLaren Art Centre, Barrie, Ontario

McMaster Museum of Art, McMaster University, Hamilton, Ontario

McMichael Canadian Art Collection, Kleinburg, Ontario

Mount Sinai Hospital, Toronto, Ontario

Musée d'art contemporain de Montréal, Quebec

Musée d'art de Joliette, Quebec

Musée des beaux-arts de Montréal, Quebec

Museum London, Ontario

Museum of Modern Art, New York City, New York

National Arts Centre, Ottawa, Ontario

National Gallery of Canada, Ottawa, Ontario

New Orleans Foundation, Louisiana

Northwestern Michigan College, Traverse City

Olympia & York Centre, Toronto, Ontario

Palm Springs Art Museum, California

Ravinia Park, Chicago, Illinois

Rodman Hall Art Centre, Brock University, St. Catharines, Ontario

Shaw Festival, Niagara-on-the-Lake, Ontario

Simon Fraser University Gallery, Burnaby, British Columbia

Smith College Museum of Art, Northampton, Massachusetts

Snite Museum of Art, University of Notre Dame, South Bend, Indiana

Solomon R. Guggenheim Museum, New York City, New York

Storm King Art Center, New Windsor, New York

Stratford Festival Theatre, Ontario

Sun Life Financial Building, Toronto, Ontario

TD Bank Building, Toronto

Temple Emanu-El, Palm Beach, Florida

The Robert McLaughlin Gallery, Oshawa, Ontario

Tufts University Art Gallery, Medford, Massachusetts

Université de Montréal, Quebec

University of Chicago, Illinois

University of Lethbridge Art Gallery, Alberta

University of Toronto Art Centre, Ontario

University of Windsor, Ontario

Vancouver Art Gallery, British Columbia

Victoria College, University of Toronto, Ontario

Wayne State University, Detroit, Michigan

Western Michigan University, Kalamazoo, Michigan

Windsor Sculpture Park, Ontario

International

Academy of Fine Arts, Kolkata, India

Bibliothèque nationale de France, Paris

City of Beer Sheva, Israel

Fondation Jean et Suzanne Planque, Lausanne, Switzerland

Galleria d'Arte Moderna, Legnano, Italy

Haifa Museum of Art, Israel

Israel Museum, Jerusalem

Kröller-Müller Museum, Otterlo, Netherlands

Kunstmuseum Basel, Switzerland

Middenplantsoen, Utrecht, Netherlands

Musée d'Art Moderne de la Ville de Paris, France

Musée de la Sculpture en Plein Air, Paris, France

Museo Internazionale d'Arte Contemporanea, Florence, Italy

Museum Boijmans Van Beuningen, Rotterdam, Netherlands

National Museum of Contemporary Art, Seoul, Korea

Olympic Park, Seoul, Korea

Reviers, Normandy, France

St. Peter's College, University of Oxford, England

Tate, London, England

Tel Aviv Museum of Art, Israel

Weizmann Institute of Science, Rehovot, Israel

Selected Bibliography

Marcel Janco. Introduction to *Oil Paintings in Relief, Watercolours and Drawings*. Tel Aviv: Z.O.A. House, 1958.

Theodore Allen Heinrich. Introduction to *Etrog: Painting on Wood/Sculptures/Drawings*. Toronto: Gallery Moos, 1959.

Natalie Edgar. Introduction to *Etrog: Sculpture/Oil on Wood/Gouaches/Prints/Drawings/Exhibition*. Waterbury, Connecticut: Lewis Gallery, 1960.

James Goldworthy. Introduction to *New Sculpture and Oils on Wood by Etrog*. Toronto: Gallery Moos, 1961.

William J. Withrow. Introduction to *Sorel Etrog: Sculpture*. New York: Rose Fried Gallery, 1963.

Theodore Allen Heinrich. Introduction to *Etrog*. Toronto: Gallery Moos; Los Angeles: Felix Landau Gallery; Montreal: Galerie Dresdnere, 1965.

Gustave von Groschwitz. Introduction to *Sorel Etrog: Recent Sculpture*. New York: Pierre Matisse Gallery, 1965.

Enzo Pagani. Introduction to *Sorel Etrog*. Milan: Galleria Pagani del Grattacielo, 1966.

Sorel Etrog and Claude Aveline. *L'oiseau qui n'existe pas*. Venice: Edition del Cavallino, 1967.

Will Grohmann. Introduction to *Sorel Etrog*. Berlin: Galerie Springer; Rome: Galleria Schneider, 1967.

William J. Withrow, with preface by Sir Philip Hendy. *Sorel Etrog: Sculpture*. Toronto: Wilfeld Publications, 1967.

Jean-Luc Daval. Introduction to *Etrog*. Geneva: Gallery Georges Moos, 1968.

Theodore Allen Heinrich. *The Painted Constructions 1952–1960 of Sorel Etrog*. Berne: Switzerland: Staempfli et Cie, 1968.

Carlo L. Ragghianti. Introduction to *Sorel Etrog, 1958–1968*. Florence: Palazzo Strozzi, 1968.

Sorel Etrog and Eugène Ionesco. *Chocs*. New York: Martha Jackson Gallery, 1969.

Alan Jarvis. Introduction to *Sorel Etrog*. Dallas: Valley House Gallery, 1969.

Alan Toff. Introduction to *Sorel Etrog: One Decade*. Toronto: Art Gallery of Ontario, 1969.

Mario Amaya. Introduction to *Etrog*. Toronto: Dunkelman Gallery, 1970.

Eugène Ionesco. Introduction to *Etrog*. London: Hanover Gallery, 1970.

Leo Rosshandler. Introduction to *Sorel Etrog: Paintings, Pastels and Drawings*. Toronto: Dunkelman Gallery, 1971.

Gianlorenzo Mellini. Introduction to *Sorel Etrog*. Montreal: Dominion Gallery, 1972.

George W. Staempfli. Introduction to *Sorel Etrog: New Sculpture*. New York: Staempfli, 1972.

Marshall McLuhan. Introduction to *Sorel Etrog: Recent Works*. Toronto: Marlborough Godard; Montreal: La Galerie Mira Godard; New York: Marlborough Gallery, 1977.

Jean-Marie Benoist. Introduction to *Sorel Etrog*. Paris: Centre Culturel Canadien, 1978.

Sorel Etrog and Claude Aveline. *L'oiseau qui n'existe pas*, trans. George Buchanan. Paris: Editions Daniel Jacomet, 1978.

Sorel Etrog. "Dream Chamber: Joyce and the Dada Circus, A Collage," in Robert O'Driscoll, ed. *Dream Chamber/About Roaratorio*. Toronto: Black Brick Press; Dublin: Dolmen Press, 1982.

Sorel Etrog and Samuel Beckett. *Imagination Dead Imagine*. London: John Calder Publishers, 1982.

Sorel Etrog. "Hinges: A Play," in John Calder, ed. *New Writing and Writers 20*. London: John Calder Publishers; New York: Riverrun Press, 1983.

Sorel Etrog. *The Kite/Le Cerf-Volant*. London: John Calder Publishers, 1984.

Sorel Etrog. "From Sorel Etrog," in *As No Other Dare Fail: For Samuel Beckett on His 80th Birthday*. London: John Calder Publishers, 1986.

Leo Rosshandler. Introduction to *Sorel Etrog: New Paintings*. Montreal: Dominion Gallery, 1989.

Sorel Etrog. *Dream Chamber: Joyce and the Dada Circus. A Collage*. Toronto: Exile Editions, 1996.

Barry Lord and Bridget Tan. *Essays for The Cult of the Head: Sculptures by Sorel Etrog*. Singapore: Singapore Art Museum, 1997.

Gary Michael Dault. Introduction to *Sorel Etrog: Composites*. Toronto Christopher Cutts Gallery, 2000.

Pierre Restany. *Sorel Etrog*. Munich; London; New York: Prestel, 2001.

The Art Gallery of Ontario is partially funded by the Ontario Ministry of Culture. Additional operating support is received from the Volunteers of the Art Gallery of Ontario, City of Toronto, the Department of Canadian Heritage, and the Canada Council for the Arts.

This catalogue is published in conjunction with the exhibition

Sorel Etrog
Art Gallery of Ontario
April 27–September 29, 2013

Contemporary programming at the Art Gallery of Ontario is supported by

Canada Council for the Arts   Conseil des Arts du Canada

Art Gallery of Ontario
317 Dundas Street West
Toronto, Ontario
Canada M5T 1G4
www.ago.net

Library and Archives Canada Cataloguing in Publication

Ihor Holubizky

Sorel Etrog : five decades / Matthew Teitelbaum, Ihor Holubizky, Gary Michael Dault.

Includes bibliographical references. Catalogue of an exhibition held at the Art Gallery of Ontario, Toronto, Ont. from April 27–Sept. 29, 2013.

1. Etrog, Sorel, 1933–
—Exhibitions.
I. Holubizky, Ihor, 1952–
II. Dault, Gary Michael
III. Etrog, Sorel, 1933–
IV. Art Gallery of Ontario
V. Title.

N6549.E864A4 2013
709.2   C2013-901288-5

ISBN 978-1-894243-73-5

Abridged exerpts and images were taken from the following texts:

Page 93: Preface to William J. Withrow. *Sorel Etrog*. Toronto: Wilfeld Publications, 1967. Text by Sir Philip Hendy reprinted with permission of Sorel Etrog.

Pages 94–99: Theodore Allen Heinrich. *The painted constructions 1952–1960 of Sorel Etrog*. Berne, Switzerland: Staempfli + Cie, 1968. Text by Theodore Allen Heinrich reprinted with permission of Sorel Etrog.

Pages 100–101: William J. Withrow. *Sorel Etrog*. Toronto: Wilfeld Publications, 1967. Text reprinted courtesy of William J. Withrow.

Page 104: Image of Pablo Picasso's *Guernica* © Picasso Estate/SODRAC (2013)

Pages 106–108, 110–111: Marshall McLuhan. *Sorel Etrog: Images from the Film* Spiral. Toronto: Exile Editions, 1987. Text by Marshall McLuhan reprinted courtesy of the Estate of Marshall and Corinne McLuhan.

The publisher has made every effort to trace and contact copyright holders of the works reproduced in this book, and will be glad to correct in subsequent editions any errors or omissions that are brought to its attention.

All photography by the AGO, except for the following:

Cover: L. Brown
Pages 2–3: Paul Smith
Page 7: Anthony Hayman
Page 8: Leslie Shurgin
Pages 14–15: Courtesy of Sorel Etrog
Page 19: Herb Levart
Page 20: Aurelio Amendola
Pages 21–24: Aurelio Amendola
Page 25: Courtesy of Sorel Etrog
Page 28: Anthony Hayman
Page 32: Courtesy of Sorel Etrog
Page 33: Courtesy of Kröller-Müller Museum
Page 36: Vi Cross
Page 40: Photographic Bureau, Dartmouth College
Page 42: Michel Nguyen
Page 50: John Mahler, Toronto Star
Page 51: Foto Frugoni, Firenze
Page 53: Courtesy of Sorel Etrog
Page 64: Lika Etrog
Page 72: Foto Frugoni, Firenze
Page 75: Courtesy of Sorel Etrog
Pages 76–77: Aurelio Amendola
Page 82: Courtesy of Sorel Etrog
Page 85: Courtesy of Sorel Etrog
Page 128: Herb Levart

Production Credits

Sorel Etrog
Art Gallery of Ontario
April 27–September 29, 2013

Exhibition

Guest Curatorial Consultant
Ihor Holubizky

Curatorial Assistant, Canadian
Gregory Humeniuk

Interpretive Planner
David Wistow

Project Manager
Laura Comerford

Curatorial Administrative Assistant
Samantha Benjamin

Exhibition Services Manager
George Bartosik

Production Coordinator, Design Studio
Malene Hjorngaard

Conservators
Lisa Ellis
Sherry Phillips
Joan Weir

Collection Care Specialist
John Williams

Exhibition Designer
Kristina Ljubanovic

Interactive Designer
Tharan Parameshwaran

Graphic Designer
Aleksandra Grzywaczewska

Production Coordinator, Exhibition Services
Charles Kettle

Installation Coordinator
Brian Groombridge

Registrar
Curtis Strilchuk

Traffic Coordinator
Dale Mahar

Development
Lisa Landreth

Communications
Laura Banks

Social Media
Meagan Campbell

Media Producers
Barbara Arsenault
Danny Winchester

Book

Editor
Ihor Holubizky

Managing Editor
Jim Shedden

Copy Editor
Daniel Naccarato

Editorial Assistant
Claire Crighton

Designer
Lauren Wickware

Photographers
Craig Boyko
Ian Lefebvre
Dean Tomlinson
Sean Weaver

Image Rights and Reproduction Coordinator
Syvalya Elchen

Prepress and Printing
Andora Graphics Inc.

Overleaf: Etrog in his New York studio, 1959–1960

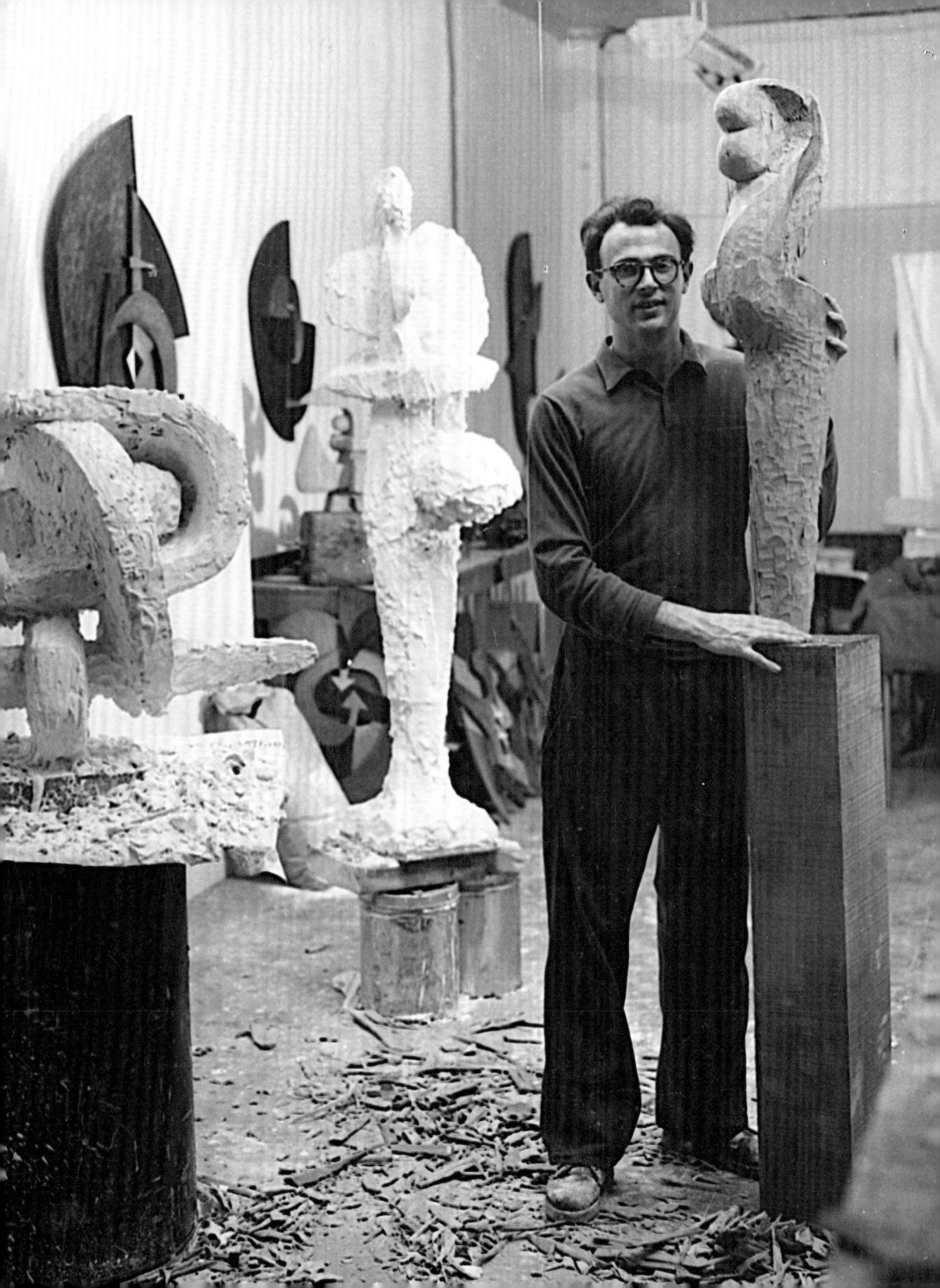